GUIDELINES FOR
EARLY LEARNING
IN CHILD CARE
HOME SETTINGS

Publishing Information

Guidelines for Early Learning in Child Care Home Settings was developed by the Child Development Division of the California Department of Education (CDE), under contract with the American Institutes for Research (AIR), the California Child Care Resource and Referral Network (CCCRRN), and the WestEd Center for Child and Family Studies (WestEd). The document was edited by John McLean, working in cooperation with Tom Cole, Consultant, Child Development Division. It was prepared for printing by the staff of CDE Press: Cheryl McDonald created and prepared the cover and interior design; Jeannette Reyes typeset the document. It was published by the California Department of Education, 1430 N Street, Sacramento, CA 95814-5901. The document was distributed under the provisions of the Library Distribution Act and *Government Code* Section 11096.

© 2010 by the California Department of Education
All rights reserved

ISBN 978-0-8011-1699-5

Ordering Information

Copies of this publication are available for sale from the California Department of Education. For pricing and ordering information, please visit http://www. cde.ca.gov/re/pn/rc/, or contact the CDE Press Sales Office:

CDE Press Sales Office
1430 N Street, Suite 3207
Sacramento, CA 95814-5901
Telephone (toll-free): 1-800-995-4099
Fax: 916-323-0823

Notice

The guidance in *Guidelines for Early Learning in Child Care Home Settings* is not binding on local educational agencies or other entities. Except for the statutes, regulations, and court decisions that are referenced herein, the document is exemplary, and compliance with it is not mandatory. (See *Education Code* Section 33308.5.)

Contents

A Message from the State Superintendent of Public Instruction

There is growing recognition in California and across the nation of the importance of high-quality early care and education in preparing children for success in school and life.

Brain research over the last decade has documented the influence of early experiences upon children's social, emotional, and cognitive development. Based on evidence from neurobiology and the behavioral and social sciences, we now know that what happens in the first five years of life is critical to a young child's development. Effective early care and education can provide a foundation that will support a child into adulthood.

In addition, there is an increasing body of research showing that young children are far more capable learners than once believed, and that good educational experiences in the early years can have a positive impact on later learning in school. While some preschool-age children attend center-based programs, many more young children receive important early experiences in family child care and license-exempt child care settings. *Guidelines for Early Learning in Child Care Home Settings* focuses on the special role that licensed family child care and license-exempt providers play in educating the children they serve, and it offers guidance to help providers create positive, nurturing environments for the children in their care.

This publication relies on content from a previous California Department of Education publication aimed at center-based programs—*Prekindergarten Learning and Development Guidelines*—to address home-based care settings. Because many home-based care settings serve both preschool-age children and younger children in mixed-age group settings, the document also includes guidance that is specific to caring for infants and toddlers.

I hope this publication helps you strengthen relationships with the children and families you serve, develop a home-based curriculum that will enhance children's learning and development across domains, and ensure that your home is both a caring and learning environment. I wish you success in your professional development and with your work in providing high-quality home-based care for young children.

Jack O'Connell

JACK O'CONNELL
State Superintendent of Public Instruction

Acknowledgments

The development of *Guidelines for Early Learning in Child Care Home Settings* required the collaboration of many people, including an advisory panel of early care and education experts specializing in family child care and license-exempt settings; a stakeholder group of home-based child care providers, community college instructors, child care advocates, and trainers of home-based caregivers; a writing team from the American Institutes for Research (AIR) that worked with the California Child Care Resource and Referral Network (CCCRRN) and the WestEd Center for Child and Family Studies (WestEd); staff members of the California Department of Education's Child Development Division; and other key contributors.

Note: The names, titles, and affiliations of the individuals listed in these Acknowledgments were current at the time the publication was developed.

Advisory Panel

Deborah Eaton, Director of Accreditation, National Association for Family Child Care

Janet Gonzalez-Mena, Early Childhood Education/Child Development Consultant and Author

Diane Harkins, Program Director, Center for Human Services, University of California, Davis

Jean Monroe, Early Childhood Education/Child Development Consultant

Laurie Prusso, Child Development Instructor, Modesto Junior College

June Solnit Sale, Early Childhood Education/Child Development Consultant and Author

Wendy Wayne, Former Executive Director, First 5 Kern County

Stakeholder Group

Debra Boles, Program Director, YMCA Childcare Resource Service

David Crummey, Director of Children's Services, Human Response Network

Donna Daly-Petersen, Former President, California Association for Family Child Care

Ellen Flanagan, Former Family Child Care Provider

Gil Guevara, City of Oxnard Housing Authority

Rita Hatchett, Family Child Care Provider

Judy Ishiura, PITC Infant/Toddler Specialist Coordinator, WestEd

Rosemarie Kennedy, Former Family Child Care Provider

Leatrice Knox, Family Child Care Provider

Lillian Neely, Child Development Instructor

Maria Rios, Family Child Care Provider

Toni Robertson, Family Child Care Provider and UC Davis Extension Instructor

Andrea Scheib, Family Child Care Provider and Child Development Instructor

Anh Kim Tran, Program Specialist, Bananas Resource and Referral Agency

Annette Villareal, Family Child Care Provider

Sheila Wills, Coordinator, License-Exempt Assistance Project (LEAP), Crystal Stairs Resource and Referral Agency

Manuel Kichi Wong, Early Childhood Education Instructor, City College of San Francisco

American Institutes for Research

San Mateo, California

Primary staff members:

Jennifer Anthony, Deputy Project Director

Susan Muenchow, Project Director

Deborah Parrish, Principal Investigator

Other staff members who assisted with the project were **Connie Liu, Gabriele Phillips, Carmella Schaecher,** and a team of technical and content editors.

California Child Care Resource and Referral Network

Jacqueline Lowe, Central/Southern Manager and Central Valley Regional Coordinator

Patricia Siegel, Executive Director

WestEd Center for Child and Family Studies

Sausalito, California

Deborah Greenwald, Senior Program Associate

Peter Mangione, Codirector

California Department of Education

Gail Brodie, Consultant, Quality Improvement Office, Child Development Division

Tom Cole, Consultant, Quality Improvement Office, Child Development Division

Cecelia Fisher-Dahms, Administrator, Quality Improvement Office, Child Development Division

Camille Maben, Director, Child Development Division

Rick Miller, Deputy Superintendent, P-16 Policy and Information Branch

Anthony Monreal, Former Deputy Superintendent

Gwen Stephens, Former Assistant Director, Child Development Division

Center for Health Training

Rebecca Malia Ramler, Former Project Manager

Desired Results *access* Project

Anne Kuschner, Project Director, Desired Results *access* Project,
Napa County Office of Education

Focus Groups

Five focus groups—in Fresno, Los Angeles, Chico, San Diego, and San Francisco—were assembled and managed by **Rebecca Malia Ramler** of the Center for Health Training. Focus group participants were licensed and license-exempt home-based child care providers.

Photographers

Jennifer Anthony
Miriam Chernow
Keith Gaudet
Teresa Gelerter
Amy Merickel
Hemmie Wang
Sara Webb-Schmitz

Additional Contributors

Steven Anthony, Kindergarten Teacher
Olga King, Olga King Family Child Care Home
Stacy Merickel

Introduction

SERVING AS A HOME-BASED CHILD CARE PROVIDER IS AN
IMPORTANT JOB—one that requires hard work, creativity,
flexibility, and genuine concern for children and their families.
In California, there are several types of home-based child care
settings, including "family, friend, and neighbor care" that does
not require a license; family child care homes licensed by the
state; and licensed settings that are also accredited by the
National Association for Family Child Care (NAFCC).
Whether you operate a licensed family child care home,
care for your grandchildren, or are a provider accredited by
a national organization, you have an opportunity to make
a positive and lasting impact on the lives of the children
and families in your care.

As you read *Guidelines for Early Learning in Child Care Home Settings,* you may want to think about why you are a home-based child care provider. Perhaps you think the home offers the best setting for working with young children. Maybe you want to use your teaching skills in a setting that allows you to work at home and care for your own children. Or you may want to help a family member or neighbor by caring for their children. Regardless of the reasons you became a home-based provider, the guidelines in this book were developed to help you improve your service to children and their families and to improve the quality of your work life.

Development of the Guidelines

In 2000, the California Department of Education (CDE) published *Prekindergarten Learning and Development Guidelines (Prekindergarten Guidelines)* to provide guidance to preschool directors and teachers on building high-quality prekindergarten programs. The *Prekindergarten Guidelines* addressed multiple areas of child development: language; thinking skills; and social, emotional, and physical development. However, they focused primarily on school- and center-based programs.

Recognizing that many children receive their early care and education in home-based settings, the CDE developed *Guidelines for Early Learning in Child Care Home Settings* specifically for family child care and exempt-care providers. This document covers the same topics as those in the *Prekindergarten Guidelines*, but it also addresses the specific concerns that home-based providers face every day as they strive to nurture and teach the children in their care. Additionally, it addresses the reality that many family child care and license-exempt providers serve infants and toddlers side by side with preschool-age children.

The development of *Guidelines for Early Learning in Child Care Home Settings* relied on extensive input from providers—the people who are most familiar with home-based child care. The process was guided by an advisory group composed of early care and education specialists, early childhood education instructors from community colleges, and practitioners who provide support to family child care and exempt-care providers; and by a stakeholder group consisting of family child care and exempt-care providers, family child care association leaders, trainers, and others who provide support to home-based providers. The CDE hopes that the extensive involvement of these specialists and providers in the formation of this publication has resulted in practical, state-of-the-art information.

How the Guidelines Can Benefit the Children in Your Care

The suggestions and guidance in this publication are meant to assist you in many ways with the children for whom you provide care.

The Guidelines will help you:

- Provide learning experiences for preschool children, infants, and toddlers in mixed-age group settings that are common in home-based care.
- Promote meaningful conversation with children, develop their vocabularies, and encourage their interest in books and stories.
- Interest children in daily home activities that involve problem solving, measuring, sorting, classifying, and other skills that serve as building blocks for future learning in math and science.
- Include children with disabilities and other special needs in your home-based setting, and get help for those children when needed.
- Show respect and appreciation for the home languages and cultures of children (and their families) whose backgrounds differ from yours.

How the Guidelines Can Improve Your Service to Families

One of the strengths of home-based child care is that it enhances the opportunity to get to know children in the context of their families. By understanding and respecting the primary role of the family in the lives of young children, and by supporting the family in times of celebration as well as stress, you strengthen a child's social and emotional development.

The Guidelines will help you:

- Explain to families how, on a daily basis, you promote language development and thinking skills in a natural home setting by talking with children, preparing their meals, and playing with them.
- Communicate with parents and other family members and learn how to involve them in home-based learning and care activities.

How the Guidelines Can Improve Your Work Life

Working as a home-based child care provider is a demanding job. Whether you are a licensed family child care provider or an exempt provider, you may wish you had more interaction with other providers (and other adults), help with business practices, and additional training or education.

The Guidelines offer suggestions about how to:

- Receive support from and meet other providers by joining or organizing a family child care association and by connecting with other organizations.

- Pursue training and professional development opportunities that are appropriate for home-based providers and that suit your work hours.
- Provide high-quality care by incorporating best business practices and by having a plan for program development or improvements to your home.

Early Childhood Experiences and the Learning Process

Research shows that early childhood experiences—particularly in the first five years of a child's life—may have a profound effect on a child's development and on his or her capacity to learn in the future. The development of a young child's brain involves a complicated blend of the child's genetic makeup and environmental factors such as behavioral experiences and nutrition.[1] Additionally, for most young children in the United States, child care settings are the places where they first learn to interact with other children, form relationships with adults outside their immediate families, and receive important input for early learning and language development.[2]

Preparing young children for kindergarten

Many children lack key skills when they enter school. Kindergarten teachers often report that children would be better prepared for school if they had prekindergarten experiences focusing on social and emotional aspects of learning in addition to activities focusing on language development and other skills. Teachers also report that it can be very difficult to help children who lack confidence or who struggle with cooperation and self-control.[3] Home-based child care can offer positive experiences that help children's social, emotional, cognitive, and physical development.

Benefits of high-quality early childhood settings

As a home-based child care provider you have a unique opportunity to contribute to the future success of the children in your care. The quality of care that you provide—the language that each child hears, the way in which you respond to a child's words and actions, and the attention that you give to each child—influences children in many ways. Your daily approach to child care affects:

- The quality of the relationships that the children in your care form, both now and in the future.
- The way the children learn to talk and listen—and the size of each child's vocabulary.
- Their ability to reason and exercise self-control.
- Their motivation to learn and their approach to learning when they enter school.

A growing body of research confirms that high-quality child care and early education help prepare children for school. Participation in high-quality child development settings has short-term and long-term benefits. Children who are most at risk of school failure—for example, those whose parents have little education, who are dual-language learners, or whose mothers are depressed—show the most dramatic gains from high-quality programs, but the quality of the care makes a difference for all children.[4]

Short-term benefits

In the short term, children in high-quality early childhood programs:
- Have better language ability and fewer behavior problems.[5]
- Score significantly better in language development, print awareness, and mathematics than children in lower-quality programs.[6]
- Show significant cognitive gains during early childhood compared with children in lower-quality programs.[7]
- Enter kindergarten with skills needed to handle school tasks successfully.[8]

Long-term benefits

In the long term, children in high-quality early childhood programs:
- Are less likely to be retained in a grade.
- Have fewer years of special education.
- Are less likely to drop out of high school.[9]
- Have higher rates of high school graduation and lower rates of juvenile arrest.[10]

Every dollar invested in high-quality early childhood programs for children from low-income families has been estimated to save $7 in future expenditures for special education, delinquency, welfare, and lost taxes.[11] Other research shows that early interventions for disadvantaged children result in 15 to 17 percent returns for each dollar invested.[12] In addition, researchers have estimated that in California, a one-year, high-quality preschool program available to all children, regardless of family income, would ultimately save $2.62 for every dollar invested.[13]

Benefits of high-quality, home-based child care

The findings presented above are based on studies conducted in center- or school-based early childhood programs, which are fundamentally different from home-based settings. However, research also shows the benefits of home-based care and the importance of high quality in those settings. Home-based child care is able to meet the needs of children, families, and communities. It is particularly helpful to families that have recently immigrated to the United States because those families may have the opportunity to choose a provider with a matching cultural and linguistic background—and the care offered in a culturally supportive environment may strengthen the sense of security and self-confidence in young children.[14] Home-based child care settings also offer families more flexibility in finding child care with mixed-age groups, allowing siblings of different ages to be together. Finally, home-based settings frequently offer lower ratios of children to adults than center-based programs—and small group sizes foster the health, safety, and comfort of children by strengthening the primary-care relationship.[15]

Importance of high-quality programs

Program quality in home-based child care settings—just as in center-based care—is critical to improved outcomes for children. Children in high-quality settings:

- Have better language skills than children who attend lower-quality family child care homes.[16]
- Are more sociable, know more words, and understand more that is communicated to them.[17]
- Have more secure attachments to providers than children who receive lower-quality care, because the providers tend to be more sensitive and responsive to the children's needs.[18]

In family child care, caregiver training is the best predictor of the quality of the care.[19] *The Family Child Care Training Study* found that training of family child care providers contributes to improvements in quality and to progress in children's emotional development.[20] Training, participation in support networks, and the amount of schooling undertaken by a provider explain more than two-thirds of the variation in family child care practices.[21]

Mixed-age groups

Home-based child care providers rarely care for a single age group; they typically care for children in mixed-age groups—a combination of infants, toddlers, preschoolers, and school-age children.

Mixed-age groupings can be challenging. It takes time and guidance for younger and older children to learn how to interact with each other in group settings. As a home-based child care provider, you play an important role in anticipating and responding to challenges as they arise. For example, if an older child has a block tower toppled by a curious infant, the way in which you respond to the older child's anger can help that child learn to regulate his or her emotions. Or the way you adapt when you have a young infant in your care who needs freedom of movement, but who must be kept safe as well, helps her to understand your "cues" as she seeks support and guidance while exploring her environment. Challenges such as these occur in mixed-age groups, and your responses to these situations provide children with guidance on handling their emotions, impulses, and differences with others.

Working with mixed-age groups also requires that providers be flexible and creative. There are times when infants and toddlers need to be separated from older children to have quiet time with adults. Similarly, older children sometimes need opportunities to focus on special activities without interference from younger children. Child care providers need to be creative to arrange activities that are tailored for the mixed ages of children in their care.

Benefits of mixed-age groups

Although mixed-age groups present challenges to home-based child care providers, they also offer significant benefits to children, families, and providers. Mixed-age settings:

- Can feel more like "family" environments in which infants and toddlers have the opportunity to observe older children, and older children often enjoy being with infants and toddlers.
- Provide children with opportunities to learn about patience, empathy, and understanding. For example, older children may be asked to slow down for younger children in a group; to be supportive as infants and toddlers learn to crawl, walk, or dress themselves; and to be tolerant when younger children become tired or frustrated. In turn, younger children watch and learn from the behavior of the older children.
- Promote social participation and acceptance. Younger children are more likely than same-age peers to accept an older child who is socially less mature. In addition, younger children can participate in complex activities organized by their older playmates and can learn how to initiate their own activities in the future.[22]
- Give providers continuous teaching and learning opportunities. Each day, home-based child care providers have the opportunity to offer age-appropriate guidance to the children in their care—such as showing younger children how to explore their environment while accepting limitations, and teaching older children to use their more advanced skills in positive, constructive ways. Providers can also learn how to fulfill different roles for different age groups simultaneously.

Other Perspectives on Home-Based Child Care

In the eyes of many children, families, child care providers, and kindergarten teachers, home-based child care settings offer distinct advantages over school- and center-based programs. The following quotes are just a few examples of people's firsthand experiences with home-based child care.

A Child's View
Why is home-based child care special?

"I've never talked so much to somebody in my whole life as I do with Ms. Ramos. I haven't watched television in two whole months! I don't get bored here."

[Child's name withheld]

A Parent's Perspective
Advantages of home-based care

"I chose family child care because I like the smaller groups and the family atmosphere. I feel my child gets the advantages of more personal attention and learns without pressure. She also learns how to relate and cooperate with children in different age groups."

—Athena Tessman, parent
(quote provided by Donna Daly-Peterson,
California Association for Family Child Care)

A Child Care Provider's View
Benefits of home-based care

"Family child care offers the critical, individualized care that children need. Children know that *I* will be the one to open the door each day and say, 'Good morning! I'm so happy to see you.' And they know that in the evening, I will be there to say, 'Bye-bye. I'll be waiting for you tomorrow.' Children feel secure because they know that when their parents bring them to the door each day, I—not a substitute—will be there to greet them. This security makes them think, *I can learn anything, just throw it at me and I'll show you.*"

—Leatrice Knox,
family child care provider;
Vallejo, California

Teachers' Perspectives
What should children learn in home-based child care settings?

"The most important thing a child care provider can do is to make sure children have high self-esteem and a 'can-do' attitude."

—Alice Kawasaki,
elementary school teacher;
Sunnyvale, California

"Kindergarten is a major introduction to the educational world and also to the social world. Providers need to teach children interaction skills. In other words, children need to learn how to deal appropriately with both adults and other children in social situations. They need to be talked to *and* with. Most importantly, they need *human*—not electronic—interaction."

—Steven Anthony,
elementary school teacher;
Sunnyvale, California

Document Organization

Guidelines for Early Learning in Child Care Home Settings is divided into five chapters:

Chapter 1. The Home Based Child Care Provider: Roles and Relationships

Chapter 2. The Home as a Caring and Learning Environment

Chapter 3. Developing a Home-Based Curriculum

Chapter 4. Professional Development for Home-Based Child Care Providers

Chapter 5. Home-Based Child Care as Part of an Early Learning System

Chapters 1 through 4 begin with an introduction and are broken down into sections. The guidelines presented are unique to each section, and each section starts with the following topics:

- Why Is This Important?
- Remember That Young Children…
- Keys to Effective Home-Based Child Care
- Considerations When Infants and Toddlers Are Present
- Guidelines in This Section

Each guideline includes "Practices"—practical suggestions (including many specific examples) for home-based child care providers to follow as they work with children and families each day. Although the primary focus of this publication is on preschool-age children, ages three to five, the document also offers practices for settings that include infants and toddlers. It should be noted that although some providers care for school-age children in addition to preschoolers, infants, and toddlers, the document does not address the integration of school-age children with preschool children. Finally, for ease of reference, Appendix D presents a summary of the guidelines in this publication.

Summary

Guidelines for Early Learning in Child Care Home Settings was developed for you, the home-based child care provider. The guidelines in this book center on the principle that warm, attentive, high-quality care in the early years of a child's life can provide a solid foundation for all future learning—and that your role as a home-based child care provider is vital to the well-being of each child in your care. The CDE hopes this publication improves the quality of your work life and enriches the lives of the children and families with whom you interact each day.

Notes

1. National Research Council and Institute of Medicine, page 185.
2. Ibid., page 297.
3. Lewit and Baker 1995; Rimm-Kaufman et al. 2000.
4. Gormley et al. 2004.
5. Bowman et al. 2001.
6. Bryant et al. 2003.
7. Burchinal and Ramey 1989; Layzer et al. 1993; Campbell and Ramey 1994; National Academy Press 1990.
8. Howes and Hamilton 1993.
9. Karoly 2005.
10. Reynolds et al. 2001.
11. Berruta-Clement et al. 1984; Schweinhart and Weikart 1997; Reynolds et al. 2001.
12. Heckman 2006.
13. Karoly and Bigelow 2005.
14. Schnur and Koffler 1995.
15. American Academy of Pediatrics et al. 2002.
16. Goelman and Pence 1987.
17. Kontos 1994.
18. Kontos et al. 1995.
19. Burchinal et al. 2002.
20. Galinsky, Howes, and Kontos 1995.
21. Fischer and Eheart 1991.
22. Katz et al. 1990.

The Home-Based Child Care Provider: Roles and Relationships

*A*S WITH ALL EARLY CHILDHOOD EDUCATORS, home-based child care providers serve in multiple roles: as caregivers, teachers, and family partners. But as a home-based provider, you care for children in the warmth and comfort of a home setting, frequently overseeing children of different ages with varied strengths, needs, and interests. You have the opportunity to form close relationships with each child—or, if you are related to the children in your care, to strengthen family ties. You also have the opportunity to encourage children's learning and to strengthen partnerships with the families of the children in your care.

As a *caregiver*, your relationships with children and their families lay the foundation for much of their experiences in your home. You have the opportunity to create a warm, nurturing environment that supports children's social, emotional, cognitive, and physical development. To be effective, you need to enjoy young children, and you need many talents: observation skills, imagination, creativity, the ability to listen, and the ability to identify and support each child's unique needs and interests.

You also serve as a *teacher* to the children in your care. To be an effective teacher, it is important to address all areas of a child's development: cognitive (thinking) skills; language and literacy; and social, emotional, and physical development. Whether children learn about liquids and solids during sand and water play or increase their language skills through rhyming and word-play activities, it is important to watch their progress toward the learning goals you set for them. By observing children's progress, you will know when to make changes to your home setting and when to change your efforts to help the children learn. Teachers must adjust their styles and expectations based on each child's abilities and development—especially when caring for children in mixed-age groups, who learn in different ways and at different speeds. Throughout this publication you will find discussion about the differences in teaching and caring for children in mixed-age groups.

Finally, you are a *partner* with the families of the children in your care. An effective home-based child care provider works with the whole family as well as with the individual child. As you visit with family members when children are dropped off and picked up each day, and during other activities that include families, there are many opportunities for genuine partnerships to develop. Families can provide helpful insights and share information to support their child's growth and development.

The Home-Based Child Care Provider as Caregiver

Why Is This Important?

As a *caregiver,* you set the emotional climate of your home setting. The quality of your relationships with the children will help shape how they learn and feel about themselves, other people, and the world at large. Through relationships, children learn about themselves, about other people's feelings and expectations, and about the importance of cooperation and sharing. Home-based providers often care for the same children over extended time periods—in some instances, several years—and therefore have an opportunity to provide the continuity of care that is essential to children's emotional well-being.

Remember That Young Children . . .

- Who have positive relationships with caregivers make easier transitions from home to child care.
- Who have positive, nurturing relationships with caregivers are confident and secure when exploring new situations and when facing learning challenges.
- Who have nurturing relationships and responsive social environments have a better chance of succeeding in school.
- Benefit from ongoing care provided by a nurturing child care provider.

Keys to Effective Home-Based Child Care

- Be sincere and comfortable with children and enjoy their company.
- Demonstrate that you care about each child, and show affection in ways that take into consideration the uniqueness of each child.
- Look at daily learning activities and routines as opportunities to strengthen bonds with children and to provide individual attention.
- Understand that caring and teaching are closely related.

Considerations When Infants and Toddlers Are Present

Responsive care for infants and toddlers means following each child's unique rhythms and styles in order to promote well-being and a healthy sense of self. Successful caregivers adapt their expectations of, and interaction with, each child accordingly. While responsive caregiving is important for all age groups, it is especially important for infants and toddlers.

As stated previously, many home-based providers and children stay together for several years. All children—especially infants and toddlers—benefit from enduring relationships with responsive caregivers.

14

CHAPTER 1
The Home-Based
Child Care Provider:
Roles and
Relationships

The Home-Based
Child Care Provider
as Caregiver

1. Create a caring and nurturing environment where positive social and emotional development can take place.
2. Use caregiving routines as opportunities to meet children's social, emotional, and physical needs and to respond to their interests and abilities.

THE HOME-BASED CHILD CARE PROVIDER AS CAREGIVER

Create a caring and nurturing environment where positive social and emotional development can take place.

Make sure that all children—including those who have cultural backgrounds that are different from yours—feel cared for and safe. Create an environment of cooperation and mutual respect, showing children positive ways to resolve conflicts. Ask yourself what it would feel like to be a child in your home, and remember to be sensitive to cultural and language differences. Communicate with family members about ways to help children feel at ease in your home.

Social and emotional development are central to a child's learning capacity. The children in your care will learn best if they feel safe and comfortable with you, their caregiver, and when their physical needs are met.

Practices That Promote Nurturing Environments

- Remember that your words and actions show children that you enjoy being with them.
- Show affection for each child in ways that are comfortable for you and the child.
- Communicate with each child's family members about their beliefs and practices in order to better understand and provide for every child.
- Think about ways to express that you care about and respect all children.
- Respond to a child's crying as quickly and effectively as possible.
- Help children understand their emotions by giving names to feelings: *"That really seems to make you happy,"* or *"You seem angry right now."*

When infants and toddlers are present

Although all children need unhurried time, infants and toddlers need more time than older children for each activity.

15

CHAPTER 1
The Home-Based
Child Care Provider:
Roles and
Relationships

The Home-Based
Child Care Provider
as Caregiver

Active Listening with Children[*]

Listening carefully and nonjudgmentally to children helps validate their thoughts and feelings and contributes to their self-esteem. By listening attentively, you model a very important way of relating positively to others. This is a skill children learn best by example.

Active listening involves responding with body language—especially facial expressions—in addition to words. Your facial expressions can show children that you are listening carefully, responding to the thoughts and feelings behind a child's words. One way to demonstrate active listening is to drop to a child's height and maintain eye contact.

There are three steps in the active-listening process:

1. **Receive the message.** The child sends a message in words, manner, tone, or body expression: "I'm going to the library this weekend!"

2. **Reflect the message.** You reflect the feelings or thoughts behind the message and check to see if you are correct: "You seem to be pretty excited about going to the library with your dad." This tells the child that you are listening carefully.

3. **Confirm the message.** The child affirms your feedback ("Yes, I love the library!"), or denies it and tries to send a clearer message ("No, I don't like the library"). This helps you confirm exactly what the child is telling you.

---

*Adapted from Chalufour et al. 1988.

2

THE HOME-BASED CHILD CARE PROVIDER AS CAREGIVER

Use caregiving routines as opportunities to meet children's social, emotional, and physical needs and to respond to their interests and abilities.

Routines are consistent, repeated approaches to caregiving and other activities. For children, routines are a vital part of the day. The predictability of routines comforts children, makes it easier for them to trust their caregiver, and supports cooperative behavior. For example, knowing what to expect during arrival and pickup times, or during meals and naptimes, can be very calming for children. Even the language that accompanies a routine—for instance, *"Let's put all the toys away before we eat lunch"*—can reinforce a child's trust in his or her caregiver.

Having a routine doesn't necessarily mean that an activity occurs at the same time each day. As a home-based child care provider, you may have a different schedule each day, but your basic routines for approaching activities should be consistent. Approach routines with a positive attitude and

16

CHAPTER 1
The Home-Based
Child Care Provider:
Roles and
Relationships

The Home-Based
Child Care Provider
as Caregiver

know that they are important times for learning, sharing, and building trust. Because caregiving routines require close contact, they provide opportunities for one-to-one connections with each child every day.

Practices That Facilitate Caregiving Routines

- View routines as opportunities to nurture all children, to be sensitive to their individual needs, and to listen, learn, share, and care.
- Think of routines as chances to have one-to-one communication, to establish cooperative relationships, and to help each child feel a sense of connection and belonging in your home.

Examples of routines that may help daily activities run more smoothly

- Humming the same lullaby each time you diaper a baby
- Hanging up jackets on individual coat hooks and saying each child's name when doing so
- Asking children to sing a special song as they go to the bathroom to brush their teeth
- Singing a song before meals
- Providing special "quiet time" books for children who finish their meals before others
- Washing hands after toileting
- Reading a story before naptimes
- Greeting family members upon arrival and departure

When infants and toddlers are present

- Respond to their interest in personal-care routines and allow them to be active participants. For example, wait for toddlers to raise their arms before changing their shirts.
- Make sure that older children are engaged in safe play, in places where you can observe them, while tending to younger children's more frequent needs.
- Encourage older children to assist with caregiving routines for younger children. For example, if a preschooler is interested in helping, he can do so in small ways such as getting a clean diaper from the infant's bag or by showing a younger child how to wash her hands.
- Take advantage of younger children's more frequent naps to work with older children on learning activities.

The Home-Based Child Care Provider as Teacher

Why Is This Important?

Everyone who interacts with a young child is in some sense a *teacher.* The more you know about how children grow and learn, the more you will be able to take advantage of teachable moments that occur each day.

Having information about how well the children in your care are progressing can help you plan your day. You want the children in your care to feel successful and confident, but you also want to offer experiences that will help them develop further. In addition, by communicating with family members and by monitoring the children's progress, you can identify children with special needs or challenges.

Remember That Young Children . . .

- Are individuals with different capacities and learning styles.
- Are active and self-motivated learners.
- Thrive and grow in environments that foster their individual skills, learning abilities, and developmental progress.

Keys to Effective Home-Based Child Care

- Strive to create an environment that is interesting but not overwhelming. Develop learning experiences that are challenging but not frustrating.
- Pay attention to learning activities and experiences that are especially engaging for children, and note the ways in which a particular activity may be frustrating.
- Be familiar with different observation methods that help you understand the progress and development of individual children and of the group, and that increase your understanding of children's interests and abilities.
- Learn more about child development by attending conferences, reading, taking courses, and participating in other training opportunities.
- Recognize the importance of face-to-face interaction as opposed to more one-sided modes of communication such as television and computer usage.

Considerations When Infants and Toddlers Are Present

Infants and toddlers do not separate teaching from caregiving—and you do not have to separate those activities, either. Teaching and caregiving often occur simultaneously. When you read a book to a toddler or give a bottle to an infant in your arms, the child is learning. The manner in which you listen to and respond to the child and match the child's pace are important aspects of caregiving and teaching. A toddler may learn that reading is

18

CHAPTER 1
The Home-Based
Child Care Provider:
Roles and
Relationships

The Home-Based
Child Care Provider
as Teacher

pleasurable, and an infant may learn that gazing into your eyes and listening to your voice while drinking milk is reassuring and comforting.

To facilitate learning among infants and toddlers, observe their behavior and interests. Provide materials and spaces that match their interests. Avoid activities that require infants and toddlers to perform specific tasks, and limit efforts to guide their play unless they need redirection for safety reasons. Instead, encourage natural curiosity by observing infants and toddlers and by letting them follow their own interests.

GUIDELINES IN THIS SECTION

1. Understand children's needs and capabilities. Pay attention to their behavior to provide responsive, individualized care.
2. Honor and encourage each child's curiosity and creativity, and make learning fun.
3. Balance adult-initiated and child-initiated learning activities and experiences.
4. Observe children regularly to support their growth and development.
5. Observe children in natural and familiar settings and during routines. Use multiple sources of information to get a complete picture of each child.
6. Keep families informed about, and involved in, observations and records of their children.

THE HOME-BASED CHILD CARE PROVIDER AS TEACHER

Understand children's needs and capabilities. Pay attention to their behavior to provide responsive, individualized care.

Understanding how young children think, feel, and reason is critical. When you give children interesting problems and learning experiences, you are helping them develop their cognitive (thinking) skills. Learn about young children by observing them, by talking with family members, and by participating in informal and formal education. Set realistic expectations of what children can do. Carefully prepare the learning environment and be responsive to children's natural curiosity about the world.

Not all children will be ready for an activity at the same time. Know when children need time to play by themselves and when the emphasis should be on cooperating within a group. Give children the time they need to watch, think about, and approach new experiences while you provide security and appropriate support. Respect each child's need to move away from an activity, approach it in a new way, or be encouraged to continue. Recognize that the goal is not just to get children to do what *you* want them

19

CHAPTER 1
The Home-Based
Child Care Provider:
Roles and
Relationships

The Home-Based
Child Care Provider
as Teacher

to do; children have different abilities, so it is more important to understand what children can and need to do at any particular time.

Practices That Foster Understanding

- Use a variety of learning approaches—such as experimentation, inquiry, play, and exploration—to guide children's learning.
- Help children become self-motivated thinkers by asking open-ended questions and by inviting follow-up comments or questions.
- Recognize signs of stress in children's behavior, communicate with family members about your observations, and respond in ways that help children reduce stress.
- Know that trial and error nurture and encourage creativity; however, some children may need help if they have made several unsuccessful attempts to solve a problem.
- Observe a child at various times of the day—when the child is alone, with others, at play, during routines, and during transitions.
- Reflect on your observations. Use them to guide your interaction with each child.
- Be aware of individual differences in children. Some children "look before leaping," and others leap first. When a child chooses to watch an activity, that can be a form of participation.
- Remember that children's learning is multisensory; understand that some children may learn more easily by hearing rather than seeing, or vice versa.

When infants and toddlers are present

- Respond to their nonverbal cues (gaze, moods, body movements) and notice the way they respond to your verbal and nonverbal cues.
- Understand that they may need more time than older children to think about what you have said and to respond to you.
- Remember that some two-year-olds may look physically like three-year-olds, but you should not expect younger children to act older than they are. For example, it is not realistic to expect two-year-olds to sit for extended periods or to stay seated at table activities designed for older children.

THE HOME-BASED CHILD CARE PROVIDER AS TEACHER

Honor and encourage each child's curiosity and creativity, and make learning fun.

Young children are active learners who are naturally curious about their environment, and there are many ways to support them as they learn. Observe children's behavior (including verbal and nonverbal cues) to learn

20

CHAPTER 1
The Home-Based
Child Care Provider:
Roles and
Relationships

The Home-Based
Child Care Provider
as Teacher

about their interests. Encourage them to learn about and try new activities. Ask them to make several attempts to solve a problem before they seek help—for example, when working on a challenging puzzle or art project. Teach children appropriate ways to express frustration if they have difficulty accomplishing tasks; after all, learning how to handle frustration is an important life skill. You can help children enjoy and expand their interests, develop creativity and persistence, and learn new skills.

Practices That Encourage Curiosity and Creativity

- Observe children to learn about their interests. Provide opportunities for them to explore those interests.
- Establish special times when children can ask questions. This can help nurture their curiosity.
- Provide time when children can share and talk about items that are important to them.
- Schedule regular "listening time." Tell stories to the children, have them listen to music, and offer them opportunities to tell their own stories or talk about personal experiences.
- Encourage children to create new things from familiar materials. For instance, you could have the children use milk cartons, tape, and magic markers to make pretend cameras.
- Plan long-term projects. Some examples are watering seeds regularly, recording plant growth on a chart each day, and using an outdoor thermometer to record daily temperatures.

When infants and toddlers are present

- Encourage older children to observe and respect infants' and toddlers' choices and interests.
- Allow infants and toddlers to follow their own rhythms of focus and interest. As long as they are safe, avoid interrupting their concentration as they play and explore.

More "face time," less "screen time"

The American Academy of Pediatrics states that even one hour of screen time (watching television and DVDs, playing video games, or using computers) per day is a lot for preschoolers.[1] Television viewing in childhood and adolescence is associated with poor fitness, smoking, being overweight, and elevated cholesterol in adulthood.[2] Furthermore, children who watch television violence may become numb to violence, accept violence as a way to solve problems, imitate what they see, or identify with victims or victimizers.[3] Positive, loving interaction between you and the children in your care is a good way for the children to envision a peaceful, nurturing world.

21

CHAPTER 1
The Home-Based
Child Care Provider:
Roles and
Relationships

The Home-Based
Child Care Provider
as Teacher

THE HOME-BASED CHILD CARE PROVIDER AS TEACHER

3 Balance adult-initiated and child-initiated learning activities and experiences.

It is important to offer a balance between adult-initiated and child-initiated activities. A planned art project is an example of an adult-initiated activity. Child-initiated activities—for example, playing with building blocks during free time—are chosen and started by children. When planning and implementing learning activities for young children, ask yourself how much direct involvement, guidance, or explicit instruction is needed to make the activity most beneficial for children's learning. Your plans may be influenced by the nature of each activity; the personality, skills, and interests of the children involved; or even the time of day.

Practices That Promote a Balance of Activities

- Understand that, depending on the child's age and developmental level, only minimal guidance may be necessary for many open-ended activities.
- Make sure materials are safe and age-appropriate and that there is always adult supervision.
- Be flexible. An activity that started out as child-initiated may need your guidance if children have difficulty focusing on or understanding what to do. Similarly, an adult-initiated activity may turn into a child-initiated activity once the children's understanding and comfort level grow.
- Give children opportunities throughout the day to make choices and explore their own interests.
- Build relationships with children through positive interaction.

When infants and toddlers are present

Remember that adult-initiated activities consist of many daily caregiving routines. Diapering, mealtimes, and other daily events provide opportunities for cooperation and closeness with a child.

4 THE HOME-BASED CHILD CARE PROVIDER AS TEACHER
Observe children regularly to support their growth and development.

The primary goal of observation and documentation in a home-based setting is to understand and support all areas of a child's development. Make objective observations. Be sure to avoid labeling or categorizing children, because doing so is risky and can seriously limit the children's opportunities to reach their potential.

22

CHAPTER 1
The Home-Based
Child Care Provider:
Roles and
Relationships

The Home-Based
Child Care Provider
as Teacher

Practices That Facilitate Observation and Documentation

- Understand that observing children's behavior is an important part of early care and education.
- Ensure that observation is a daily practice. Observe children at different points throughout the day—during group and individual play, routines and caregiving activities, and transition times.
- Use your observations to plan activities that enhance the developmental progress and school readiness of individual children. Make changes based on what you learn over time.
- Collect samples of children's drawings, paintings, and writing.
- Try different ways of recording your observations to determine what works best for you. For instance, you might use a notepad, digital recorder, or camera.
- Discuss your observations with the child's family.
- Watch for signs of developmental problems, and know where and how to refer families to specialists for a complete assessment or evaluation when appropriate.
- Talk with other providers about alternative strategies for observing children.
- Participate in training that covers different ways to observe children. Contact resource and referral (R&R) agencies, family child care associations, or community colleges to find out about training opportunities.

5 THE HOME-BASED CHILD CARE PROVIDER AS TEACHER

Observe children in natural and familiar settings and during routines. Use multiple sources of information to get a complete picture of each child.

Note how children behave when they are alone, with other children, with their families, and with you throughout the day—during active and free play, organized activities, and caregiving routines. Setting up activities just for the sake of observation can make children feel that they are being tested, and watching them in new or unfamiliar environments may frighten them or prevent them from behaving normally. Additionally, children may behave differently in other homes and environments than they do in your home. Getting input from different people involved in a child's life will provide the most complete and balanced picture of each child's development.

Practices for Gathering Information About Children

- Learn about children by carefully watching them, listening to them, and studying their work.
  - Ask children questions that encourage them to describe what they are thinking.

23

CHAPTER 1
The Home-Based
Child Care Provider:
Roles and
Relationships

The Home-Based
Child Care Provider
as Teacher

- Listen to them as they talk with others informally and when they speak during group discussions.
- Study the work (projects, writing, drawings) of preschool-age children. Ask them to tell you about their work; for example, you might ask, *"Can you tell me a story about this colorful picture you've drawn?"*

- Ask parents and family members what their children do at home, what they see as their children's strengths, and if they have any concerns.
- Use different sources of information to answer questions about the child's development; include your observations, the family's observations, examples of the child's work, and other sources.
- Talk with families about how you observe and track children's progress and school readiness. Discuss any concerns you might have in a gentle, nonthreatening manner—away from the children.
- Treat children's information with respect and confidentiality.

When infants and toddlers are present

Notice how the younger children handle problems that arise (e.g., how they retrieve dropped toys, get around obstacles, or move around other children in small spaces).

Early Warning Signs That a Child in Your Care May Need Help*

A preschool-age child who exhibits any of the following behavior may need help:

✓ Does not pay attention or stay focused on an activity for as long a time as other children of the same age

✓ Avoids or rarely makes eye contact with others

✓ Gets unusually frustrated when trying to do simple tasks that most children of the same age can do

✓ Often acts out; appears to be very stubborn or aggressive

✓ Acts extremely shy or withdrawn

✓ Does not like to be touched

✓ Treats other children, animals, or objects cruelly or destructively

✓ Tends to break things frequently

✓ Displays violent behavior (e.g., tantrums, screaming, fighting, or hitting other children) on a regular basis

✓ Stares into space, rocks body, or talks to self more often than other children of the same age

✓ Often bangs head against an object, floor, or wall

---

*Adapted from California Department of Education 1999a.

24

CHAPTER 1
The Home-Based
Child Care Provider:
Roles and
Relationships

The Home-Based
Child Care Provider
as Teacher

Early Warning Signs That a Child in Your Care May Need Help
(continued)

✓ Does not recognize dangerous situations such as walking in traffic or jumping from high places

✓ Tends to be sick often; complains of headaches or stomachaches

✓ Has sleeping, feeding, eating, or toileting problems

✓ Is overly impulsive, active, or distractable

✓ Does not respond to discipline as well as children of the same age

✓ Has difficulty putting thoughts, actions, and movements together

✓ Does not seek approval from family members or caregivers

If you observe a preschooler with any of these warning signs, keep notes on the child's behavior. Discuss your observations with the child's family; Appendix C ("Talking with Parents When Concerns Arise") presents an in-depth look at how to do that. If appropriate, the family can contact their local school district or the special education program of their county office of education. Representatives of these agencies may schedule an assessment to see if the child qualifies for services. The child's parents or legal guardians must give written permission for the child to be tested and to receive special education. All services are confidential and provided at no cost to the family. For further information, contact the California Department of Education's Special Education Division at 916-445-4613.

A child from birth to age three who exhibits any of the following behavior may need help:

✓ By age six months, rarely makes sounds like cooing or gurgling

✓ Is unusually quiet

✓ Does not shake head to indicate "no"

✓ By age one, does not say mama or dada

✓ By age two, rarely names family members and/or common objects

✓ By age two, does not speak in two-word phrases

✓ By age two, does not point to objects or people to express wants or needs

✓ By age three, does not follow simple directions or speak in three- or four-word sentences

✓ By age three, does not know last name, gender, or common rhymes

If you have concerns about a child who is under age three, call the California Department of Developmental Services (DDS) at 1-800-515-2229. You will be provided with information on resources in your community such as the Family Resource Center or the nearest DDS regional center. For a directory of regional centers, visit the following DDS Web site: http://www.dds.ca.gov/rc/rclist.cfm.

25

CHAPTER 1
The Home-Based
Child Care Provider:
Roles and
Relationships

The Home-Based
Child Care Provider
as Teacher

6 THE HOME-BASED CHILD CARE PROVIDER AS TEACHER

Keep families informed about, and involved in, observations and records of their children.

Parents and family members need to be fully informed and aware of the observations and documentation being kept at the child care setting. Remember that these records are protected by privacy laws and must be kept confidential. Information about the child's behavior at home and in other places outside your child care home should be sought from family members, as this knowledge can be helpful when making observations.

It is often difficult to deal with families and parents who are facing the possibility that their child has a disability or other special needs. Families tend to be very protective of their children and therefore should be respected and handled delicately. You may wish to consult with professionals and other home-based child care providers for guidance on how to talk with families so each child's unique needs can be addressed. Additionally, Appendix C provides helpful information on this topic.

Practices That Promote Two-Way Communication with Families

- Talk with families about your observations of their children, and be sure to mention each child's strengths.
- Talk with families about their observations of their children; ask them what they feel is unique about their children and whether they have any concerns about their children's development.
- Use your observations (and each family's) to try various approaches to learning and communicating—and discuss each child's progress with family members.
- Establish a "cubby" or special place for each child where families can view their children's artwork and other projects. Additionally, display artwork in other places where children and their family members can see it.
- Consider different ways of sharing information. Daily communication may be convenient, but it is inappropriate and disrespectful to discuss observations in front of a child. Weekly or biweekly e-mail updates that can be read in private may be better options.
- Listen to each family's comments, concerns, and observations. Families will appreciate this.
- Contact your local R&R agency and community college about classes and workshops covering appropriate instruments, techniques, and observation methods for all children—including children with disabilities or other special needs.

The Home-Based Child Care Provider as Family Partner

Why Is This Important?

Part of your job as a home-based child care provider is to serve as a *family partner.* It is important to develop a sense of collaboration between you and each child's family members; when you have good rapport with a child's family, the child is more likely to feel secure in your home and enjoy positive experiences while in your care.

Some families may feel threatened by their children's connection to you. However, most families appreciate exchanging ideas, insights, and news with someone who is closely involved with their child because it positively influences the child's growth and development. You can help families prepare their children for future school success—but as a caregiver, your role is to supplement the parental role, not replace it.

Keys to Effective Home-Based Child Care

- Honor cultural differences and communicate closely with families to learn about their beliefs, values, and desires for their children. You play an important role in making family members feel welcome and in learning from them about their children.
- Share with families your knowledge of appropriate learning activities and experiences for children. Emphasize the many ways in which children's interaction with adults at home can enhance school achievement.
- Encourage family members to become involved with the child care home and to form and strengthen relationships with you.

Considerations When Infants and Toddlers Are Present

Caring for infants and toddlers frequently causes heightened emotions in family members and caregivers. The intense desire to protect young children can sometimes cause a family to feel that a provider is not doing a good job of caring for their child—or vice versa. Because of these protective urges, make time for frequent two-way conversations with family members about their feelings, ideas, and concerns regarding their child. When conflicts arise, gather from the family as much information as possible before reacting. Take time to think about solutions, and ask other child care providers for feedback and suggestions.

GUIDELINES IN THIS SECTION

1. Encourage families to talk with you about their ideas for supporting their children's learning and about working with you to prepare their children for school.

27

CHAPTER 1
The Home-Based
Child Care Provider:
Roles and
Relationships

The Home-Based
Child Care Provider
as Family Partner

2. Create an environment in which families feel comfortable about speaking up for their children.

3. Share information with families about activities and experiences in your home, and encourage them to continue these activities in their homes.

4. Establish partnerships with families to strengthen what children learn about math, reading, science, motor skills, and the arts.

5. Recognize that family members and adults other than parents may play a role in promoting children's development.

6. Support families in other ways, especially by connecting them with resources in their communities.

THE HOME-BASED CHILD CARE PROVIDER AS FAMILY PARTNER
Encourage families to talk with you about their ideas for supporting their children's learning and about working with you to prepare their children for school.

A successful way to involve families is to ask for and discuss their ideas for supporting their children's education, and to work together to prepare the children for school. Working with family members to define shared goals helps strengthen the partnership between you and each family. When there are cultural and language differences, work together to find ways to communicate. It is important to recognize differences in communication styles and to communicate openly with families about cultural practices.

Practices for Collaborating with Families to Support Children's Learning

- Acknowledge that families have goals for their children and strategies to achieve those goals. Recognize that every family is part of a larger social and cultural context. Be aware of your own beliefs and values as you communicate with families.

- Make it clear to parents and family members that you understand and respect their goals and concerns. This does not mean you must implement whatever a family desires. In some cases, you may need to negotiate with families to reach agreement on specific points.

- Ask families to share the ways they provide care and promote learning at home. For example, if a mother sings a particular lullaby to her children before they fall asleep, ask her to teach you the song. Incorporate the families' positive approaches to caregiving and learning to ensure consistency between your home and the children's homes. This is particularly important when children are not yet able to talk or to share what they do at home.

28

CHAPTER 1
The Home-Based
Child Care Provider:
Roles and
Relationships

The Home-Based
Child Care Provider
as Family Partner

- Set up regular times for in-depth discussions with families. If pickup times are not convenient for those discussions, you might try a different method such as calling family members in the evening.
- Consider each family's concerns and beliefs when setting up learning activities and experiences.
- Respect each family's concerns and beliefs about using different materials. For example, to accommodate families who do not want their children to get dirty, you might provide smocks or large shirts for the children. As another example, some families believe it is wasteful to create artwork from food. You could provide substitute materials to accommodate those families.
- Share with families your observations about their children. Provide feedback about the children's projects and activities.
- Make communication logs easily accessible so family members can share information or offer suggestions. Be sure to protect the confidentiality of these records.

THE HOME-BASED CHILD CARE PROVIDER AS FAMILY PARTNER

Create an environment in which families feel comfortable about speaking up for their children.

In order for families to feel included and empowered, you must be able to communicate and collaborate effectively, have confidence in each other, and perceive each other as caring individuals dedicated to the well-being of children.

Practices to Help Families Feel Included and Empowered

- Establish trust with family members by learning about each family's cultural and other preferences and by incorporating those preferences into daily care and education. Work with families to ensure you provide care and education that is culturally consistent with what the child is learning at home.
- Acknowledge parents and family members as individuals, and greet them and their children each day.
- Encourage families to visit your home at any mutually acceptable time.
- Encourage family members to share their areas of expertise with the other children and families in your care.
- Solicit help from families when addressing problems that their children may be having in your child care setting.
- Invite families to participate in some of the learning activities and experiences you offer to their children.
- Talk with family members regularly—not just when you have problems with a child. Make space and time available for private, one-on-one meetings.

29

CHAPTER 1
The Home-Based
Child Care Provider:
Roles and
Relationships

The Home-Based
Child Care Provider
as Family Partner

- Establish and communicate appropriate limits so that your needs and those of your family are respected and valued.
- Work to establish a routine that is satisfactory for each family and for you.

 **3 THE HOME-BASED CHILD CARE PROVIDER AS FAMILY PARTNER**

Share information with families about activities and experiences in your home, and encourage them to continue these activities in their homes.

The key to building successful partnerships with families is to share the educational information and ideas that are important to you. Regular communication with the child's family will help reinforce and support what the children learn in your home.

Practices That Educate and Inform Families

- Inform families regularly about the purpose and benefits of the learning activities and experiences in your home.
- Suggest a variety of information and resources for parent and family education—in various media (print, audio, video) and in the home languages of each family, if applicable.
- Make the environment welcoming to families, with displays of schedules, recent learning activities and experiences, or planned activities.
- Send newsletters, notes, or e-mails to family members to inform them about what their children are doing and learning.
- Show family members that you support their relationships with their children. For instance, you could place photos of family members in play areas.

When infants and toddlers are present

Inform families that infants and toddlers will be involved in daily activities but will participate differently than older children. Infants and toddlers will be allowed to join activities at their own pace and according to their unique developmental stages.

30

CHAPTER 1
The Home-Based
Child Care Provider:
Roles and
Relationships

The Home-Based
Child Care Provider
as Family Partner

THE HOME-BASED CHILD CARE PROVIDER AS FAMILY PARTNER

Establish partnerships with families to strengthen what children learn about math, reading, science, motor skills, and the arts.

Discuss with families age-appropriate expectations for learning math, language and literacy, science, health, physical activity, and the arts. Communicate regularly with each family about their child's progress and the ways they can support learning in all of the domains.

Practices That Foster Partnerships to Support Learning

- Offer letters, newsletters, or other materials to families so they can help their children with preschool concepts.
- Encourage parents and family members to talk with their children about ideas in math, reading, science, physical development, and the arts—and to share information with each other and with you about how they support each of these domains of learning at home.
- Talk with families about activities that their children enjoy so that these activities can be repeated and reinforced at home—for example, by using music activities to teach art appreciation and math concepts, by setting the table to teach counting and shapes, and so on.
- Ask families to participate in activities in your home so they will know how to repeat the activities in their homes.
- Provide families with regular updates about their children's progress and development in all areas.

When infants and toddlers are present

Inform families that younger children's interests and abilities are just as important as those of older children. Younger children learn in different ways and at a different pace than older children, but they still learn concepts in each of these areas.

THE HOME-BASED CHILD CARE PROVIDER AS FAMILY PARTNER

Recognize that family members and adults other than parents may play a role in promoting children's development.

In many cases, children—even if they live with their parents—receive some care from relatives or other adults, and they may have most of their daily interaction with siblings. Regardless of who serves as the primary caregiver, members of the extended family may be important sources of guidance, information, and support.

31

CHAPTER 1
The Home-Based
Child Care Provider:
Roles and
Relationships

The Home-Based
Child Care Provider
as Family Partner

Practices That Promote Inclusion of All Family Members

- Be careful about how you refer to children's families, and do not assume that all families are alike. To become more familiar with a family situation, talk informally with whoever brings the child to the program in the morning. These conversations may lead to written communication or telephone conversations with appropriate family members and other caregivers when necessary.
- Acknowledge the variety of family structures by:
  - Identifying the child's primary caregiver(s).
  - Inviting all significant family members to participate in daily routines and special events.
  - Recognizing how siblings and other family members may be engaging in informal educational experiences with the child at home.
  - Demonstrating acceptance of all types of family groupings and using educational materials that include nontraditional families.
  - Gathering information about families at initial meetings.

6 THE HOME-BASED CHILD CARE PROVIDER AS FAMILY PARTNER
Support families in other ways, especially by connecting them with resources in their communities.

When families are successful at meeting their children's basic needs for food, shelter, and clothing, they are more likely to support their children's learning. You have the opportunity to support families by linking them with resources in their communities.

Practices That Support Families in Other Ways

- View your role as serving the child's whole family.
- Know how to obtain current information about relevant community programs and services for families, and know how to make appropriate referrals.
- Inform families about local opportunities for young children—such as story time at a library, educational opportunities, and recreational programs offered at parks and community centers.
- Share information about educational opportunities for parents and family members, such as gaining literacy skills, earning a general educational development (GED) credential, finding employment, or becoming skilled in the use of technology.*
- Make space available to place or hang pictures of children with their families.

*A *GED credential* is the official term for what people often refer to as "a GED." For more information about GED credentials, visit the American Council on Education Web site at http://www.acenet.edu/.

32

CHAPTER 1
The Home-Based
Child Care Provider:
Roles and
Relationships

The Home-Based
Child Care Provider
as Family Partner

Helping Families Enter Child Care*

Visits with families and their children are opportunities to get acquainted

- Observe family members and their children as they interact.

- Let family members and their children observe you as you interact with the other children in your care.

- Let children observe you as you engage in friendly conversation with their parents or other family members.

- When meeting a child for the first time, make some safe, indirect contact with the child. For example, you might offer a toy or food.

Interviews with parents and family members clarify expectations

- Find out how each child is cared for at home.

- Explain how you provide basic care and how you deal with crying, biting, and so on.

- Lay a foundation for open communication.

The entry interview is a time to solidify agreements

- Review your home's child care policies.

- Make a transition plan. Does a child need several preliminary visits before coming to child care regularly? Could the child stay for only an hour or two on his or her first day? When and how should part-time care become full-time?

- Review ways in which families and their children can prepare for a transition to child care.

Tips for handling the first day

- Have a special place, or "cubby," for each child's belongings. An individual welcome sign (for instance, on a chalkboard) is a nice touch, too.

- Invite the family members to sit with their child but not to entertain the child or other children. This will ease the transition from the family's care to your care.

- When a child first arrives, avoid direct eye contact, touching, and talking directly to the child.

- Talk with the family member(s). Use the child's name (pronounced correctly) while remaining at a respectable distance.

- Offer a toy and use it as a common focus or bridge between you and the child.

*Adapted from Zetes 1998.

33

CHAPTER 1
The Home-Based
Child Care Provider:
Roles and
Relationships

The Home-Based
Child Care Provider
as Family Partner

- Help the family member(s) recognize an appropriate time to say good-bye.
- Help the child close the door or say good-bye from a window.
- Be available to hold and comfort the child.

Help parents and family members with the separation from their children

- Separation can be very emotional for parents and family members.
- If a child cries at the point of separation, some parents and family members worry. Other families worry if their children do not cry. Assure family members that crying is usually brief.
- Acknowledge how difficult it can be to leave a child.
- Make sure the family members understand how important it is to say good-bye and to say when they will return—to build the child's trust that family members will not leave them unexpectedly.
- Invite family members to telephone during the day to check in.
- When talking with parents and family members at pickup time, be honest about how the day went.
- Help each child reconnect with his or her family members at pickup time. Remind the children that their family members have returned as promised.

How to Balance Everyone's Needs When a New Baby Arrives

A new baby can bring a whirlwind of emotions to everyone in the child's family—and to the other children in your care. The new mother may feel proud, protective, excited, and anxious. Older siblings may feel a combination of pride, excitement, and jealousy. The other children in your care may feel curious, excited, and somewhat jealous as well. As a home-based child care provider you have an opportunity to make the arrival of a baby easier for everyone.

VIGNETTE

A New Baby Arrives in a Child Care Home

The new baby. Jed's new baby sister, 12-week-old Lina, is coming to Ms. Arnett's child care home for the first time this morning. Jed is three years old and has been coming to Ms. Arnett's child care home since he was as young as Lina. Jed is very excited about the other children seeing his baby sister for the first time. He feels proud and protective of Lina, and sometimes a little jealous of all the attention she gets. Lina's mom, Rhonda, hands the new baby to Ms. Arnett, who sits on a couch and holds the child.

34

CHAPTER 1
The Home-Based
Child Care Provider:
Roles and
Relationships

The Home-Based
Child Care Provider
as Family Partner

How to Balance Everyone's Needs When a New Baby Arrives
(continued)

The new mother. Rhonda is fussing with blankets and the baby's diaper bag as she gets ready to leave Lina for the first time. With tears in her eyes, Rhonda looks at Ms. Arnett and says, "It's not any easier with the second child!" Even though Rhonda has known Ms. Arnett for years and trusts her, she is still having a hard time this morning. Ms. Arnett understands that Rhonda has strong protective feelings for her children and doesn't take it personally that Rhonda seems concerned about her baby's safety. She pats Rhonda on the arm and says, "I promise you that I'll protect both of your children." Ms. Arnett smiles warmly and promises to call Rhonda at naptime to report on the morning.

The new big brother. Rhonda has a final request before she leaves: "Jed might want to help you with diapering Lina. He gets a little too excited, though, and sometimes I ask him to go play until I'm done changing her." Jed looks down at the baby and frowns a bit. Lina coos and smiles at Jed. He lights up and reaches out to touch his sister's face. Rhonda reaches out to stop him, but Ms. Arnett gently guides Jed's hand to Lina's shoulder. Jed and Ms. Arnett stroke Lina gently. Ms. Arnett asks Jed, "Do you think she likes that?" Jed nods his head. Then Ms. Arnett says, "Lina, do you like that when we touch you softly? Your mama and your brother love you so much!" Rhonda relaxes a bit and leans to kiss Jed and Lina good-bye.

The other children in the child care home. Because Ms. Arnett wants to help all the children see that Lina is a thinking, feeling person, she asks, "Lina, would you like to come outside and see our pretty garden?" Lina's eyes widen and she kicks her legs. Ms. Arnett nods to Lina, then turns to the other children and asks, "Do you think Lina would like to see the garden we planted?" The children respond quickly, each with a different answer: "She wants a bottle!" "She's too little!" "What if bugs hop on her?" Then Ms. Arnett says, "My goodness! What caring children you are! I think you will have lots of help from the children, Lina!" She turns to the older children and asks, "Is that right?" The children nod vigorously, with big smiles on their faces.

Notes

1. Healy 1998.
2. Hancox et al. 2004.
3. American Academy of Child and Adolescent Psychiatry 2002.

CHAPTER 2

The Home as a Caring and Learning Environment

*I*T IS IMPORTANT FOR YOU AND YOUR HOME ENVIRONMENT to make a positive first impression on the children and families in your care. Children and their families feel welcome when they are greeted with a warm smile; a clean, organized environment; and an assortment of engaging materials. One of your most important jobs is to create a home environment that helps children of different ages feel safe and comfortable. The surroundings should also show respect for the different cultures of the children in your care and should welcome children and families who have disabilities or other special needs.

Welcoming Children into a Safe and Healthy Home

Why Is This Important?

Your home environment can provide structure for children's experiences and can support routines throughout the day. A child-friendly home environment helps to limit disorganization and conflict and allows children to focus on specific learning activities. Establishing a safe, healthy, and organized home environment allows you to have more time for positive interaction with children as they play and learn.

Remember That Young Children . . .

- Experience a sense of belonging, order, and security in a safe, healthy, and organized home environment.
- Thrive in an environment that is safe for every developmental stage, which may differ from a child's chronological age.

Keys to Effective Home-Based Child Care

- *Physical space.* There should be enough space for all children, including those with physical challenges, to move freely and easily in your home.
- *Lighting and color.* Make sure there is plenty of light in your home. Appropriate colors (especially on walls) create a warm, cheerful, and welcoming atmosphere.
- *Texture.* Provide a variety of textures to create a stimulating environment for children. Toys, art supplies, furniture, floor coverings, animals, foods, and other items contribute different textures that heighten children's awareness of the world around them.
- *Visuals and sounds.* The sights and sounds in your home influence the way children learn and the way they interact with others. Strive to create an environment in which children are exposed to different types of visuals and sounds.
- *Sanitation.* Your home should be cleaned and sanitized frequently. It is especially important to clean bathrooms, eating and play areas, toys, and other materials used by the children in your care.
- *Safety.* Make sure your home is safe for everyone: for you, the children, and the children's family members.

Considerations When Infants and Toddlers Are Present

- Clean toys and surfaces regularly. This is especially critical for younger children, who often put objects in their mouths.
- Use low-pile carpets and secured rugs to provide safe, stable surfaces for children who are beginning to crawl and walk.

37

CHAPTER 2
The Home as a
Caring and Learning
Environment

Welcoming
Children into a
Safe and Healthy
Home

- Put away small objects that may present choking hazards to younger children.
- Be mindful of immunization requirements.
- Remember that the kitchen can be an especially dangerous area for infants and toddlers.
- Provide furniture, equipment, and materials that are safe and comfortable for infants and toddlers—for example, chairs that allow the children to rest their feet on the floor when sitting.

GUIDELINES IN THIS SECTION

1. Prepare and arrange your home in ways that welcome children and foster learning.
2. Focus on preventing illness and injuries.
3. Emphasize and model proper nutrition.
4. Provide interest areas, materials, and activities that are engaging and age-appropriate.

WELCOMING CHILDREN INTO A SAFE AND HEALTHY HOME
Prepare and arrange your home in ways that welcome children and foster learning.*

Every home has its own "feel," its own atmosphere—and your home's physical environment has a big impact on the quality of child care you provide. Young children need an environment that is carefully and thoughtfully organized. Your home should be inviting, functional, and free of clutter so the children will not be distracted easily. By paying attention to health and safety factors; the arrangement of space and furniture; the lighting, colors, and sounds in your home; and other elements; you can create a safe, comfortable environment that promotes learning.

Practices to Create a Welcoming Home That Facilitates Learning

- Provide as much fresh air and natural light as possible; both will help children stay alert and maintain good health.
- Make your home safe and welcoming for all children, including those who have special needs.
- Offer tidy, open, and well-organized spaces where children can play and interact with each other. Also, try to limit children's exposure to disruptive noise.
- Store toys and supplies where children will have easy access to them. Using low, open shelving is a good way to do this.

---

*Adapted from Zetes 1998.

38

CHAPTER 2
The Home as a
Caring and Learning
Environment

Welcoming
Children into a
Safe and Healthy
Home

- Arrange areas so that you can easily see or hear all children as they participate in activities.
- Make sure that the furniture, toys, and other materials in your home are sized appropriately for the children in your care.
- Use a variety of colors—for example, with wall paint, posters, and other materials—to create a cheerful atmosphere that appeals to the senses. Shades of blue and green can be very calming, while bright colors such as purple, orange, yellow, and red tend to be more stimulating.
- Create separate "interest areas" that offer a variety of learning opportunities. For example, you could set up areas offering age-appropriate activities in early reading and writing, art, science, and drama (pretend play). You can use crates, containers, tables, screens, and cupboards as area dividers.
- Provide comfortable seating in play areas. By including comfortable seats for adults, you can foster adult–child interaction.
- Check all usable space. Is there a room or an area in your home that could be converted into a play space? Will you allow children to have access to bedrooms for naps or playtime?
- Decide which rooms and areas in your home will be available to children and those that will be off-limits. Use safety latches or doorknob covers to close off rooms that you do not wish to use for child care. An extended portable gate (not an accordion type) can keep children out of areas that have no doors. Make sure the children and your family members are aware of the boundaries.
- Determine the extent to which your home will focus on child care. Some home-based child care providers choose to keep their home mainly as an adult-oriented environment that has basic childproofing and a few baskets of toys. Other providers create settings that are more child-centered. Ultimately, the way in which you balance living space and child care is a personal choice involving you and your family members.

When infants and toddlers are present

- Provide areas on the floor or ground where infants and toddlers can be safe and comfortable. Using mats, blankets, and rugs can be helpful.
- Make sure children have adequate space to move about freely and easily; doing so will help them learn how to use their bodies.
- Avoid using restrictive equipment such as swings, walkers, and infant seats.
- Designate an appropriate place in your home where mothers can nurse their babies.

39

CHAPTER 2
The Home as a
Caring and Learning
Environment

Welcoming
Children into a
Safe and Healthy
Home

2

WELCOMING CHILDREN INTO A SAFE AND HEALTHY HOME
Focus on preventing illness and injuries.

Health and safety considerations are an important part of every child care setting. As a home-based child care provider, it is important to teach and model appropriate health habits and practices and to provide a safe environment at all times. There are many steps you can take to protect the children in your care (and yourself) from infectious diseases and injuries. Some of those steps involve keeping your home clean, knowing how to handle and dispose of various materials, being familiar with first aid practices, and managing other aspects of your home's environment.

Practices That Promote Health and Safety

The following practices can help you limit the occurrence of illnesses and injuries in your home.

Sanitation

- Make sure that you and the children in your care practice frequent hand washing. Use soap and water, or alcohol-based hand sanitizers containing at least 60 percent alcohol. Wash hands after diapering or toileting children; before eating snacks and meals; after sneezing or blowing the nose; before and after administering first aid; after handling bodily fluids of any kind; and in other instances as appropriate.
- Regularly clean and disinfect bathrooms, toys, diapering areas, play areas, floors and other surfaces, bedding, and other materials that you and the children use each day.
- Dust and vacuum your home regularly to limit potential breathing problems, allergic reactions, or asthma attacks. Be sure to talk with families about any sensitivity or allergies their children may have (reactions to dust, pet hair, chemicals, and so on).

Handling and disposing of materials

- Wear protective, latex-free gloves when you come in contact with blood or bodily fluids that contain blood, or when children have cuts, scratches, or rashes involving breaks in the skin. Note that many adults and children are allergic to latex.
- Properly dispose of any items that come in contact with blood or other bodily fluids.
- Soft items such as diapers, bandages, clothing, and others can be disposed of in securely tied plastic bags. If a child's care requires sharp items such as lancets (for finger sticks), or needles and syringes, the items should be disposed of in hard-sided, OSHA-approved containers.

40

CHAPTER 2
The Home as a
Caring and Learning
Environment

Welcoming
Children into a
Safe and Healthy
Home

First aid

- Keep a readily accessible first aid kit. The kit should contain items such as sterile bandages and gauze pads, packets of antibiotic ointment and antiseptic wipes, an instant cold pack, first aid tape, scissors and tweezers, an oral thermometer, and a first aid instruction booklet. The first aid kit should be kept out of reach of children.
- Attend pediatric first aid training classes to learn how to handle incidents such as choking, fainting, cuts and scrapes, nosebleeds, and insect bites. Learning how to perform Rescue Breathing is especially valuable.*

Managing the physical environment

- Conduct daily health and safety checks of your home. Address any potential hazards that you find.
- Always provide adult supervision of the children in your care. Be sure that the level of supervision is appropriate for each child's age and developmental stage as well as for the activities that children are involved in. In addition, guide children in the safe use of outside toys and equipment.
- Keep all equipment and materials in good condition. Make sure items are clean, sturdy, and have no missing parts.
- Store all potentially dangerous items such as medications, cleaning supplies, and tools in secure locations where children cannot reach them.
- Cover electrical outlets, block off fireplaces, lock pool gates, and address any other potential hazards in your home.
- If you have pets, be aware that some children might be allergic to or fearful of them. Always ensure that the children's health and safety are your first priority.
- If you have plants in your home, make sure they are not poisonous.
- Do not smoke and do not drink alcohol while caring for children.

Other considerations

- Talk with families about when it is and when it is not acceptable for children with various illnesses and symptoms—such as colds, fevers, coughs, and so on—to be in your home. Be sure each parent or family member understands your expectations.
- Discuss with families the need for their children to receive regular health checkups. It is also a good idea for you to visit your doctor regularly.
- Protect your back against potential strain. Bend at your knees when lifting children or when picking up toys from the floor, and be sure to carry heavy objects close to your body. Additionally, stretch your muscles periodically.

*For more information about Rescue Breathing, visit the Centers for Disease Control and Prevention Web site: http://www.cdc.gov/.

41

CHAPTER 2
The Home as a
Caring and Learning
Environment

Welcoming
Children into a
Safe and Healthy
Home

When infants and toddlers are present

Remember that infants and toddlers are particularly vulnerable to communicable diseases. Take the following precautions to protect their health and safety while you care for them:

- When feeding solid foods to very young children, cut the food into bite-size pieces to prevent choking—and do not allow older children to share their food with younger children. Taking these steps will limit the spread of foodborne illnesses and will minimize choking hazards for the younger children.

- Change diapers in a safe, clean place where you can easily see or hear all of the other children in your care.

How Children Catch Colds*

Colds are caused by viruses—and more than 200 different cold viruses have been identified. Cold viruses commonly settle and multiply in humans, causing stuffy noses, sneezing, sore throats, coughs, and headaches.

When a body fights a cold, it develops some immunity to that specific virus—but that leaves at least 199 other viruses to fight! As children go through life, they build immunity to viruses one by one. However, a child can get a cold from the same virus more than once, even though immunity is usually building and subsequent bouts with the same virus tend to be milder and shorter.

A person who has a cold can transmit the virus to another person through very casual contact such as coughing, sneezing, or even breathing or talking near someone. Cold viruses also spread through touching. Children sometimes cough into their hands and then touch other children's hands when playing games and so forth. The viruses then spread through hand-to-mouth contact. Because many viruses remain active for several hours, children can catch colds by touching a toy, crayon, table, or other item that was recently handled by a sick child.

All of these facts may add to your stress as a caregiver, causing you to clean surfaces constantly and monitor child-to-child contact somewhat obsessively—but you cannot clean and monitor at all times. For you and the children in your care to have a normal life, you will have to settle for being cautious. There are steps you can take to limit the spread of germs in your child care setting. Make sure that all people in your household wash their hands with soap and water frequently and thoroughly; doing so will reduce the chances of virus transmission. In addition, when children are old

*Adapted from Solnit Sale 1998a.

42

CHAPTER 2
The Home as a
Caring and Learning
Environment

Welcoming
Children into a
Safe and Healthy
Home

How Children Catch Colds *(continued)*

enough, teach them to cough and sneeze into tissues or their upper-sleeve areas (not their hands). Teach them also to keep their hands away from their faces, where germs are numerous. Finally, although colds are most contagious when noses are runny, you should be aware that children shed virus cells before symptoms appear and for up to three weeks after the onset of symptoms.

3 WELCOMING CHILDREN INTO A SAFE AND HEALTHY HOME
Emphasize and model proper nutrition.

Providing a variety of healthy, nutritious foods gives children the energy they need to learn, grow, and socialize. Modeling proper nutrition is just as important; a balanced diet will give you energy, focus, and stamina, and the children will learn good habits by watching you.

Practices That Encourage Healthy Eating Habits

- Be aware of the United States Department of Agriculture (USDA) Food Guide Pyramid and children's individual nutritional needs.* The pyramid provides guidance on making smart choices from every food group, getting the most nutrition out of calories, and staying within daily calorie needs.
- Serve a sufficient amount of nutritious food to children. Ensure that meals or snacks are available at least every two to three hours and that drinking water is always available. Do not overwhelm children with large portions of food.
- Get a list of children's food allergies from their parents or family members and avoid serving foods that cause allergic reactions. If one child's allergies are so severe that he or she breaks out in hives when coming into contact with specific foods (such as peanut products), do not serve those foods to any of the children.
- Be mindful of and select foods that are representative or respectful of each child's culture. For instance, some Asian American children may be accustomed to eating rice porridge for breakfast, while some Hispanic children may prefer tortillas and eggs in the morning.
- Store, prepare, and serve food in a sanitary manner.
- Learn about the USDA-sponsored Child and Adult Care Food Program (CACFP), which serves nutritious meals and snacks to eligible children

---

*The official name of the USDA Food Guide Pyramid is "MyPyramid." For more information, visit http://www.mypyramid.gov.

43

CHAPTER 2
The Home as a
Caring and Learning
Environment

Welcoming
Children into a
Safe and Healthy
Home

and adults who receive care at participating child care centers, day care homes, and adult day care centers. Further information about the CACFP is available at http://www.cde.ca.gov/ls/nu/cc/ccc.asp and in Chapter 4.

- Eat healthy, nutritious foods so you can set a good example for the children.

When infants and toddlers are present

- Provide time and space for mothers to nurse or bottle-feed their children before they leave your home.
- Hold infants and toddlers in your arms when bottle-feeding.
- Keep a record for families of what their children have eaten throughout the day. If you participate in the CACFP, there are specific recordkeeping requirements.

4 WELCOMING CHILDREN INTO A SAFE AND HEALTHY HOME
Provide interest areas, materials, and activities that are engaging and age-appropriate.

Young children need stimulating environments to help them learn and grow. By offering a variety of engaging, age-appropriate interest areas, materials, and activities, you can help the children in your care develop valuable social and individual skills. A wide range of activities and materials foster interaction, group and individual play, creativity, imagination, exploration, and problem solving.

When activities and materials are planned and selected, consider the physical, social, emotional, and intellectual level of each child. Providing age- and developmentally appropriate experiences will help children feel comfortable in your home and will allow them to grow according to their unique developmental stages.

Practices to Create an Environment that Fosters Growth and Learning

Interest areas

- Offer two to four distinct interest areas focusing on themes such as reading; art projects; games; music; drama; playing with toys, blocks, or play dough; and others.
- Provide variety to support different learning goals and opportunities. For example, an area focusing on sign or label making can help support early reading and writing.

44

CHAPTER 2
The Home as a
Caring and Learning
Environment

Welcoming
Children into a
Safe and Healthy
Home

- Change or alternate the areas periodically, making adjustments to stimulate learning and to respond to children's evolving interests.
- If possible, set up outdoor areas in addition to indoor areas.
- Offer areas where children can play by themselves but still be within your line of sight.

Materials

- Provide materials that can be used in many different ways; examples include play dough and blocks.
- Use strategies such as labeling—in English and in the children's home languages, if applicable—to help children select materials and return them to their proper locations. For example, a bucket of pens could have a label taped to it with a picture of pens and the word "Pens" written in large, bold letters.
- Group materials that are used together in logical ways. For instance, you could create separate containers for blocks, vehicles (cars, trucks, boats), animals, action figures, and so on.
- Provide duplicates of some toys and materials to allow more than one child to play with similar items simultaneously. This can help children play together and can limit arguments among children.
- Pay attention to the colors and textures of materials in each interest area. Offer as much variety as possible.
- Vary the materials and toys periodically to maintain children's interest and to account for the children's evolving skills. To reduce costs, you might be able to borrow materials from toy-lending libraries. Always remember to clean and disinfect any materials you borrow before using or returning them.
- Offer materials that are both realistic and that encourage imaginative play. Provide clothing and props so children can engage in pretend play.
- Use materials that are commonly found in homes to expand the children's learning. For example, use the kitchen for science experiments or use photos and artwork displayed on your walls to tell stories.

Activities

- Provide opportunities for active and quiet play. As examples, you could offer jumping, climbing, and dancing for active play, and puzzles, painting, and reading for quiet play.
- Provide regular opportunities for outdoor play. If outdoor space is limited, look for other locations in your community (such as parks) where you can offer activities.
- Allow children to participate in activities with as little disruption to themselves or other children as possible.

45

CHAPTER 2
The Home as a
Caring and Learning
Environment

Welcoming
Children into a
Safe and Healthy
Home

When infants and toddlers are present

- Provide board books for reading, and make sure other materials such as paints and play dough are nontoxic.
- Ensure that shelving is placed at appropriate heights. Preschoolers should be able to reach toys and materials without assistance, but younger children should not.

Preparing for Each Day

Before the children arrive at your home each day, it is important to prepare yourself and your home. Thoughtful preparation and self-care can help make your days go more smoothly. One way to get ready for your day is to eat a nutritious breakfast; doing so will give you the energy and focus you need to provide high-quality care to the children. Some providers find it helpful to engage in early-morning meditation, stretching, yoga, or other exercise (such as walking, jogging, or biking). Remember that *you* are your home's most important asset! Your health is just as important as the children's health.

As covered earlier in this chapter, be sure to conduct daily inspections of toys, equipment, and other materials in and around your home. *Do any toys have missing or broken parts? Are there any small objects or other potential choking hazards within easy reach of infants and toddlers?* (You might have to get down on your hands and knees to do a thorough inspection.)

When children arrive each morning, make quick observations about their physical and emotional state—and ask questions of the family members if you feel you need to. *Did the children get enough sleep? Do they appear to be suffering from seasonal allergies or cold symptoms? Are there any special circumstances you should know about that might affect their behavior?* Getting answers to questions such as these will allow you to provide the best care possible.

Cleaning Up*

How do you get children to pick up toys and clean up after themselves? Each home-based child care provider has a different approach. Here are some suggestions:

1. **Consider each child's age when setting your expectations for cleanup.** Expect more from a four-year-old than from a toddler. A toddler can be expected to put some things (such as plastic blocks) into the places or containers where they belong, but you should be

---

*Adapted from Gonzalez-Mena 1993.

46

CHAPTER 2

The Home as a
Caring and Learning
Environment

Welcoming
Children into a
Safe and Healthy
Home

Cleaning Up *(continued)*

aware that he or she may have the urge to dump or throw them again. On the other hand, a four-year-old can be expected to put away one group of toys and then help clean up others as well.

2. **Keep your environment orderly.** Cleaning up is easier when items have designated storage places, and children develop a sense of order when their environment is well organized.

3. **Keep a manageable amount of toys out at one time.** Too many toys can overwhelm and distract children, and fewer toys require less cleanup.

4. **Make a game out of the cleanup process.** Putting things back in their proper places can give children the same joy as working a puzzle. Some children do not even know that cleanup is a chore! Show the children that cleaning up can be fun.

5. **Pick up after yourself.** Modeling good cleanup habits and a positive attitude can help the children develop their own good habits.

Home-based child care providers have different views on cleaning up toys and materials. Some providers expect children to clean up continuously, while others are willing to let clutter accumulate as long as the children are involved in constructive activities. Cleanup times may be ongoing, or they may be scheduled events—for example, before lunch and at the end of the day. Either approach is acceptable.

Some providers see a need for children to be involved in ongoing projects and are willing to suspend cleanup in specific areas. For instance, you might place a "Please Save" sign on a child's block structure to allow the child to work on the structure at a later time—but that could pose a problem if other children want to use the blocks. You could manage the situation by talking with the other children and by redirecting them to different activities so the creator of the block structure can feel respected and valued. Always acknowledge and respect each child's feelings and help the children work out solutions together.

It is important to involve children in the cleanup process. If you clean up your home by yourself after the children leave for the day, you add to your daily workload and you miss opportunities to teach the children about responsibility.

Addressing Cultural Diversity

Why Is This Important?

Each home-based child care setting has its own rules and customs. The culture of your child care home is different from that of each child's home, and the differences may be more pronounced if your ethnicity, native language, economic level, or country of birth are not the same as those of the children in your care. Building respect for cultural differences is an important part of providing a nurturing environment where children can thrive.

Remember That Young Children . . .

- Come from a wide variety of religious, ethnic, linguistic, cultural, and economic backgrounds.
- May not have equal access to resources because of family, economic, or political circumstances. Multiple approaches may be needed to offer equal learning opportunities to all children.

Keys to Effective Home-Based Child Care

- Be aware of your own cultural background and any biases that you might have about other cultures or populations.
- Understand that belonging to a community gives children a fundamental sense of security. Use that cultural base to strengthen their self-esteem and their feelings of being connected to others.
- Demonstrate an active interest in and acceptance of each child's cultural background, and consciously avoid and discourage actions that are disrespectful of children's cultural backgrounds and communities.
- Strive to create bridges of understanding and communication between you and any families whose culture, language, economic level, or country of birth differ from yours.

Considerations When Infants and Toddlers Are Present

It is especially important to establish two-way communication with families about how they care for infants. Families may have very different approaches to feeding and diapering babies, toilet learning, and hygiene. As a professional, it is your responsibility to initiate conversations with families and to communicate with them frequently, even when differences arise. Listen carefully to parents and other family members; together you can find ways to care for all children in a manner that is consistent with their experiences at home. Remember that family members and providers alike tend to have a strong desire to protect young children. Honor the fact that this desire is even stronger for a family than it is for you.

48

CHAPTER 2
The Home as a
Caring and Learning
Environment

Addressing Cultural
Diversity

Toilet learning is handled in different ways throughout the world. In some cultures, toilet learning may begin when a child is only a few months old, and in others, families may not begin the training until a child is about three years old. Adult approaches to this vary: some adults are proactive about the training; others initiate the training only when they feel their child is ready. Be aware of your own preferences, expectations, and limits as you communicate with families about their feelings on this subject.

GUIDELINES IN THIS SECTION

1. Respect and show appreciation for all individuals and cultures, making the acceptance of diversity a central theme in your child care environment.
2. Understand your cultural beliefs and practices, and be aware of how your feelings and ideas about other cultures, ethnicities, communities, and religions affect the care you provide.
3. Learn about the history, beliefs, and practices of the children and families you serve.
4. To the extent possible, use caregiving practices that are consistent with children's experiences in their own homes.
5. Provide materials that reflect the characteristics, values, and practices of diverse cultural groups.
6. Teach children what to do when they experience social injustice, bias, and prejudice.

ADDRESSING CULTURAL DIVERSITY

Respect and show appreciation for all individuals and cultures, making the acceptance of diversity a central theme in your child care environment.

A basic attitude of mutual respect is essential for creating a positive and accepting home-based child care environment. This statement applies to ethnically and culturally diverse child care settings *and* to settings where people have the same or similar cultural backgrounds.

Practices to Emphasize the Importance of Respecting All People

- Encourage all children to appreciate and respect others—to be considerate of other people's beliefs and feelings and of the different ways in which people express themselves.
- Seek awareness and understanding of your own culture, as this is the first step toward appreciating and honoring other cultures.
- Seek information about the cultures of families and children in your care. Talk with the families and explore other resources, such as workshops and

49

CHAPTER 2
The Home as a
Caring and Learning
Environment

Addressing Cultural
Diversity

courses on cultural diversity offered by your local resource and referral agency or community college.

- Talk with children about experiences in their lives. As they talk, listen for and discuss examples illustrating similarities and differences in the traditions, practices, roles of family members, and family structures that are represented in their cultures and communities.

- Encourage children to understand how their words (according to age) and behavior affect others. Emphasize mutual respect and sensitivity. Additionally, model fairness as a central concept. *"We should all respect each other and ourselves"* is a cardinal rule.

- Talk honestly about similarities and differences without making judgments.

- Deal honestly with children's questions and observations about differences they observe in other people; acceptance of others is encouraged.

- Incorporate materials from and discussions about many cultures and linguistic backgrounds—not just those of the children currently in your care.

- When teaching children about different cultures, focus on everyday activities as well as special occasions. Use more than a "tourist approach" in which children learn only about other people's holidays, heroes, customs, and special events; explore common beliefs and everyday routines.

- Find ways to enjoy experiences that include all children and that are based on different cultural practices.

- Be sensitive to the cultures of children and families who have disabilities or other special needs.

- Learn and use greetings and other key words from the home languages of the families you serve.

When infants and toddlers are present

Understand that children first identify with what is familiar before they appreciate how others are different.

2 ADDRESSING CULTURAL DIVERSITY
Understand your cultural beliefs and practices, and be aware of how your feelings and ideas about other cultures, ethnicities, communities, and religions affect the care you provide.

Before you can understand other people's beliefs, practices, and traditions, you must be aware of and understand your own. Having that awareness can help you be more open to people who are different from you.

50

CHAPTER 2
The Home as a
Caring and Learning
Environment

Addressing Cultural
Diversity

Practices That Promote Cultural Understanding

- Identify and understand the beliefs of your culture, religion (if applicable), and community. Recognize that this is an ongoing process.
- Recognize also that what may feel normal and comfortable to you may seem strange and uncomfortable to some children and their families—and vice versa. For example, people often have different preferences and views about foods they eat, how foods are eaten, body language, ways of greeting one another, showing affection, and so on.
- Understand that certain messages might be confusing to a child whose beliefs are different from your own. Identify the cultural messages that your home, family, manner, language, and values are sending to each of the children in your care. Ask someone from another culture to help identify the messages that your home environment is sending, and ask for opinions about things you might need to change to be more inclusive of different cultures.
- Understand that your feelings about sensitive topics such as religion, politics, and sexual orientation may differ from those of the families you serve. When children ask questions about potentially controversial topics, keep these differences in mind when you answer.

Through culture, children gain a feeling of belonging and a sense of who they are; what is important in life; what is right and wrong; how to care for themselves and others; and what to celebrate, eat, and wear.

What is "Culture"?*

Everyone has a culture. Culture is made up of all those factors in your environment that are accepted by the group as the norm, or the expectation. Culture includes beliefs, attitudes, and practices. The foundation of many cultures rests upon accepted beliefs or myths. Culture includes people's views on the following subjects:

- Ways of relating to one's elders
- Behavior between boys and girls
- Roles of women and men
- Ownership of property
- Prohibition of certain kinds of behavior
- Childrearing practices such as discipline, toilet learning, feeding, and bathing
- Expectations about behavior at various ages
- Attitudes toward different types of people
- Rites of passage

*WestEd: The Program for Infant/Toddler Care (PITC) 1997.

51

CHAPTER 2
The Home as a
Caring and Learning
Environment

Addressing Cultural
Diversity

- Birth and marriage ceremonies
- The meaning of death and ways of dealing with death
- Food and mealtimes
- School and activities
- Organization and cleanliness

3 ADDRESSING CULTURAL DIVERSITY
Learn about the history, beliefs, and practices of the children and families you serve.

When you take time to learn about each family's history, beliefs, and practices, everyone benefits. Talk with families, seek opportunities to visit their homes, gather information about their culture, and get to know extended family members. If you make efforts such as these, children and their families will feel appreciated and understood, and you will better understand why children behave as they do.

Practices to Help You Understand the Children in Your Care

- Talk with families frequently about the ways in which they care for their children at home. Discuss aspects of the children's behavior and learning that are important to each family.
- Ask parents and families about their cultural practices. Talk with them to ensure you have an accurate understanding of their beliefs and values.
- Seek opportunities to visit the homes and communities of the families you serve; this will show families that you care about them and their children. For example, you might visit a newborn sibling, attend a family barbeque, or offer to coordinate a potluck dinner held alternately at different families' homes. Even a few minutes of your time can make children and families feel special.
- Encourage families to bring to your home various objects or materials that reflect their culture—to show to children, leave on display, or use as teaching tools. Ask parents and family members to share stories, demonstrate how to make crafts or cook special foods, or sing songs.
- Make efforts to respect and be responsive to every family's values. When there are differences between a child's home culture and yours, try to accommodate the child's needs or wishes. For example, some people believe that children should maintain a clean physical appearance at all times when attending school. As a result, some children are reluctant to engage in learning activities and experiences such as painting or outdoor play that may soil their clothing. For an activity such as painting, you

52

CHAPTER 2
The Home as a
Caring and Learning
Environment

Addressing Cultural
Diversity

might provide extra clothes for the children (such as big T-shirts) so their family members will not get upset and so the children will not be singled out.

- Recognize when your values conflict with a family's values, and address these conflicts promptly. For example, if you disagree with a family about how to manage toilet learning, you might approach the situation by saying, *"We have different ideas about toilet learning. What can we do to make sure everyone is happy?"*

ADDRESSING CULTURAL DIVERSITY

4 To the extent possible, use caregiving practices that are consistent with children's experiences in their own homes.

When you follow the form of caregiving that children experience at home—for example, incorporating familiar ways of using language—the children are likely to feel more secure and comfortable. However, there are times when it may be difficult to attain cultural consistency between a child's home and your child care setting, or you may feel that it is beneficial to introduce new strategies and practices. Whenever your approaches or practices differ from what a child experiences at home, communicate with the child's family members to make them aware of those differences.

Practices That Facilitate Consistency of Care

- Understand that children may have different ways of speaking and listening based on what is acceptable in their culture. For example, in some cultures, interrupting someone who is speaking, or looking at the person straight in the eyes, are considered rude. In other cultures that behavior is acceptable or even expected.
- Recognize that some cultures emphasize individual initiative, while others place a higher value on being a member of a group. Children from families that value individual initiative may be more prepared to assert their own opinions and less prepared to cooperate with others.
- Acknowledge that cultural groups have different views about the responsibilities of the family and of home-based child care providers in helping children acquire skills and knowledge. For example, some families may believe that you are the best person to help their children develop an interest in reading and writing. Other families may feel that it is their responsibility to introduce their children to those experiences.
- Have a clear understanding of cultural differences regarding discipline. Some forms of discipline are never appropriate. For instance, although you cannot use corporal punishment—and licensing regulations prohibit

53

CHAPTER 2
The Home as a
Caring and Learning
Environment

Addressing Cultural
Diversity

it—understand that some families will use it at home. Instead of judging the home behavior, talk with family members about how you approach discipline and how that approach supports a child's learning and development. Always strive to provide positive guidance for children.

- Make sure that meals and snacks reflect diverse cultures and traditions. Be aware of and maintain the dietary restrictions and mealtime practices of various cultures when preparing and serving meals.

- Understand that some families—especially new immigrants—are eager for their children to learn English. As English is used, incorporate the child's home language whenever possible and ensure that the children can be understood, feel valued, have their needs met, and have the opportunity to develop fluency. In this way, you will support the children's early-language experiences as they learn English. Books that incorporate English learning with children's home languages and practices may help providers who are unfamiliar with a particular culture or language.

When infants and toddlers are present

Communicate with families about their expectations for diapering and toileting. Sometimes you will have to negotiate with them about the approaches you use. You might need to consider issues such as the health-and-safety rules in your home, or group and individual needs.

5 ADDRESSING CULTURAL DIVERSITY
Provide materials that reflect the characteristics, values, and practices of diverse cultural groups.

In order to align your home with the cultures of children's families and communities, you need to ensure that the materials and activities you choose reflect each child's neighborhood and world. Books, music, food, artwork created by the children, pictures displayed in your home, activities, visitors and guests, and field trips should reflect the cultures and ethnicities of the children in your care as well as children from other cultures and backgrounds.

Practices That Promote Authentic Examples of Culture

- Ask families and children to bring in photographs that show the children and their family members participating in familiar learning activities and experiences. If possible, photocopy those pictures and use them to explore similarities and differences among individuals and groups.

- Encourage families and children to bring items from home—such as empty food and shoe boxes and articles of clothing—for pretend play.

54

CHAPTER 2
The Home as a
Caring and Learning
Environment

Addressing Cultural
Diversity

- Use books that provide accurate, modern portrayals of diverse groups. For example, use books that show Native Americans living in urban communities and wearing clothing other than that worn for traditional ceremonies and celebrations. Books showing traditional Native American communities in an authentic context may be provided as well. If or when you encounter cultural stereotypes in books or other media, discuss those stereotypes with the children.
- Invite family members or other adults representing different cultural backgrounds to come to your home to share personal or cultural stories or assist with learning activities that are representative of their group.
- Provide books and other reading materials that encourage children to discover not only linguistic, ethnic, and cultural differences, but also those related to age and ability. Materials should also feature nontraditional gender roles.
- Represent the diversity of children's families and communities in your visual displays, pictures on walls, and children's artwork.
- Reflect and value diversity by providing familiar and culturally appropriate props and materials. For example, the pretend-play area might include cooking utensils and materials that reflect the cultural makeup of the children in the program; you could include chopsticks to show Asian influences, or bowls made from gourds to reflect African culture.

Promoting Cultural Pride Among the Children in Your Care

You can foster cultural pride in your child care home setting by:

- Asking children to bring in a family photo album to share at circle time. Pictures of family members, everyday activities, and celebrations will reinforce the idea that all people have similarities and differences. Some children live in single-parent homes, others live with their grandparents, and some live with an aunt or uncle. Each family unit has its own traditions and routines.

- Introducing children to music and dance from different cultural and linguistic backgrounds. If children are comfortable doing so, invite them to share a song or dance that they enjoy with their families. In addition, ask family members to come into your home to share a song, play an instrument, or teach a dance.

- Cooking and preparing foods from different cultural and ethnic backgrounds. Introduce foods, words, techniques, tools, and utensils as you cook. For example, if you prepare Mexican food, use a *maquina tortilladora* (tortilla press) to make tortillas, a *molcajete* (stone and pestle) to grind chiles and make masa, and a *comal* (griddle) to make tortillas and to blister chiles. Invite family members to cook or help you cook.

55

CHAPTER 2
The Home as a
Caring and Learning
Environment

Addressing Cultural
Diversity

- Asking children to share clothes that people from their culture wear for everyday and special occasions. Explain that all cultures have special clothes for celebrations, and that all have everyday clothes for school, work, and relaxation.

- Inviting children to send postcards to your home when they take day-trips and vacations. They could do this when they visit local sites such as zoos or museums, or when they travel to faraway destinations. Show the children that each child's experiences are unique and valuable.

6 ADDRESSING CULTURAL DIVERSITY
Teach children what to do when they experience social injustice, bias, and prejudice.

Create an environment that discourages bias and promotes acceptance of others and respect for diversity. Whether or not children are able to talk about social injustice, bias, and prejudice, they learn about those attitudes at an early age. Children act out and express the biases of their society—biases related to gender, race, ethnicity, economic level, and disability.

Practices That Foster Positive Responses to Bias

Teach children to appreciate and respect people's similarities and differences. Understand the difference between being prejudiced and being curious about others; many children in your care will be learning about and experiencing cultural differences for the first time, and they will be curious about the differences they see. For example, when children make remarks about different colors and shades of skin, reinforce the message that all people have similarities and differences. Use books and other resources that show people of different cultures and backgrounds.

Use a multicultural approach in your home. A multicultural approach incorporates perspectives, materials, foods, and toys from different cultural and linguistic backgrounds. It might include learning activities and experiences such as sharing stories about children's daily routines and practices; using materials that reflect the characteristics and practices of different cultural groups (such as dolls of different ethnicities and "play foods" from different cultures); and tasting foods from various cultures.

Use an antibias approach in your home. An antibias approach avoids stereotypes, prejudice, and discrimination that are based on race, culture, ethnicity, class, gender, age, or physical ability. Examples of gender-based stereotypes include statements such as *"You throw like a girl,"* or *"Boys don't take care of babies."* An antibias approach might include letting all children,

56

CHAPTER 2
The Home as a
Caring and Learning
Environment

Addressing Cultural
Diversity

regardless of gender, take turns assuming different roles in pretend play: father, mother, doctor, professional race car driver, teacher, pilot, and so on. Providing books that show women in nontraditional career roles or that show men changing diapers could support that approach. Another antibias approach might include choosing outdoor activities in which all children—regardless of gender or ability—can participate and excel. For example, if one of the children in your care uses a wheelchair, you could offer a modified basketball game in which the children shoot balls into a garbage can.

Teach children how to respond to situations that make them feel uncomfortable or that cause them emotional pain. You could teach them a simple statement such as *"I don't like it when you say that to me."*

When infants and toddlers are present

Recognize and encourage older children's attempts to be inclusive, accepting, and understanding.

Including Children with Disabilities or Other Special Needs

Why Is This Important?

Supporting the rights of children to participate fully in their communities includes access to home-based child care. Make sure that your home environment supports individual differences and lets all children demonstrate their strengths and skills. In an inclusive environment, children can interact with and befriend other children who have diverse backgrounds and abilities.

Remember That Young Children . . .

- Thrive in child care settings where adults aim to meet the needs of every child.
- Learn to appreciate and accept different people and cultures by being in inclusive environments.

Keys to Effective Home-Based Child Care

- Make sure all children have access to a learning environment that promotes their growth and development.
- Know that it may be necessary to adjust daily routines and to adapt learning activities to support children with special needs.
- Listen to and collaborate with family members and specialists.
- Participate in training so you can provide an optimal learning environment for young children.

57

CHAPTER 2
The Home as a
Caring and Learning
Environment

Including Children
with Disabilities
or Other Special
Needs

Considerations When Infants and Toddlers Are Present

Infants and toddlers may have disabilities or other special needs that have not been identified yet. You might be the first person to notice something about a child that needs further evaluation. There are many resources available to help you communicate with family members about concerns, provide information for referrals, and integrate any resulting interventions into your child care setting. You can be an important source of comfort and information for a family.

In the area of disabilities, terminology differs according to the age of the children in your care. For children from birth to age two, early intervention services—in the form of Individualized Family Service Plans (IFSPs)—are available to children under Part C of the Individuals with Disabilities Education Act (IDEA).* For children and youths from age three to twenty-one, Part B of the IDEA provides special education services through Individualized Education Programs (IEPs).

GUIDELINES IN THIS SECTION

1. Actively support the concept of inclusion by creating an environment in which all children and families feel welcome.
2. Partner with families by communicating frequently and by exchanging resources.
3. Be a part of the educational team that develops and implements IFSPs and IEPs for eligible children.
4. Work with family members and specialists to support children's daily learning activities, experiences, and environments.
5. Develop strategies to include children who have disabilities or other special needs by participating in training and by talking with family members and specialists.

INCLUDING CHILDREN WITH DISABILITIES OR OTHER SPECIAL NEEDS

Actively support the concept of inclusion by creating an environment in which all children and families feel welcome.

Children with disabilities or other special needs have a lot in common with typically developing children. All children—regardless of their health status, developmental stage, abilities, or limitations—want to be loved and accepted. When you plan learning activities and experiences for the children and consider your overall approach to child care, take into account each child's personality, learning goals, needs, and interests. Each child is unique, and all families want their children to be in a nurturing environment.

---

*For more information about the Individuals with Disabilities Education Act, visit the following United States Department of Education Web site: http://idea.ed.gov/.

58

CHAPTER 2
The Home as a
Caring and Learning
Environment

Including Children
with Disabilities
or Other Special
Needs

Inclusive child care benefits all children and families. With the resources, technical assistance, and support necessary to adapt curriculum, instruction, and observations, you can successfully include all children in your child care setting. In an inclusive environment, children and families learn about acceptance and appreciation of individual differences. When you make inclusion an important priority, everyone will feel welcome in your home.

Practices to Help All Children and Families Feel Included

- Make sure every child has full access to materials and activities in your home.
- Be aware of and comply with state and federal laws and regulations pertaining to children with disabilities. See Appendix B for more information.
- Encourage positive interaction and friendship among all children by adapting your home, curriculum, and instructional practices when needed.
- Provide books in your home that represent people with disabilities or other special needs. Additionally, make sure you offer inclusive toys and activities.
- Share with families your approach to including children who have disabilities or special needs.

2 INCLUDING CHILDREN WITH DISABILITIES OR OTHER SPECIAL NEEDS
Partner with families by communicating frequently and by exchanging resources.

In high-quality, home-based child care, early intervention is most effective when you work with families in a respectful partnership to assess a child's strengths and needs, to make decisions, and to set goals for the child's learning and development.*

Practices That Facilitate Effective Communication

- During initial conversations with the family of a child who has a disability or other special needs, be especially open, sensitive, and caring.
- Build trust with the families of children who have disabilities or other special needs. Be available consistently, exchange significant information, maintain a safe home, protect confidentiality, show genuine concern for each child, and demonstrate that you value the family's input.
- Communicate daily with families. Exchanging a notebook with information about the child is an effective strategy for establishing ongoing communication.
- Listen actively to families to obtain information about children with disabilities or other special needs. Ask open-ended questions that cannot

*California Department of Education 1996.

59

CHAPTER 2
The Home as a
Caring and Learning
Environment

**Including Children
with Disabilities
or Other Special
Needs**

be answered yes or no—such as, "What do you do at home to encourage your child to talk?"

- Help families connect with community supports, resources, and services. There may be times when you need to seek assistance from knowledgeable, experienced specialists to address the needs of a child with disabilities or other special needs. Refer families to appropriate specialists and community resources, such as resource and referral agencies, family resource centers, local school districts, or county offices of education.
- Offer families opportunities to talk with other families about child development, parenting, or other concerns.
- Seek information and training to help you address the needs of children in your care—and always consult with families and specialists involved in a child's care.
- When communicating with families about children with disabilities or other special needs, explore and respect the family's cultural preferences.

3 INCLUDING CHILDREN WITH DISABILITIES OR OTHER SPECIAL NEEDS
Be a part of the educational team that develops and implements IFSPs and IEPs for eligible children.

Children and youths from age three to twenty-one who qualify for special education services must have an IEP developed by an interdisciplinary team. As required by state and federal laws, the IEP contains clearly identified goals and objectives that are regularly monitored. As required by the federal IDEA, the interdisciplinary team must include the child's parents or guardians in addition to special education professionals, and may include the home-based child care provider.

The emphasis on a cooperative, team approach has many benefits, including mutual support and communication. For many children with disabilities or other special needs, routines, learning activities, and experiences often require minimal modifications. For example, you may already serve children who have language delays or learning disabilities. The IEP teams can help you meet the individual child care goals and needs of those children. Cooperative teams can also help you establish daily activities and routines that meet the needs of all children—not just those with disabilities or other special needs.

Practices That Encourage Collaboration with Interdisciplinary Teams

- Focus on helping children with disabilities or other special needs on a daily basis. For example, a child's IEP may include regular peer interaction as a way to support the development of language skills. In this case, you could encourage the other children in your home to communicate regularly with this child.

60

CHAPTER 2
The Home as a
Caring and Learning
Environment

Including Children
with Disabilities
or Other Special
Needs

- Understand that some IEPs may include ideas and approaches that can benefit all children in your home. For example, to interact with children who have poor vision, you may need to emphasize oral directions and information rather than visuals such as drawings, photos, or cues from your facial expressions and body language. Additional information and direction can help each child in your home.
- For each child with a disability or other special needs, work on the child's goals during daily routines and activities, and keep records of the child's progress.

When infants and toddlers are present

Let families know that you are willing to take an active role in supporting IFSPs.

All About IFSPS and IEPS*

What is an IFSP? An Individualized Family Service Plan, or IFSP, is a process for assisting families and professionals in the delivery of early intervention services to infants and toddlers (birth to age three). The IFSP describes the services, providers, locations where services are given, and goals pertaining to each child and family. The process includes family members, teachers, and other professionals, and it involves the delivery of family-focused services in "natural" environments—which include home and community settings.

What is an IEP? An Individualized Education Program, or IEP, is a written plan for the delivery of special education services to children and youths from age three to twenty-one. The IEP includes statements that address a child's present level of educational performance and overall functioning; annual goals; short-term instructional objectives; specific educational services needed; dates of service; participation in regular education programs; and procedures for evaluating the child's progress. The IEP must be signed by the child's parents or legal guardians and by the educational personnel working with the child, including the regular teacher.

Children with IEPs: who may provide services?

The following is a partial list of specialists who may provide services to children with special needs:

- Physical therapists
- Occupational therapists
- Speech and language therapists
- Vision specialists
- Orientation and mobility specialists

- Audiologists
- Health or medical personnel
- Psychologists
- Learning disabilities specialists

*Center for Human Services 2002.

61

CHAPTER 2
The Home as a
Caring and Learning
Environment

Including Children
with Disabilities
or Other Special
Needs

INCLUDING CHILDREN WITH DISABILITIES OR OTHER SPECIAL NEEDS

4 Work with family members and specialists to support children's daily learning activities, experiences, and environments.

The most effective way for you to provide high-quality care to children with disabilities or other special needs is to form a partnership with family members and specialists. Children with disabilities and other special needs often require modifications to their educational environments or to the instructional activities and experiences in which they participate. Some children with special needs may also require therapeutic services that are provided directly by a specialist—such as a speech-language pathologist, occupational therapist, or physical therapist. Family members and specialists can often recommend ways of teaching and caring that take into account the individual needs of children.

Practices That Facilitate Specialized Support

- If adaptations or modifications are needed, work with family members and specialists to support a child in his or her daily activities and experiences in your home. For example, specialists and family members may supply you with special materials or equipment to use in the home, or they may show you how to break down an activity into smaller steps so that a child can learn more easily.
- Be aware of visual and auditory stimuli (sights and sounds) in your home and the role they play in supporting or detracting from the learning environment for each child. For example, bright lights and loud music can cause stress in some children.
- Provide opportunities that support children's independence. Observe children to determine and provide the level of help or guidance they need.
- Create ways to include all children in daily routines and learning activities. Assess the environment regularly to ensure that all children have access to activities, toys, materials, and social interaction. This is especially important for children who have limited fine or gross motor skills.
- Identify adaptations to your home that may be needed for a child to participate in learning activities. For instance, you might need to adjust the height of a sand table to accommodate a child in a wheelchair. Incorporate adaptations and special procedures to support each child.
- Make sure indoor and outdoor pathways are as wide as possible and free of barriers.
- Assess your home's visual environment to determine if it enhances learning through the use of color and lighting. If necessary, make specific accommodations for children with visual impairments.

62

CHAPTER 2
The Home as a
Caring and Learning
Environment

Including Children
with Disabilities
or Other Special
Needs

5

INCLUDING CHILDREN WITH DISABILITIES OR OTHER SPECIAL NEEDS

Develop strategies to include children who have disabilities or other special needs by participating in training and by talking with family members and specialists.

Inclusion of all children requires thoughtful planning. Take advantage of opportunities for training and reflection so you can develop the skills and understanding that children with special needs may require. Seek information about specialized resource agencies and professionals. Set aside time to talk and work with families and specialists; you have valuable information to share about each child's daily routine, behavior, likes, and dislikes.

Practices to Help You Include Children with Disabilities or Other Special Needs

- Participate in a variety of professional development opportunities—such as family child care association meetings, workshops and training offered by your local resource and referral agency, and community college courses—to learn about and discuss the best ways to help children with disabilities or other special needs.

- If you believe that a child may have special needs, talk with family members and refer them to your local school district for an assessment. See Appendix C for more information.

- Work with families and specialists to develop IFSPs and IEPs; plan instructional strategies; monitor individual children's progress on a regular basis; and identify supplies, equipment, and adaptations needed by children with special needs. Communication is essential; child care providers, families, and specialists all have important knowledge about children.

- Offer your family child care home environment as a place where specialists can perform assessments or provide therapy for the child.

- Make it a high priority to meet with parents and family members. If necessary, make special arrangements to accommodate parents' schedules. Be sure to coordinate your goals with the families' goals for their children. When you meet with family members, gather information about how they care for their child at home and how they feel about their child's growth and development. Address concerns and celebrate successes.

CHAPTER 3
Developing a Home-Based Curriculum

*T*HE IDEA OF A CURRICULUM IS OFTEN ASSOCIATED WITH SCHOOLS, but every home-based child care setting needs a curriculum as well. A curriculum includes all of the activities and experiences that you offer to the children in your care—especially planned activities that focus on learning. Developing a curriculum involves each of the following actions:

- Planning daily learning activities and experiences
- Recognizing the importance of play as a learning activity
- Selecting toys and materials
- Setting goals for learning and development based on each child's individual needs and abilities
- Providing regular opportunities for movement and exercise
- Organizing the space in your home
- Building upon children's daily discoveries to explore further learning and development activities
- Cultivating caring relationships with the children and their families, and involving families in the planning of developmentally appropriate activities

The Role of Play

Play is central to children's development, and opportunities for both structured and spontaneous play are important. Play is a unique way for children to learn about their world and themselves. It also helps children see how they fit into their world.

Children's spontaneous play can be a rich source of ideas for the development of a curriculum. For example, if you observe a group of children repeatedly engaging in imaginary play about an animal's illness or hospitalization, you might decide to convert a playhouse area into a veterinary clinic for a week or two.

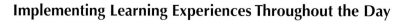

While involved in imaginary play, children are challenged to meet the language, problem-solving, and social competencies of their more sophisticated peers. When play is interesting and important to children, they are eager to learn new words, physical skills, and social behaviors that will allow them to stay involved in the activity. For instance, many three-year-olds have not yet mastered socially appropriate ways to enter into play with other children. As a sensitive and observant home-based child care provider, you can help children learn how to join others in play. However, be sure to respect the right of older children to play with their peers, and always ensure the safety of infants and toddlers by keeping them away from small, potentially hazardous toys and items.

Implementing Learning Experiences Throughout the Day

In home-based child care settings, everyday learning experiences often encompass many areas of development, such as cognitive, social, physical, linguistic, or creative development. For example, child care providers often involve children in the preparation and distribution of snacks because they know these tasks can promote social, emotional, and physical development in addition to skills in mathematics, science, language, literacy, and health.

Rather than plan a social development or math activity, providers can integrate those aspects of development into everyday chores, free play, and conversation. Games and other activities can cover multiple subjects and areas of development. For example, a simple baking activity can teach children math concepts as they measure ingredients; science concepts as they watch liquids transform into solids; and nutrition concepts as they learn how their bodies use the final food product to give them energy. In this same activity, children can also learn about teamwork, sequencing (by following the steps of a recipe), patience, following directions, and a sense of accomplishment. By offering fun, interesting activities, you can create an integrated curriculum that allows children to explore their world with their, bodies, minds, and senses.

Following the Children's Interests

Children's spontaneous day-to-day discoveries, interests, and questions—as well as their learning goals, activities, and experiences—can help you develop an effective curriculum. For instance, if the children exhibit a sudden fascination with the feel and texture of oranges, you could adapt your curriculum to help the children explore their curiosity. You might teach them about how and where oranges grow—which combines elements of science and geography. You could also present nutrition information to show that eating oranges promotes growth and overall health. Additionally, you could develop the children's mathematics skills by having them count oranges in various exercises, and you could promote literacy by reading and sharing books that feature oranges. Infants and toddlers could be included as well. Toddlers might like to carry baskets of oranges; peel and taste them; or help make orange juice. All of these experiences would provide the children with interesting, real-world learning opportunities.

When you incorporate children's ideas into their learning goals, you enhance the children's self-confidence and self-esteem in important ways. Children will see that you respect their thinking and value their questions. Over time, this approach will help the children become confident, self-directed learners.

The Basis for Early Learning

An effective home-based child care curriculum aims to prepare young children for kindergarten and the primary grades; it helps children develop impulse control, foundational language, literacy, reasoning, and mathematic skills and it increases their self-esteem. Children learn these skills largely in the context of play, daily routines, and projects that encourage exploration.

At times, it is appropriate for home-based child care providers to use focused learning activities—or more formal types of instruction—to meet learning goals. For example, if you observe the need for greater emphasis on literacy or language development, you might lead children in alphabet songs or games that demonstrate connections between alphabetical letters and their corresponding sounds.

The Meaning of a Curriculum for Infants and Toddlers

A curriculum for infants and toddlers is rooted in your responsive relationships with the children and their families. Daily caregiving routines such as feeding and diapering are the foundation of curriculum for infants and toddlers. The warm, responsive relationship a baby or toddler experiences with you provides her with a secure base from which she can venture out to explore the world. When she knows she can count on you to care for her, she can explore, return, reconnect, and move out from you again. Your ability to understand and respond to her nonverbal communication—such as eye contact, facial expressions, and touch—is very important. For young children, the world is new. Every moment is a learning moment. During the first three years of their lives, infants and toddlers gain a foundation for lifelong learning through their relationships and their exploration.

For infants and toddlers, learning and development are tied together. From a baby's view point, play and learning do not consist of separate areas such as math and language. Discoveries occur simultaneously. For instance, an infant may learn over time that the word and mathematical concept *more* can be used to get more food. This learning occurs as the infant communicates with her caregiver, who responds by providing more of what the infant wants. Thus, the learning is linked with development because the infant experiences the emotional satisfaction of being understood, the physical enjoyment of eating more food, and the social success of communicating with another person—all at the same time.

Some providers try to apply a preschool curriculum to infants and toddlers. This can be frustrating for children and their family members, and it may have a negative impact on some children's desire to learn. Remember that infants and toddlers do not yet function in groups the way older children do; rather, they pursue individual interests. Be sure not to pressure infants and toddlers to act older than they are. Understanding that infants and toddlers are at different developmental stages than preschool-age children is an essential part of developing a successful curriculum.

The guidelines in this chapter focus on three- and four-year-old children, but—as with the rest of the document—the chapter also contains considerations for infants and toddlers. For more information about infant and toddler curriculum content, refer to the CDE publications *Infant/Toddler Learning and Development Program Guidelines* (2006) and the *California Infant/Toddler Learning and Development Foundations* (2009). You can learn more about these publications at http://www.cde.ca.gov/re/pn/rc. Additionally, visit the Program for Infant/Toddler Care (PITC) Web site at http://www.pitc.org.

Using the Guidelines to Develop a Home-Based Curriculum

The sections and guidelines in this chapter target specific areas of development: social and emotional development; language and literacy; mathematics; cognitive development (thinking skills); creativity and self-expression; and physical and motor development. Although the suggested activities emphasize distinct content areas, keep in mind that in home-based child care settings, learning activities and experiences often involve multiple aspects of development.

Discoveries of Infancy*

Infants and toddlers constantly gather and process information. They uncover mysteries many times each day, learning from what they see, hear, feel, taste, and touch. Infants and toddlers learn about their world by making discoveries in each of the following areas.

Learning Schemes

Learning schemes are the building blocks for discovery during infancy. By using schemes such as banging, reaching, and mouthing, children gain valuable knowledge. This development helps children discover how objects are best used and how to use objects in new and interesting ways.

Cause and Effect

As infants develop, they begin to understand that events and outcomes are caused. They learn that:

- They can cause things to happen either with their own bodies or through their own actions.
- Other people and objects can cause things to happen.
- Specific parts of objects—such as wheels, light switches, knobs, and buttons on cameras—can cause specific effects.

Use of Tools

A tool is anything a child can use to accomplish what he or she wants. Some of the tools infants use are crying, objects, their hands, and their caregivers. Infants learn to extend their power through the use of tools. They learn that a tool is a means to an end.

Object Permanence

For infants, "out of sight" often means "out of mind." When they are born, infants do not know about the permanence of objects. They make this important discovery gradually, through repeated experiences with the same objects (such as feeding bottles) and the same people in their lives (especially parents). Infants learn that things exist even though objects may be out of sight.

Understanding Space

Much of early learning involves issues of distance, movement, and perspective. Infants learn about spatial relationships by bumping into things, squeezing into tight spaces, and seeing things from different angles. In a sense, infants and toddlers at play are young scientists, busily investigating the physical universe. For example,

---

*Adapted from Lally et al. 1992.

Discoveries of Infancy *(continued)*

they find out about: (1) relative size, when they try to fit an object into a container; (2) gravity, as they watch toy cars roll down a slide; and (3) balance, as they try to stack objects of different shapes and sizes.

Imitation

One of the most powerful learning devices that infants and toddlers use is imitation. It fosters the development of communication and a broad range of other skills. Even the youngest infants learn by trying to match other people's actions. At every stage of infancy, children repeat and practice what they see, and their imitations become increasingly complex and purposeful over time. By doing the same things over and over again, children make those actions their own.

 # Social and Emotional Development

Why Is This Important?

Social and emotional development form the cornerstones of all other types of development. They directly contribute to language and thinking skills, and they lay the foundation for early learning.

Many social and emotional skills are required of young children as they venture out into the world beyond their homes and families. They learn more about who they are as individuals and how to get along with others. Your home provides many opportunities for children to develop and practice social and emotional skills such as:

- Sharing the attention of an adult with other children.
- Waiting and taking turns.
- Learning how to make friends.
- Playing and working cooperatively.
- Learning about similarities and differences.

Remember That Young Children . . .

- Are learning about who they are as individuals, as members of a family, and as members of cultural groups.
- Are discovering how to interact with teachers, other adults, and peers, and how to develop good relationships.
- Are finding ways to regulate their emotions and behaviors.
- Are learning how to care about other people's feelings and to express their own feelings in appropriate ways.

69

CHAPTER 3
Developing a
Home-Based
Curriculum

Social and Emotional
Development

- Are discovering how to trust other children and adults.
- Are learning problem-solving techniques.

Keys to Effective Home-Based Child Care

- Create a climate of cooperation, mutual respect, and acceptance.
- Ensure that all children feel safe and cared for.
- Help children learn that they are accountable for what they say and do, and for how they treat others.
- Teach the children positive ways to resolve conflict.
- Encourage the children's internal sense of self-regulation.
- Understand that guiding young children toward appropriate social behavior takes time and patience, but it can be one of your most rewarding accomplishments.

Considerations When Infants and Toddlers Are Present

It is essential for infants to develop a sense of trust. Long before they can learn to regulate their own behavior, infants have to learn that someone will respond to their cries for help. They seek secure connections with family members and caregivers, and they search for consistent love and caring. Similarly, toddlers make efforts each day to deepen and maintain emotional ties.

Relationships create the context for early learning—and the essence of the infant/toddler curriculum is found in daily caregiving routines such as diapering, dressing, feeding, napping, and even wiping a child's nose. These routines offer rich opportunities for gaining a child's attention and cooperation, which is an important early step for socialization, guidance, learning, and deepening relationships.

GUIDELINES IN THIS SECTION

1. Help each child develop a sense of self-esteem and self-confidence.
2. Be responsive to each child's emotional needs.
3. Teach children to express their emotions in socially acceptable ways.
4. Consider children's social and cultural backgrounds when interpreting their preferences and behaviors.
5. Help children form and maintain satisfying relationships with one another and with adults.
6. Help each child feel valued and included.
7. Understand that the goal of guidance and discipline is to promote greater social and emotional competence.
8. Create a sense of safety, security, and predictability through the culture, environment, and routines of your home.
9. Guide children's social behavior in the context of daily learning activities and experiences.

70

CHAPTER 3
Developing a
Home-Based
Curriculum

Social and Emotional
Development

SOCIAL AND EMOTIONAL DEVELOPMENT

Help each child develop a sense of self-esteem and self-confidence.

As young children's personalities develop, they begin to think in new ways about who they are. Preschool-age children begin to evaluate themselves as doing well or poorly in meeting the expectations of their family, friends, and society as a whole. They test their own capabilities by choosing the social, intellectual, physical, and creative learning activities and experiences that interest them. Infants and toddlers gain a sense of security and identity through their experiences in relationships.

You can support young children's self-esteem by respecting their capabilities, offering them choices in a structured setting, and setting appropriate expectations for their behavior. You can help infants and toddlers develop a positive sense of self by responding promptly and consistently to their needs. You can also support toddlers by encouraging them as they participate in daily activities.

Practices That Encourage Healthy Self-Esteem

- Recognize children's efforts and achievements. For example, compliment children when they exhibit desirable behaviors such as sharing toys.
- Emphasize the importance of relationships and connectedness, recognizing that this is an essential aspect of supporting a sense of self-worth.
- Decide when it is important to intervene in children's interactions—for example, when there is immediate physical danger—and when children should be allowed to work out issues and problems on their own. Exercising good judgment in this area will help children learn to express emotions and interact with others appropriately.
- Recognize your own feelings about self-worth, and ask the children's families about their values. In some families and cultures a sense of self-esteem is very important; other families and cultures place more emphasis on group identity.

Activities and Experiences

- Offer children worthwhile and appropriately challenging learning activities and experiences. This will foster their cognitive, physical, social, and emotional development.
- Allow children to choose activities, and be flexible about the duration of the activities. Allow the children to change activities according to their interests and attention spans.
- Encourage preschool children's pretend play to help them explore their understanding of different roles and behaviors.

71

CHAPTER 3
Developing a
Home-Based
Curriculum

Social and Emotional
Development

2 SOCIAL AND EMOTIONAL DEVELOPMENT
Be responsive to each child's emotional needs.

To promote healthy emotional development, providers must be aware of children's feelings, acknowledge those feelings as natural and acceptable, and respond with empathy and compassion. When you listen to and share children's joys, sorrows, and worries, everyone benefits. Children who are fearful, angry, or overly excited may have difficulty expressing themselves and connecting with others. Your emotional support can help children resolve troubled feelings and ensure that your home is a positive, social place where children can learn, thrive, and grow.

Practices That Facilitate Responsive Caregiving

- Respect each child's feelings, and tell all of the children in your home that feelings are important.
- Respond to children's emotions promptly and consistently. Based on the child's developmental age and personality, decide when and when not to intervene.
- Recognize and respect the family's belief system about the extent to which people should share and discuss feelings.
- Express a welcoming attitude in your voice and gestures.
- Be sensitive to each child's personality and manner of expressing emotions. Discourage name-calling and put-downs.
- Show interest in what children say and do.
- Help children make connections among events, feelings associated with the events, and behaviors that may reflect those feelings.
- Encourage children to share their emotions with you: joy, sorrow, worry, excitement, anger, and so on.
- Help children identify their own and others' feelings with words such as *surprised, excited, happy, upset, angry, sad,* or *scared.* Additionally, label these emotions when talking to infants and toddlers; for instance, *"I think you're crying because you're scared."* Be careful not to project your own feelings onto the children *(I'm sad, so the children must be, too.).*
- Communicate closely with family members about their child's emotional needs, particularly if the child seems to be having a hard time and appears to need additional support or comfort from you.
- Be aware of individual and culturally different ways of expressing emotions. For example, in some cultures, talking loudly or yelling might be frowned upon, while in other cultures it may be typical.

Activities and Experiences

Read and tell stories that help children explore their feelings.

72

CHAPTER 3
Developing a
Home-Based
Curriculum

Social and Emotional
Development

SOCIAL AND EMOTIONAL DEVELOPMENT
3 Teach children to express their emotions in socially acceptable ways.

Helping children learn how to express feelings in appropriate ways is an important task. Teach preschool-age children to consider other people's views, see connections between feelings and behaviors, and develop effective coping strategies.

Practices That Promote Appropriate Emotional Expression

- When children struggle with concepts or lack words to express their feelings, suggest and model appropriate ways of expressing oneself.
- Affirm each child's emotions and show the children how to express their feelings appropriately. Teach children the difference between feelings and actions; for instance, explain that it is okay to feel angry but it is not okay to hit others.
- Encourage empathy by pointing out to children the observable effects of their behavior on other children.
- When children express their emotions, avoid gender stereotyping—such as telling a child that "big boys don't cry" or that "nice girls don't yell."
- Teach the children that adults also have emotions, and model the expression of those emotions: *"I feel sad that our fish died."*
- Be available to help a child who is overwhelmed by his or her emotions.
- Be prepared to repeat and clarify guidance as necessary.
- Allow authentic expression of feelings by listening and by offering support and comfort.

Activities and Experiences

Encourage children to express their emotions through art. For example, ask children to paint a picture of how they are feeling that day, or to draw a self-portrait. These can be positive, healing activities.

When infants and toddlers are present

Provide older children with opportunities to model appropriate behavior and conflict-resolution practices.

SOCIAL AND EMOTIONAL DEVELOPMENT
4 Consider children's social and cultural backgrounds when interpreting their preferences and behaviors.

Children live in communities that have various cultures and ethnicities. Regular discussion and interaction with families will help you understand their expectations and practices. It will also help you support children's social and emotional learning in culturally sensitive ways.

73

CHAPTER 3
Developing a
Home-Based
Curriculum

Social and Emotional
Development

Practices for Nurturing Cultural Sensitivity

- When children first enter your care, talk with families about their cultural and social practices, especially those involving eating, sleeping, toileting, and discipline. For instance, if a child does not eat beef or pork because of religious or cultural beliefs, ask the family to share their preferences with you. This can give you a better understanding of the child.
- Maintain ongoing communication with parents and family members to ensure you have a good understanding of their culture. Remember that everyone has a culture, and culture includes religion, ethnicity, family traditions, and family composition.
- Understand that your own culture and lifestyle affect how you define appropriate and inappropriate behavior (concerning physical contact, ways of communicating and expressing emotion, and so forth). Behavior that feels normal to you may seem strange or inappropriate to someone else, and vice versa.
- Talk with families about their children's daily social and emotional experiences. Discuss what is happening in your home and the child's home, acknowledge any major changes that are happening in the child's life, and always remember to emphasize the positive. Be sure to respect each family's confidentiality and privacy.

Activities and Experiences

- Integrate children's cultural backgrounds into your home. Include learning activities, toys and materials, and social events that children experience with their families.
- Invite families to share materials that reflect their cultural background.

5 SOCIAL AND EMOTIONAL DEVELOPMENT
Help children form and maintain satisfying relationships with one another and with adults.

To adapt successfully in group settings, children need to form trusting relationships with adults and children outside their family. Your home may offer the first opportunity for a child to develop supportive relationships.

A young child's attachment to a primary caregiver is often more stable than his or her attachments to peers, although both types of attachments can change quickly. Young children need guidance and many opportunities to learn how to make and keep friends. They must be able to understand other children's views, and they need to practice the give-and-take required in friendships. Young children's friendships are based primarily on shared interests and on learning activities and experiences.

74

CHAPTER 3
Developing a
Home-Based
Curriculum

Social and Emotional
Development

Practices That Foster Healthy Relationships

- Pay attention to the ways that your actions model positive relationships for the children.
- Take time each day to talk individually with each child; do so during and apart from learning activities and experiences.
- Talk with families about the friendships their children develop in your home. This can help families foster those friendships outside your home.
- Model, encourage, and support authenticity in relationships.
- Make sure your actions reflect your words. For example, if you tell a child, *"I'll be with you in a minute,"* be certain you can fulfill your promise.
- Remember that providing a structured, predictable environment will help children develop trusting relationships.

Activities and Experiences

- Offer many opportunities for preschool-age children to work in pairs and small groups.
- Encourage interaction among children who display different social abilities. Create opportunities for them to perform small tasks and chores together so they can learn social skills from one another.
- Offer children opportunities to interact with other adults, including other children's family members and visitors to your home. You could also arrange events such as trips to local police or fire stations to provide other opportunities.

When infants and toddlers are present

Encourage older children to be kind, nurturing, and helpful while also respecting infants' and toddlers' choices. For instance, *"I know you want to share your teddy bear with Jess, but she's crawling away. I wonder what she will choose to do now."*

SOCIAL AND EMOTIONAL DEVELOPMENT
Help each child feel valued and included.

Children develop social understanding and competence as they work and play together. Young children often need adult guidance to understand the positive and negative impact of their behavior on individual children and the group.

When you ask one child to assist another child—to answer a question, share knowledge, or help with a task—children begin to realize that everyone has something to contribute. Children build self-esteem when they are praised for specific activities or accomplishments. In mixed-age groups, older children often like to help provide care for younger children. When children see that their own behavior can affect other children positively, they gain social competence and develop a sense of belonging.

75

CHAPTER 3
Developing a
Home-Based
Curriculum

Social and Emotional
Development

Practices to Encourage a Sense of Belonging

- Model appropriate and respectful social behavior.
- Give children specific, descriptive feedback on the positive impact of their pro-social behavior: *"You made room for Max on the bench, and now all of you are sitting together! May I take your picture?"*
- Provide each child with opportunities to take leadership roles. One way to do this is to designate a daily helper, giving each child a chance to assume that role.
- Refer children's requests for adult help to capable peers (when appropriate).

Activities and Experiences

- Provide older children with opportunities to assist with tasks.
- Offer older children opportunities for group play, including role playing and pretend play. Organize simple games that teach and encourage cooperation.
- Help children succeed in group situations—for instance, on outdoor play equipment or in a playhouse. Encourage them to use words, take turns, and ask questions. Be aware that many younger children do not understand the concept of taking turns.
- Allow children to "read" picture books to other children or to provide peers with other types of help.

When infants and toddlers are present

- Understand that infants and toddlers often need more time than older children to eat, wash their hands, move from one place to another, and perform other tasks.
- Help young children become aware of other people. Show them that interaction with others is important.

7 SOCIAL AND EMOTIONAL DEVELOPMENT
Understand that the goal of guidance and discipline is to promote greater social and emotional competence.

One of your roles as a child care provider is to teach children how to act in socially responsible ways, even when adults are not around to monitor their behavior. When young children experience the personal and social benefits of behaving in acceptable ways, they are more likely to choose and exhibit good behavior.

Help children recognize the benefits of good behavior. Teach them to express their feelings and resolve problems appropriately, and to use acceptable language. Compliment and encourage children when they demonstrate

76

CHAPTER 3
Developing a
Home-Based
Curriculum

Social and Emotional
Development

socially responsible behavior. Occasions when children display inappropriate behavior can be excellent teaching opportunities. Remember that you should never use corporal punishment to discipline a child; doing so will hurt a child physically and can damage a child emotionally. Corporal punishment can also diminish a child's motivation to act in socially responsible ways.

Practices to Promote Social and Emotional Competence

- Recognize and encourage children's positive social behaviors. Describe for children the types of behavior you want them to display.
- Listen patiently when children explain their inappropriate behaviors. A good practice is to take them aside, one on one, to avoid embarrassing them. Do not allow any behavior that could harm a child. Instead, offer children alternative, acceptable ways to express their feelings or meet their needs. For instance, you might give children pillows to punch or stacking rings to bite.
- Acknowledge feelings that often accompany children's inappropriate behavior. Help children understand the impact of their words and behavior on themselves and others.
- Be aware of any discrepancies between your approach to discipline and the approach of the child's family. Explain that you will not use corporal punishment even if a family authorizes you to do so.
- Help children work out problems with as little adult intervention as possible. Depending on the ages and developmental levels of the children, avoid acting as a referee.
- When you discipline children, give them time to calm down (appropriate to age) and to sort through their feelings. Instead of placing children in "time out" in a corner or another room, engage them in activities that allow them to calm down while remaining part of the group.
- Reaffirm a child's connection to you and to the group after an incident that requires disciplinary intervention. Tell the child that he or she is loved, valued, and accepted.

When infants and toddlers are present

- Remember that infants and toddlers may not be able to explain their behavior. Look for the reasons behind inappropriate behaviors and seek possible solutions. For example, some nonverbal toddlers may bite because they are frustrated with their inability to speak. Teaching these children simple sign language might be one way to relieve their frustration.*

---

*For further discussion on sign language, refer to the "Language and Literacy" section that appears later in this chapter.

77

CHAPTER 3
Developing a
Home-Based
Curriculum

Social and Emotional
Development

- Expect that you will have to restate and reinforce limits frequently. Infants and toddlers explore their environment in part by testing limits—to see what will happen when they ignore limits. Be patient, and remember that being consistent in the way you handle inappropriate behavior will pay off; even very young children will learn that you mean what you say.

8 SOCIAL AND EMOTIONAL DEVELOPMENT
Create a sense of safety, security, and predictability through the culture, environment, and routines of your home.

Children learn best when they feel safe and cared for. A calm, organized home with familiar routines and clearly stated, consistently enforced rules provides the predictability that children need in their social and physical surroundings.

Preschool-age children are more likely to follow rules and routines when they are involved in making the rules. Similarly, when children help resolve problems that arise when rules are broken, they are more likely to exhibit good behavior and to follow established rules and routines. Encourage children to follow rules by explaining that rules are in place to ensure everyone's safety and well-being.

Practices to Create a Safe and Predictable Environment

- Provide a daily routine that is predictable—but flexible when needed—so children can anticipate the daily flow of events (outdoor play, lunch, songs, naps, and so on).
- Establish rules that are clear, age-appropriate, consistently implemented, and developed with the children's help.
- Encourage children's input on how to deal with problems involving rules, making sure that all children are heard. Help children participate in the resolution of problems instead of rushing the children into adult-directed solutions.
- Give children cues to signal transitions to new activities and experiences.
- Make orderly transitions from one activity to the next. Begin the activity in a timely way and do not require children to wait for the entire group to be ready.
- Allow sufficient time for free play and outdoor play.
- Guide behavior in ways that take into account each child's personal and developmental abilities.
- Aim to limit conflicts by arranging your home appropriately and by being readily available to children. If you notice that many conflicts occur in a particular play area, try to determine the causes, and think about ways to reduce or eliminate the conflicts. For example, you might need to rearrange furniture to provide the children with more room to move.

78

CHAPTER 3
Developing a
Home-Based
Curriculum

Social and Emotional
Development

When infants and toddlers are present

Infants and toddlers may not be able to participate in group activities from start to finish. It is developmentally appropriate for infants and toddlers to become involved in activities, move away from them, and then return to them.

SOCIAL AND EMOTIONAL DEVELOPMENT
Guide children's social behavior in the context of daily learning activities and experiences.

Children are highly motivated to interact with other children. Providing children with immediate, concrete feedback on their behavior allows them to learn new social strategies. Your input can be especially important for children who are isolated from other children because of behavior issues.

Practices to Guide Positive Social Behavior

- Tell children that you appreciate it when they cooperate during daily routines.
- Practice "optimal intervention"—which means knowing when to intervene (for example, when children are in physical danger) and when to let children solve problems on their own. To practice optimal intervention, you need to know each child well.
- Teach social development when opportunities arise each day, rather than relying on artificial, stand-alone lessons.
- Introduce learning activities and experiences with clear statements about how to treat people, and model these standards with your own behavior. Here are a few sample statements: *"Use words to let others know what you want"; "Everyone will get a turn"; "Be kind to others and treat them the way you would like to be treated"; "Be gentle";* and *"Say 'please' and 'thank you.'"*
- Regard instances of inappropriate social behavior as valuable opportunities to teach children new social strategies.

When infants and toddlers are present

- Show older children that younger children do not necessarily understand the rules of a game, and that they often claim "ownership" of specific toys for extended periods. Younger children simply follow their interests and those of other children.
- Plan activities for older children that are safe and protected from infants and toddlers. For instance, set up an activity on a high table.
- Limit or eliminate the use of swings, playpens, high chairs, or other restrictive devices. Infants learn by moving freely and making choices in an appropriate environment.

79

CHAPTER 3
Developing a
Home-Based
Curriculum

Social and Emotional
Development

Actively Communicating with Infants

How can you actively communicate with babies who are not verbal? It is often easy to distinguish between a baby's various cries and to respond appropriately. However, it can be difficult to determine what a baby wants, so it might help to vocalize your observations while directly addressing the child. For example, you might use a calm, soothing tone to say *"I can see you're upset. How can I help you? I'm here for you."* Many times, the soft tones of your voice can soothe the baby *and* you as you try to understand what a baby wants. Pay attention to an infant's cues, her eye contact with you, the position and movement of her body, and the tone of her cries. Be patient as you make efforts to read each other's cues.

When preschoolers observe your interaction with infants and toddlers, they learn a variety of lessons that include empathy and patience. Preschoolers discover that babies have emotions that are similar to their own—and as a result, preschoolers may be more willing to share your attention and help out. In fact, many preschoolers become very skilled at reading infants' cues and understanding the babies' needs and wants.

Guidelines for Resolving Conflict*

The following steps can help verbal children resolve their conflicts:

Listen
Give each child involved in the conflict a chance to talk about his or her feelings.

Define
What is each child's problem and what does each one want?

Sum up
In your words, reflect the children's feelings.

Brainstorm
Ask the children to think of possible solutions. You may want to write them down.

Evaluate
Be sure everyone's feelings are considered. Allow the children to evaluate their ideas and consider which alternatives are feasible.

Decide
Restate the problem, summarize the possible solutions, and decide on one.

Review
After living with the decision, review it. Revise it if necessary.

*Adapted from *Kids Can Cooperate,* by Elizabeth Crary. 1994. Seattle, WA: Parenting Press. http://www.parentingpress.com.

Language and Literacy Development

Why Is This Important?

During the early years of children's lives, language and literacy development have a significant impact on how well children learn to read and write when they enter school. Children are born with the capacity to develop spoken language; however, they do not reach a competent level of literacy until middle childhood, after a long, gradual process that begins in infancy.

Teachers and parents are becoming increasingly concerned about the number of children who enter school with limited language and literacy skills. A child's early experiences with parents and caregivers—and particularly the quality of care that a child receives—are key factors in determining the child's general cognitive abilities and academic achievement.[1]

Remember That Young Children . . .

- Exhibit great capacity for learning language. From ages three through five, children experience tremendous growth in language skills. Their vocabularies expand from 900 to 3,000 words, and their sentences move from simple three- or four-word utterances to complicated expressions using 12 words or more. For some children, this occurs in more than one language.
- Learn to use language to meet personal and social needs and to explore their interests. They also begin to explore what it means to be a reader and writer.

Keys to Effective Home-Based Child Care

- Offer children a language- and print-rich home that provides many opportunities to explore oral and printed communication.
- Listen to what children say, and expand upon their language to build their vocabularies. Be responsive to their attempts to communicate.
- Provide learning activities and experiences that are interesting and meaningful to children. For example, when children begin to recognize and name letters of the alphabet, an effective instructional approach is to focus on the first letter of each child's name.

Considerations When Infants and Toddlers Are Present

Language and communication develop hand in hand with trusting relationships. During the early months of life, infants are fascinated with the human voice, facial expressions, and gestures, and they repeatedly imitate their caregivers' vocalizations. As they grow, infants and toddlers practice the rhythms of speech, strings of words, and sentences they hear; they do this by themselves and with their caregivers. These are important steps in building vocabulary. Through interaction with family members and caregivers, infants learn and improve upon the give-and-take of communication.

81

CHAPTER 3
Developing a
Home-Based
Curriculum

Language and Literacy
Development

Even nonverbal babies learn communication and language skills through your body language, your words, and the words of the verbal children in your care. Practices such as "sportscasting"—announcing what you are doing as you do it—will teach words to younger children and will reinforce the words that older children already know. (Here is an example of sportscasting: *"Now I'm going to pick you up. Are you ready?"*) When you read or sing songs to a group of children, the children may learn different skills, but the important point is that each child will learn something. Younger children tend to focus on the tone and inflection of your voice, whereas older children may pay more attention to the words and the story you tell.

The term "pre-literacy" has been used to describe the learning that older infants and toddlers experience when they are able to discover and explore books, stories, and the meanings of symbols.

GUIDELINES IN THIS SECTION

1. Listen to children, talk with them, and encourage them to talk with one another.
2. Read aloud to children and share stories with them.
3. Help children notice the sounds of spoken language.
4. Provide a wide variety of printed materials.
5. Model proper speech, grammar, and communication skills.
6. Respect children's home languages.
7. Support children's language and literacy development by working closely with the children's families.

LANGUAGE AND LITERACY DEVELOPMENT

Listen to children, talk with them, and encourage them to talk with one another.

Creating a language-rich environment involves listening to children and encouraging them to talk. When you encourage communication, you pave the way for children's literacy skills. Literacy begins with language; children who are encouraged to communicate become familiar with words, stories, and conversations. When children know that an adult listens to and genuinely cares about what they say, they believe in their ability to learn.

Practices to Promote Listening and Speaking

- Encourage children to participate in conversations throughout the day. Build on their interests, and be aware of opportunities to help guide and extend their conversations.
- Help children use their own words to get their needs met, solve problems, and negotiate conflicts; you can do this by modeling words and phrases. Refrain from speaking *for* children.

82

CHAPTER 3
Developing a
Home-Based
Curriculum

Language and Literacy
Development

Activities and Experiences

- Make talking and listening a daily activity. Set aside a certain amount of time each day—apart from other activities—just to talk with and listen to children.
- Provide adequate spaces for two or more preschool-age children to work and converse together during learning activities, whether the activities are planned or spontaneous.

When infants and toddlers are present

Talk with infants and toddlers, wait for their responses, and watch for their cues—no matter how young the children are. Remember that caring, respectful communication is another way to deepen your connection with each infant.

Using Sign Language with Babies and Young Children

In recent years there has been a growing trend among families and early child care professionals to use sign language to communicate with very young children. Frequently, infants respond to and duplicate hand signals before they utter words. Signing can be fun and can help children and adults communicate. There are many resources available to teach signs to adults and infants. Infants and toddlers babble as they learn language—and because signing is a form of language, infants who are learning hand signals are likely to "babble" with their hands. Children might make up signs or use them to mean something different than what you taught. For instance, at age 15 months a child named Amy learned the hand signal for *more*. When she desperately wanted her friend, Gustavo, to get up from his nap to play, she uttered her sound for his name *(Giss)* and then signaled *more* to her caregiver. Using hand signals with children can provide many opportunities for playfulness and learning.

Research-Based Benefits of Signing

- Babies who are exposed to signs regularly and consistently at six to seven months of age can begin expressive communication by their eighth or ninth month.[2]
- Babies who use symbolic gestures understand more words, have larger vocabularies, and engage in more sophisticated play than nonsigning babies. Parents of signing babies have observed decreased frustration and increased communication in their children, and have reported enriched parent–infant bonding. Signing babies also have displayed an increased interest in books.[3]
- Presenting words in visual, kinesic (sensory), and oral ways can enhance a child's vocabulary development.[4]

For more information about sign language for infants and toddlers, visit the following Web site: http://www.sign2me.com.

CHAPTER 3
Developing a
Home-Based
Curriculum

Language and Literacy
Development

2 LANGUAGE AND LITERACY DEVELOPMENT
Read aloud to children and share stories with them.

Reading, sharing, and creating stories with children is one of the most important ways to support language development and reading competence. When you show children that books and stories can be entertaining and enjoyable, you help spark their interest in reading.

Practices to Encourage Sharing of Books and Stories

- Make reading enjoyable. Let children sit next to you, and be enthusiastic about reading. Reading to children energetically can help them develop a love for books and can stimulate their desire to learn.
- Encourage children to participate in the reading process by pointing to, asking about, and discussing pictures or words that interest them.
- Read children's favorite books over and over again; children love repetition. Ask them if they would like to share their favorite books with you and the other children.
- Share a variety of books with children: picture books (with and without words); books that incorporate different languages and cultures; fiction; and nonfiction.

Activities and Experiences

- Set aside time every day to read quietly with children, both individually and in small groups. You might try starting and ending each day with reading time. As you read, you may want to point to pictures and words—or move your finger from left to right, underneath the text, as you read each page.
- Ask children questions about each story you read. As you move through a story, pause occasionally to ask children to predict what will happen next.
- Tell creative stories in which you and the children are characters. Encourage children to respond.
- Introduce new words by reading books that are related to experiences; for example, read about jungle or savannah animals before visiting a zoo. If possible, use the child's home language as well as the dominant language of the children in your program.
- Use audiobooks to expose children to different ways of reading and interpreting stories.
- Give parents a list of books that you commonly read to the children, and let them know where they can get copies for their own home (library, bookstore, or other source).
- Make photo books that include pictures of the children, their family members, and you. Encourage older children to make and illustrate their own books.

84

CHAPTER 3
Developing a
Home-Based
Curriculum

Language and Literacy
Development

When infants and toddlers are present

- Provide sturdy board books and laminated pictures for infants and toddlers to hold and explore. You can read more advanced books with the older children.
- Protect paper books from infants and toddlers.
- Be flexible when infants and toddlers want to turn pages back and forth and flip books over.
- Remember that some younger children are more interested in books than other children are. Recognize that older children who read frequently will influence the younger children in positive ways over time. You might also pay special attention to infants and toddlers' interests (such as riding tricycles) and provide books about those topics.

3   LANGUAGE AND LITERACY DEVELOPMENT
Help children notice the sounds of spoken language.

Introducing children to the sounds of spoken language prepares them to learn how to read. Phonological awareness, or the ability to notice the sounds of language, is an essential first step. Phonological awareness begins with an awareness of words and is followed by the ability to identify syllables, onsets, rimes, and letter sounds.* It is strengthened when providers and children read poems, sing alphabet songs and nursery rhymes, and play word and sound games. Phonological awareness is a key indicator for later reading success.

Practices That Foster Phonological Awareness

The following practices can help young children develop **awareness of words**:

- Sing or create songs that incorporate children's names.
- Read poems that show children the beauty and rhythm of language. Invite preschool-age children to make up their own poems. Write down these poems on large sheets of paper so children can see their own words in print. You might have the children add illustrations to their poems to expand the activity.

---

*The onset of a syllable is the first consonant or consonant cluster—for example, the *m* in the word *map,* or the *dr* in the word *drum.* The rime of a syllable is its vowel and any ending consonants; for instance, *ap* in the word *map,* or *um* in the word *drum.* Finally, children develop awareness of the smallest abstract units of sound: phonemes. Phonemes can be represented by single letters, such as with the phonemes *c-a-t* in the word *cat,* or with two letters, such as the *ch* in *cheese;* but not all letters in a word represent a phoneme—such as the silent *e* in the word *store.* (Adapted from the *California Preschool Learning Foundations [Volume 1],* page 80; California Department of Education, Sacramento, 2008.)

85

CHAPTER 3
Developing a
Home-Based
Curriculum

Language and Literacy
Development

These practices can help children develop **awareness of syllables, onsets, and rimes:**

- Clap along to the syllables of a poem, or chant as you read the poem aloud to the children.
- Play word games with the sounds in words. For example, add or delete syllables, onsets, and rimes.

The following practices can help children develop **awareness of letter sounds:**

- Substitute different sounds for the first sound of a familiar song (e.g., "*Bow, bow, bow* your boat"). Respond when children do this spontaneously.
- Help children notice when words begin or end with the same sound; for instance, *cat, hat,* and *bat* all end with the sound of *t.* Additionally, show children what happens when one part of a word is removed. One example is to say *smile* without the *s.*
- Share with children a two-page spread from a book that has pictures of easily recognizable things: a dog, the sun, a tree, and so forth. Tell the children you are thinking about one of the images on the page, and suggest that they guess which image you are thinking about as you say the word very slowly—for example, *"ddddddddddooooooooogggg."*

Verbal Toys for Preschool-Age Children*

Rhyming words fascinate children. They are verbal toys to be repeated and repeated, rolled over the tongue, and played with again and again. Such simple joy should be encouraged. You can expand your children's experiences with rhymes and meter by creating special times to read and write poems together.

You may already have a fine collection of poetry: Mother Goose and Dr. Seuss. (You see? Rhyming can be infectious!) Many of the most popular children's classics have withstood the test of time because of their tongue-tripping rhymes. When you read them out loud, emphasize the ending rhymes so the children will tune in to them and even beat you to the punch. Listen carefully to the lyrics of their favorite songs as well, because each song is a poem. Rap songs are particularly good for teaching children to hear beats and rhymes.

Writing simple poems is easier when your mind and the children's minds are filled with poems. Once you have read children's poems or songs over and over, try creating your own with the children. Tap out the meter of a nursery rhyme so the children can hear the beat—for example, *One, two, buckle your shoe.*

*Adapted from Solnit Sale 1998b.

86

CHAPTER 3
Developing a
Home-Based
Curriculum

Language and Literacy
Development

4 LANGUAGE AND LITERACY DEVELOPMENT
Provide a wide variety of printed materials.

Young children benefit from an environment that is rich in printed materials. The idea is to bathe but not drown children in language. A print-rich environment includes the physical setup of the indoor and outdoor areas as well as the materials you offer to children.

Practices to Promote Print-Rich Environments

- Create a special reading area featuring an attractive selection of storybooks, informational books, and alphabet books. Remember that board books can be kept within reach of toddlers, but other books should be placed where toddlers do not have access to them.
- Incorporate children's printed names into daily routines; for example, post children's names and pictures next to their coat hooks or cubbies, and point out the names as the children put away their belongings.
- Display print at the children's eye level. For instance, you might put a poster in the bathroom that reminds children how to brush their teeth; you could place a laminated ABC chart in the reading area; or you might display a homemade sign that reads "You are an important person!" next to a floor-length mirror.
- Provide a variety of props that include printed letters and words. Old telephone books, order forms, and empty food cartons are just a few examples.
- Keep a variety of materials in your writing area: paper, envelopes, pencils, crayons, markers, chalkboards, whiteboards, three-dimensional letters and numbers, and so on. The writing area may be a child-size table or a kitchen table that is close to easily accessible writing materials.
- Use labels to help children recognize words and meanings. Make signs or labels for containers that hold items such as markers, paper, and crayons.

Activities and Experiences

- Ask children to talk with you about their artwork. Write down what they say, and then display words and artwork side by side.
- Provide materials that inspire children to play with the alphabet. Examples include magnetic letters for the refrigerator, alphabet play-dough cutters, and wooden alphabet puzzles.
- Make books for each child that include pictures of the children and their family members, pets, and homes. Place a photo on one side of a page, and text (written or created by the child) on the other side. Laminate and bind the books.
- Refer to Appendix F for a summary of the Preschool Learning Foundations.

87

CHAPTER 3
Developing a
Home-Based
Curriculum

Language and Literacy
Development

Pointing Out Print*

Show children that printed words are all around them by pointing out examples from everyday life.

"Jessie, that's a great T-shirt you're wearing today. It has words on it. What do you think those words say?"

"Look at the sign hanging on my wall. It says, 'Mona's Kitchen.' What do you think a sign hanging in your kitchen would say?"

Make signs and labels with the children—for projects, toys and materials, and special areas in your home.

"We need to make a sign for the fish tank. Can you help me? F-I-S-H. We need to start with F."

"Wow, you made a castle! Do you want to make a sign for your castle? Do you want the sign to say, 'Tim and Harry's castle'? Okay. T-I-M." (Say this slowly, sounding out the word. Then say the *a* sound). *"We need to start with a T."* (Say and write the letter.)

Draw the children's attention to the many ways you use printed letters and words each day.

"I'm going grocery shopping later, so I wrote this list of items I need to buy. Can you tell me how many words are on the list?"

"I want your family to know how well you're doing, so I'm sending them an e-mail."

"Here's today's newspaper. I like to read the newspaper every morning so I know what's happening in the world and the neighborhood."

"Let's go over to the computer and see if we can find out more information about butterflies."

"Look at this menu I brought from my favorite restaurant. Here are some pictures of their desserts. This one looks good. It's a cake. Let's read it: C-A-K-E" (sound out slowly).

Distinguish between children's writing and drawing.

"I like the cat you drew. She's a pretty cat. I see that you wrote your cat's name. Can you tell me your cat's name?"

---

*Adapted from U.S. Department of Education 2002.

88

CHAPTER 3
Developing a
Home-Based
Curriculum

Language and Literacy
Development

5 LANGUAGE AND LITERACY DEVELOPMENT
Model proper speech, grammar, and communication skills.

Young children learn from imitation. When you model language and literacy skills that are slightly more advanced than the children's current levels, you challenge the children to advance their skills.

For children to master emerging language and literacy skills, they need many opportunities to practice those skills. Provide these opportunities by listening carefully and responding thoughtfully to children when they speak, draw, and write. Similarly, children with speech and language difficulties—and children with significant disabilities—benefit from having you or the other children help interpret, model, or extend their intended communications. Regular activities such as sharing personal news, discussing favorite stories, or acting out your own stories let children practice specific language and literacy skills over time.

Practices to Develop Communication Skills

You can model language and literacy behaviors during conversations by using these practices:

- Listen attentively to children and check your understanding of what they have said by asking questions.
- Engage in meaningful conversations with children by following their interests, expanding on what they say, and asking increasingly difficult questions.
- Respond to grammatical errors in a child's speech by modeling the correct form, not by constantly correcting the child. For instance, if a child says *"Her took my toy!"* you could ask, *"She took your toy?"*
- Respect different communication styles and do not hurry children who may take a bit longer to formulate responses. Pause while these children think, and realize that brief periods of silence are acceptable.

Activities and Experiences

- Read a story aloud, expressively, and as you read, ask children to predict what will happen next in the story or to imagine how one of the characters might be feeling.
- Write down a child's fictional story, or the child's description of an object or event.
- Listen to a child's pretend reading or encourage his or her attempts at writing.
- Introduce the children to new words for a discussion of specific topics, such as mathematics, science, or art.

89

CHAPTER 3
Developing a
Home-Based
Curriculum

Language and Literacy
Development

- Stimulate problem solving through well-timed, open-ended questions such as *"What would you do if that happened to you?"*

When infants and toddlers are present

Take time to have group discussions that include all of the children—even infants and toddlers. Sit down and talk with the children. You might ask everyone to form a circle before you begin. Gathering and talking with the children in this way may not be easy—and it may not feel like you are having traditional conversation—but through your words, the tone and volume of your voice, and your body language, infants and toddlers will be able to understand much of what you communicate.

Talk directly to infants and wait for their responses, no matter how young they are. Speak kind words and be patient with each child. When preschoolers observe that you consistently speak with preverbal infants, they will begin to view infants as developing people who have thoughts, interests, and intelligence. Both you and the preschoolers can serve as positive role models for the infants and toddlers, showing them how to listen and communicate in kind, respectful ways.

LANGUAGE AND LITERACY DEVELOPMENT
Respect children's home languages.

Respecting children's home languages means respecting an important part of who they are—their culture, background, and ways of expressing themselves. The development of a first language serves as a foundation for learning a second language. Knowledge and use of two or more languages is a valuable asset that should be encouraged and strengthened.

Practices That Foster Respect for Home Languages

- Understand the general process of learning a second language, and know that there are individual differences in each child's rate and method of learning a second language. For example, a child might be able to process complex interactions or learning activities in his or her home language but only simple interactions in English.
- Read and share basic information with families about how children learn a first and a second language.
- Support children's learning of a first and a second language by listening carefully, following a child's lead in conversation, and showing interest in and expanding on what the child says.
- If you are proficient in a child's home language, use that language to maintain communication between you and the child's family members.

(continues on next page)

90

CHAPTER 3
Developing a
Home-Based
Curriculum

Language and Literacy
Development

- If you do not speak a child's home language, ask for help from parents or other adults who do. Ask the child's family members to teach you key words in their home language (such as *hello, good-bye, sleep, food, bathroom*).[5] Learning a few words or phrases in the child's home language will help model how to learn a second language.
- Use families as resources to understand a bilingual child's proficiency in his or her home language and in English.
- Provide opportunities for English learners to hear and use their home language during daily learning activities and experiences.

7 LANGUAGE AND LITERACY DEVELOPMENT
Support children's language and literacy development by working closely with the children's families.

Your working partnership with children's family members fosters language and literacy development. It is important to discuss a child's language and literacy interests and abilities with the family, especially if the child's home language is different from the language spoken in your home. A child's home language and literacy practices are central to his or her personal and cultural identity. When your social and cultural background differ from a child's, be especially sensitive in your communication with the child's family.

Practices That Facilitate Language and Literacy Development

- During conversations, encourage children to talk about their families and homes. Be sure to respect each family's right to confidentiality and privacy if children share sensitive information.
- Encourage all families—even those who do not speak or read English—to use oral traditions to participate in their children's English-language learning. You might ask family members to watch their children participate in storybook "reading" and then encourage each family to use the book's illustrations to retell the story at home, either in English or in the family's home language.
- Share and listen to the words families use in daily conversation. This is especially important for children who are not yet verbal.
- Model open-ended questions and conversations when families arrive to pick up their children. *Example: "Tell your mommy about the play you performed for us today!"*
- Find opportunities to practice English with children whose home language is not English. Consider taking children to reading events at local libraries.

91

CHAPTER 3
Developing a
Home-Based
Curriculum

Language and Literacy
Development

Activities and Experiences

- Create a lending library so families can borrow materials that support children's language and literacy development: books, audiobooks, educational CDs and DVDs, board games, and other appropriate materials.
- Offer children's literature written in the family's home language.
- Give families a list of books that children may read in your child care home.
- Invite older children to read to younger children, retell stories, put on plays, and set up puppet shows.

Mathematics Learning and Development

Why Is This Important?

Young children are natural mathematicians. They learn informal mathematical concepts in the context of everyday learning activities and experiences such as sorting toys and playing games. It is just as natural for young children to think mathematically as it is for them to use language.

This informal mathematical knowledge serves as a foundation for the development of formal mathematical skills in elementary school. Although children's informal math knowledge emerges naturally from birth to age five, children need adult support to build this knowledge before they enter kindergarten. In fact, there is a direct relationship between the amount of adult support that a child receives in mathematical development and the child's level of informal math knowledge—and that is why all children need support at home and in child care settings to develop fundamental mathematical knowledge.

Remember That Young Children . . .

- May already know how to count to ten or recognize some numbers. Others might not have had the opportunity to learn these skills.
- Begin to mentally calculate sums and remainders when small sets of objects increase or decrease in number. Preschool children are also able to perform simple division—for example, when they share or distribute a set of objects equally among playmates.
- Understand that properties such as mass (amount), length, and weight exist, but they do not yet know how to measure or explain these properties.
- Learn to name and create common two- and three-dimensional shapes. Older preschoolers are able to analyze the properties of shapes, such as the number of sides of a triangle.

92

CHAPTER 3
Developing a
Home-Based
Curriculum

Mathematics Learning
and Development

Keys to Effective Home-Based Child Care

- Help children learn about numbers and counting as part of their daily routine.
- Make a game out of questions such as *How many?* and *Which one is bigger?*
- Offer informal opportunities throughout your home for children to learn math (for example, by sorting, measuring, and counting objects).

Considerations When Infants and Toddlers Are Present

A "math-rich environment" is different for infants and toddlers than it is for preschoolers. Although the following guidelines focus on preschoolers, you can also help infants and toddlers develop a foundation for learning math skills. For instance, almost any object can be used in a counting exercise. Make sure your home offers a wide range of toys and materials—appropriately sized for infants and toddlers—that you can use to teach basic mathematical concepts.

GUIDELINES IN THIS SECTION

1. Create a math-rich learning environment by integrating adult-guided and child-initiated learning activities and experiences.
2. Implement activities that lay the foundation for children's success in elementary-school mathematics.
3. Identify clear, age-appropriate goals for mathematics learning and development.

1 MATHEMATICS LEARNING AND DEVELOPMENT
Create a math-rich learning environment by integrating adult-guided and child-initiated learning activities and experiences.

Math should be a part of everything in your child care setting. Use a variety of approaches to introduce young children to mathematical vocabulary and concepts. Create and facilitate situations in which

children can learn about mathematics through play, structured individual learning activities and experiences, and small-group sessions. Remember that mathematical "teachable moments" arise throughout the day, not just during formal mathematics activities.

93

CHAPTER 3
Developing a
Home-Based
Curriculum

Mathematics Learning
and Development

Practices to Recognize Teachable Moments in Mathematics

- Provide natural opportunities to learn math skills. For example, countable objects and items involving numbers can be found almost everywhere. There may be play money to count, numbers on a telephone to identify, shape molds at a sand table, or measuring cups at a water table.
- Use math language every day. Examples of mathematics vocabulary include *more, less, bigger, smaller, heavier,* and *lighter.*
- Invite children to count plates or cups when you serve lunch or snacks. Or ask children to count how many people are in your home that day.
- Point out labels, graphs, countable objects, and other math-related learning opportunities throughout your home. For instance, place a numbered picture sequence in the bathroom: *(1) Turn on the faucet; (2) Squirt soap; (3) Rub hands to make bubbles; (4) Count to ten; (5) Rinse;* and *(6) Get towel and dry hands.*
- Regularly change and provide materials that support mathematics learning: building blocks; games that teach matching skills; stacking toys; puzzles that reinforce counting and number recognition; large dice made of foam; and other items.

When infants and toddlers are present

- Recognize that you can introduce infants and toddlers to mathematical concepts such as quantity, measurement, time, and classification by teaching them words such as *before, after,* and *more;* providing them with simple nesting toys; and having them group objects by shape, color, or size.
- Understand that infants and toddlers can increase their early math understanding by putting materials together in a one-to-one correspondence—for example, by placing pom-pom balls in a muffin tin. Acknowledge and encourage the children as they gain early math skills.

Let's Talk Math*

In addition to writing numbers and learning how to count, young children need to learn words and ideas that are important to their future success in mathematics. You can help children develop early mathematics skills by following these practices:

- Use words such as *same, different, more than, less than,* and *one more* as you compare groups of objects.
- Name the *first, second, third, fourth,* and *fifth* items when you talk about things in a line or a series. For example, when cooking,

*Adapted from U.S. Department of Education 2002.

94

CHAPTER 3
Developing a
Home-Based
Curriculum

Mathematics Learning
and Development

Let's Talk Math *(continued)*

ask the children, *"What do you think the first ingredient will be? Okay, what is the second thing we should add to the bowl?"*

- Use location words: *in back of, beside, next to, between.*

- Teach children to recognize, name, and draw different shapes, and to combine some shapes to make new or bigger shapes.

- Make comparisons between objects: *taller than, smaller than.*

- Teach children to measure things with string or strips of paper, and then show them how to use items such as rulers, scales, and measuring cups to take measurements. Discuss why we need to measure things.

- Arrange groups of objects according to size—from largest to smallest, or vice versa.

- Show children how to copy patterns and to predict what will come next.

- Match objects that are alike.

- Describe similarities and differences among objects.

- Sort objects into groups according to color, shape, size, or other classification. Discuss how groups of objects are the same or different.

Mathematics Games for Two or More Children*

- Set up a mystery game involving shape recognition. Use cardboard or another material to make shapes such as circles, half-circles, triangles, squares, and rectangles. Lay out the shapes on a table, and place identical shapes in a paper bag so the children cannot see them. Ask each child, one at a time, to choose a shape from the table. Then have the child reach into the bag to identify the same shape.

- Provide the children with various small objects that have holes. Show the children how to use string to make necklaces and other jewelry with the objects. This activity gives children opportunities to practice sorting skills and to make simple patterns.

- Organize a treasure hunt. Give each child a paper bag and ask the children to find items of particular shapes that you have hidden inside or outside your home.

_____

*Adapted from Fromboluti and Rinck 1999.

95

CHAPTER 3
Developing a
Home-Based
Curriculum

Mathematics Learning
and Development

2 MATHEMATICS LEARNING AND DEVELOPMENT
Implement activities that lay the foundation for children's success in elementary-school mathematics.

A strong mathematics curriculum can enhance and strengthen children's informal mathematical abilities. It can also help build a firm foundation for the more formal learning that begins in kindergarten.

Practices to Develop Foundational Skills in Mathematics

- Consider each child's current level of mathematical knowledge, and think of ways to enrich children's knowledge and skills as they move toward kindergarten.
- Strengthen children's mathematical thinking by participating in their conversations and play. Talk about times of the day, prices, distances, and patterns, and other mathematics vocabulary and concepts.
- Help children experience math in everyday activities such as sorting the laundry or setting the table.
- Provide many types of materials to count and sort. In addition to toys and the like, you might try using items such as rocks, leaves, and twigs.
- Recognize that mathematical thinking can be strengthened throughout the day. Have the children work on puzzles; play with and identify blocks of different shapes; and compare items by using mathematical terms such as *smaller, bigger, less,* and *more.* Additionally, show the children that numbers are all around them.
- Encourage children to observe how patterns exist in everyday life, in nature, in the toys they play with, and in the clothes they wear.

Activities and Experiences

Design activities and experiences that emphasize math concepts included in the Preschool Learning Foundations, such as number sense, algebra and functions (classification and patterning), measurement, geometry, and mathematical reasoning.*

3 MATHEMATICS LEARNING AND DEVELOPMENT
Identify clear, age-appropriate goals for mathematics learning and development.

Goals for mathematics learning and development should be clearly stated, age-appropriate, continually monitored, and revised as necessary. Be aware of ways to help all children develop their mathematical thinking based on what they already know and are able to do.

---

*See Appendix F for more information about the Preschool Learning Foundations.

96

CHAPTER 3
Developing a
Home-Based
Curriculum

Mathematics Learning
and Development

Practices That Promote Appropriate Mathematics Learning

- Set clearly stated goals for mathematics learning and development, and share the goals with the children's families.
- Think about the effectiveness of the math activities and experiences that you offer in your home. Make sure the children are interested in and excited about the activities you select, and that they are progressing toward the goals you have set for them. If the children are not making progress, introduce new activities and experiences.
- Regularly observe each child's mathematical learning and development. Talk with families about their children's progress and about any problems you may observe.

Learning Mathematics Through Play*

- When cleaning up a room, ask the children to put items that belong together into two separate piles. Almost any group of things in your home can be sorted in some way. Teach the children to sort items in a specific manner but give them opportunities to think of different sorting rules as well.

- Four- and five-year olds love to play with puzzles and board games. These activities help children learn math concepts such as counting, planning ahead, thinking of and finding patterns, and understanding quantities. When you play with the children, show them the strategies you use to solve puzzles, find patterns, and so on.

- Children also enjoy playing with blocks. Because blocks have three-dimensional shapes and can be handled, children can use them to combine and change shapes. They learn to recognize geometry in the real world and they see relationships between and among shapes. By fitting one shape over another—for example, a pyramid over a cube to make a house—they can see how shapes relate to each other. As children are building things with blocks, ask them why they are using certain shapes; this question can help them think about what they are doing.

*Adapted from Fromboluti and Rinck 1999.

97

CHAPTER 3
Developing a
Home-Based
Curriculum

Mathematics Learning
and Development

- Ask the children to estimate who among them is the tallest child, and then show the children how to measure each child's height. This simple activity will help them develop an understanding of estimation, number sense, and measurement.

- Provide children with large cardboard boxes to climb in and out of. You may want to open the two ends of a box to make a tunnel for children to crawl through. Children enjoy this activity, and it gives them the opportunity to experience themselves in space.

- Children can learn about numbers and counting by playing many different games with dice and dominoes. They can practice counting, learn which numbers are bigger and smaller than others, and eventually recognize how many dots are on each die or domino just by seeing them.

DESIRED RESULTS FOR MATHEMATICS*

Desired Results Developmental Profile—Preschool (2010)©
DRDP–PS (2010)©

The Desired Results Developmental Profile—Preschool (2010)© gives teachers a means to observe children's understanding of mathematical concepts along a continuum of development.

The preschool instrument is organized into seven developmental domains. A **Domain** represents a crucial area of early learning and development for young children. Within each domain, there are several **Measures.** Each measure focuses on one aspect of development within a domain. Within each measure, there are four **Developmental Levels** that represent a continuum of development: Exploring, Developing, Building, and Integrating. **Descriptors** of the developmental levels define the behaviors expected for each level. A level is mastered if the child typically demonstrates the behaviors in that level's descriptor. Behaviors are typical if the child demonstrates them easily and confidently, consistently over time, and in different situations.

On this continuum, children at the **Exploring** level start to become familiar with a new knowledge area and, in a basic way, try out skills they are starting to learn. At the **Developing** level, children begin to demonstrate basic mastery in a knowledge and skill area. At the **Building** level, children refine and expand their knowledge and skills in an area of learning, and at the **Integrating** level, they connect the knowledge and skills they have mastered in one area with new knowledge and skills in other areas.

---

*Copyright 2010 by the California Department of Education

98

CHAPTER 3
Developing a
Home-Based
Curriculum

Mathematics Learning
and Development

DEVELOPMENTAL DOMAIN: MATH
(Mathematical Development)

Measure 33: Number sense of quantity and counting
Child uses number names to represent quantities, and counts
increasingly larger sets of objects.

Developmental Levels and Descriptors

Exploring: Recites some number names, not necessarily in order;
identifies, without counting, the number of objects in a collection
of up to three objects.

Developing: Recognizes and knows the names of some numerals;
correctly recites numbers in order, one through ten.

Building: Counts at least five objects correctly without counting
an object more than once.

Integrating: Counts at least ten objects correctly; correctly recites
numbers in order, up to 20; demonstrates understanding that the
number name of the last object counted is the total number of objects.

Examples. Each developmental level includes examples that provide
a sample of possible behaviors that might be observed for that level.
Examples are not meant to be exhaustive, nor are they intended to
be a checklist for evidence of mastery of that developmental level.
Mastery may be demonstrated with other examples also.

Following are additional measures of mathematical development for
preschool children, ages three to five:

Measure 34: Number sense of mathematical operations
Child shows increasing ability to add and subtract small quantities of
objects.

Measure 35: Classification
Child shows increasing ability to compare, match, and sort objects into
groups according to some common attribute.

Measure 36: Measurement
Child shows increasing understanding of measurable properties such as
length, weight, and capacity, and begins to quantify those properties.

Measure 37: Shapes
Child shows increasing knowledge of shapes and their characteristics.

Measure 38: Patterning
Child shows increasing ability to recognize, reproduce, and create patterns
of varying complexity.

99

CHAPTER 3
Developing a
Home-Based
Curriculum

Mathematics Learning
and Development

Desired Results Developmental Profile—Infant/Toddler (2010)©
DRDP–IT (2010)©

When infants and toddlers are present in a home care setting, their understanding of mathematical concepts is revealed by measures in the Cognitive Domain. In particular, infant/toddler (IT) Measure 28 (Number), Measure 29 (Classification and matching), and Measure 30 (Space and size) help gauge the development of individual children. In the cognitive domain, five developmental levels are used to identify children's development: Responding with Reflexes; Expanding Responses; Acting with Purpose; Discovering Ideas; and Developing Ideas.

DEVELOPMENTAL DOMAIN: COGNITIVE

IT Measure 28: Number

Child shows understanding of the concept of number or quantity.

Developmental Levels and Descriptors

Responding with Reflexes: Responds to single events or actions with reflexes.

Expanding Responses: Attends to one thing or object at a time.

Acting with Purpose: Recognizes that there are different amounts of things.

Discovering Ideas: Knows and uses simple number names, but not always correctly.

Developing Ideas: Recognizes or uses numbers to represent small amounts or to count up to a small number.

Examples. As with the preschool instrument, each developmental level in the infant/toddler instrument includes examples that might be observed for that level. Examples are not exhaustive, nor are they intended to be a checklist for evidence of mastery of that developmental level. Mastery may be demonstrated with other examples also.

Following are additional measures of mathematical development in the Infant/Toddler Cognitive Domain:

Measure 29: Classification and matching
Child compares, matches, and categorizes different people or different things.

Measure 30: Space and size
Child shows understanding of how things move in space or fit into different spaces.

Cognitive Development (Thinking Skills)

Why Is This Important?

When children develop thinking skills and general knowledge of their world, it becomes easier for them to read and learn when they enter school. You play an important role in helping children learn new information, ideas, and vocabulary. You also help them connect new information and ideas to what they already know and understand. By providing high-quality child care, you teach children to become full participants in their education.

Remember That Young Children . . .

- Learn about what things are and how they work.
- Gather and process information about the world around them.
- Extend their use of language and expand their vocabulary.
- Develop the ability to solve problems.

Keys to Effective Home-Based Child Care

- Encourage children to explore and work with familiar equipment and materials in your home.
- Cook and prepare foods to teach children about substances and changes in substances.
- Provide children with opportunities to learn about plants by planting seeds and by taking care of the growing plants.
- Help children learn about social situations and interactions through dramatic play.

Considerations When Infants and Toddlers Are Present

Infants learn in two primary ways: through relationships, and by making their own discoveries. Research on cognitive development shows that infants learn by observing and imitating people around them, and by continually inventing new and better ways of doing things. Allow infants and toddlers sufficient time to explore and work with materials. Keep in mind that infants and toddlers often repeat behaviors many times as they gather information about their environment.

GUIDELINES IN THIS SECTION

1. Build on children's natural curiosity by providing opportunities to explore social studies and science.
2. Use computers and other forms of technology appropriately.

101

CHAPTER 3
Developing a
Home-Based
Curriculum

Cognitive
Development

COGNITIVE DEVELOPMENT

Build on children's natural curiosity by providing opportunities to explore social studies and science.

Young children have an instinctive desire to explore the world. Encourage children to act on their curiosity so they can gain new knowledge. Because a young child's knowledge is tied to his or her personal experiences, your home should offer many opportunities for children to explore social studies, science, and mathematics (which was covered previously in this chapter).

For young children, the meaning of social studies is found in the cultures and communities where they live. Learning about community helpers and about the cultures of other families in the program provides a rich foundation for later learning in social studies. In the same way, young children experience science in the natural world around them. Observing weather, plants, and animals is fascinating for children. By learning about seasonal changes and about seeds and plants, caring for pets, and observing animals in the wild, children gain an early appreciation of science that will grow as they continue through elementary grades.

Practices to Encourage Learning About Communities and Cultures

- Encourage children to learn about the world around them. Talk with them about local places of interest such as libraries, schools, stores, parks, and noteworthy buildings; how the children get to and from home; how other people get from one place to another; what people do during the day; and whether members of the children's extended families live nearby or far away.
- Take children on "walking field trips" so they can learn about different aspects of your neighborhood.
- Offer children opportunities to display their artwork, writing, and other projects that show positive images of and stories about their families, friends, and acquaintances.
- Encourage children to recognize and accept similarities and differences among families.

When infants and toddlers are present

Understand that infants and toddlers have a more limited view of the world. For them, social studies consists of family members and places they know, other children in your care, their home environment, you, and your child care environment. As younger children develop familiarity with their immediate social settings, they build a foundation for later interest in other settings.

102

CHAPTER 3
Developing a
Home-Based
Curriculum

Cognitive
Development

Practices to Encourage Learning About the Natural World

- Explore the outdoors to identify and examine plants, animals, leaves, and other natural phenomena.
- Provide materials such as seeds to plant, a fish tank or terrarium, a magnifying glass, scales, and mirrors.
- Encourage children to develop and explore scientific concepts by observing natural phenomena and events. Ask them questions about what they observe, their theories for explaining what they observe, and other aspects of their discoveries.

When infants and toddlers are present

Infants and toddlers explore their environment in simple ways—for instance, by placing things in their mouths—but their methods of exploration are scientific nonetheless. Based on their daily exploration, young children make discoveries and decisions, and they modify their behavior. For example, infants may learn that a rug does not taste good. They may bite the rug several times before they make this discovery but they will assimilate their knowledge and change their behavior based on what they have learned. As a provider, you may choose to offer infants and toddlers other items to bite and explore, but what is most important is that you watch the children, understand their favorite ways of exploring, and respond to them based on your observations.

2 COGNITIVE DEVELOPMENT
Use computers and other forms of technology appropriately.

Computers, television, and other forms of technology should support—not replace—your role as a teacher. Use technology to enrich and extend children's learning activities and experiences.

Practices to Facilitate Appropriate Use of Technology

- Make sure that children's exposure to computers and television is limited.
- Remember that real life and real people are more important than the abstract world of television, computers, video games, and the like. Nothing can replace human interaction.
- Teach children about simple, interesting machines and gadgets such as CD and DVD players, electric mixers, toasters, and other devices in your home.
- Remember that most children do not understand or think about the potentially negative aspects of using computers, watching television, playing video games, or using other types of modern technology.

103

CHAPTER 3
Developing a
Home-Based
Curriculum

Cognitive
Development

- Use technology to enhance learning, and strive to achieve a balance between the use of technology and other instructional aids.
- When integrating the use of technology into your curriculum, consider each child's characteristics and needs, the families' wishes, and available resources. Choose computer software that is developmentally appropriate, open-ended, interactive, and that invites children to make choices.
- Learn how to use technology to help children with disabilities or other special needs.

When infants and toddlers are present

Understand that it can be difficult for infants and toddlers to detach their gaze from television or computer screens. Do not misinterpret this staring as a sign that the children like or need to look at television or computer screens.

Creativity and Self-Expression

Why Is This Important?

Art, music, and dramatic play contribute to the intellectual, emotional, and aesthetic life of children. The arts can also serve as an excellent means of communication.

Child development experts agree that the arts are valuable because they offer children opportunities to exercise reasoning, organization, and fine motor skills; they can show children that there are many ways to view life; and they allow children to express themselves freely. In a painting, for example, composition, color, and relationships are presented simultaneously. Children reveal their preferences, attitudes, and values in their creative works—which also reflect different aspects of the environments in which the children live.

The arts have a positive impact on the following areas of children's development:[6]

- **Academic performance.** The arts make the learning process fun. When children enjoy learning activities, they tend to improve academically.
- **Work habits.** Artistic endeavors such as drawing and painting require concentration, dedication, and experimentation, all of which can help children develop better work habits in other learning areas.
- **Creative discovery and self-expression.** The arts provide children with the freedom to express their deepest thoughts, values, and emotions in numerous ways.
- **Assessment of children's development.** Through a child's creative work, adults have tangible ways of viewing children's intellectual and emotional development.

104

CHAPTER 3
Developing a
Home-Based
Curriculum

Creativity and
Self-Expression

- **Cultural understanding.** The arts can help children gain a better understanding of their own culture and other cultures.
- **Physical development.** Art forms such as dancing, singing, drawing, painting, and sculpting help children develop fine and gross motor skills. The arts also provide children with opportunities to use excess energy and to vent emotions in positive ways.
- **Leisure.** Artistic activities make free time enjoyable and meaningful for children.

Remember That Young Children . . .

- Learn to use a variety of materials and to increase their sense of mastery and creativity through art activities. Children learn to express feelings and ideas through their artwork; they discover that talking is not the only way to express themselves.
- Can master the use of simple musical instruments such as rhythm sticks, tambourines, and drums. They also are interested in the sounds made by more complicated instruments (such as the piano, violin, and guitar), and in how those instruments are played. Children enjoy singing; making up silly, rhyming verses; learning fingerplays; and using music to tell stories and express feelings. Often they will make up songs to accompany other activities such as cleaning up or preparing to eat a snack.
- Need opportunities to move and stretch their bodies. They move constantly, wiggle, change positions, and sit in a variety of ways.

Keys to Effective Home-Based Child Care

Provide daily opportunities for children to use their imagination and creativity through a variety of learning activities and experiences. Make available a variety of materials that can be used in visual arts, dramatic play, music, and dancing; and demonstrate your appreciation of children's work by complimenting them and by displaying some of their work. Talk with the children's families about art, music, and dramatic-play activities that you offer. Additonally, share the children's artwork with their families.

Considerations When Infants and Toddlers Are Present

Infants and toddlers embody creativity and self-expression. Each of their movements and utterances is a piece of creation unfolding. Your responsiveness, communication, encouragement, and tender caregiving provide infants and toddlers with the foundation they need to grow and to express themselves freely. In some ways, you teach and model creativity and self-expression for infants and toddlers—but it is just as important to nurture and protect these young children as they exhibit their innate creativity and expressiveness.

105

CHAPTER 3
Developing a
Home-Based
Curriculum

Creativity and
Self-Expression

GUIDELINES IN THIS SECTION

1. Offer a variety of opportunities for children to use their imagination and creativity.
2. Encourage children to express their feelings through art, music, dramatic play, and dance.

CREATIVITY AND SELF-EXPRESSION

Offer a variety of opportunities for children to use their imagination and creativity.

Art, drama, and music are universal languages. They encourage many kinds of communication that complement and enhance learning in other curricular areas—such as early language and literacy, mathematics, and social development.

Practices to Encourage Creative Expression

- Introduce the children to a wide range of creative arts including music, drama, visual arts, and dance.
- Emphasize the creative process rather than final products. Stress that there are numerous ways to create artwork and to express oneself artistically. Encourage children to create their own artwork, and avoid providing samples.
- Encourage children to appreciate the arts as participants and as part of an audience. One way to do this is to make paper-bag puppets and to have children take turns acting out stories for each other.
- Use new experiences as opportunities to create art. Take children to a museum, grocery store, or pizzeria, and when you return to your home, ask the children to draw pictures or develop a short dramatic play based on something they observed.
- Share your own appreciation of the arts by singing songs, dancing with the children, playing a musical instrument or your favorite CDs, and in other ways.

Activities and Experiences

- Offer a variety of materials that foster artistic and creative expression. These might include patterns and cloth from different cultures; large containers of paint; crayons; easels; large sheets of paper; clay; modeling dough; musical instruments; clothes and hats for dramatic play; and materials from the outdoors such as flowers and leaves.
- Remember that it is not always necessary to buy materials for art projects. You can also use recycled materials and everyday objects. For example,

106

CHAPTER 3
Developing a
Home-Based
Curriculum

Creativity and
Self-Expression

hand puppets can be made out of items such as paper bags, office supplies, felt, pens, and crayons.

- Display samples of the children's artwork prominently and at the children's eye level.

2 CREATIVITY AND SELF-EXPRESSION
Encourage children to express their feelings through art, music, dramatic play, and dance.

The arts offer positive, healthy ways for children to express their emotions. When children are happy or excited they can share their joy through art, dramatic play, and dance. Often the joy that children express in a painting, play, or dance is contagious; it has the power to lift everyone's spirits. There are times when children can express themselves more effectively through art and dance than through verbal communication—especially when they experience feelings of anger, anxiety, or self-doubt. As a provider you can inspire children to express themselves through art, and you can learn from what they create.

Practices to Promote Self-Expression

- Introduce children to the comforting properties of music, dramatic play, and art. For example, when children are joyful and excited, play upbeat music to which they can dance *("Let's play this salsa music and dance together!")*. When children are tense, you might play soothing music to calm their nerves: *"Let's listen to this classical music and relax a bit."*
- Each day, pay close attention to the children's art, dramatic play, and dance. Watch for changes in their creative work to better understand their emotions. For instance, one day a girl may depict herself in a drawing as larger than life, with a broad smile across her face. On another day she might draw a picture that shows a considerably smaller image of herself—a drawing in which she is standing apart from her peers or family members. Study these details and ask children to talk with you about their artwork.
- Recognize that all forms of art can help children express their thoughts and emotions. Be accepting of all forms of the children's artwork, singing, or dramatic play—not just the work that is cheerful, pretty, or outstanding.

Activities and Experiences

- Invite children to make up a dance. Ask them to perform it for the whole group or to teach the dance to others.
- Ask the children to paint pictures (or self-portraits) of how they feel on a particular day or at a given moment. When they finish their artwork, talk with each child about his or her picture.

- Invite the children to prepare a skit or short play to perform. Ask the children to decide what the play will be about and to choose the roles they would like to play.

 ## Physical and Motor Development

Why Is This Important?

Young children have boundless energy. Channel their energy by providing them with many different opportunities to develop physically, to stay strong and healthy, and to refine their physical skills. When physical activity is a regular and enjoyable part of young children's routines, the children are more likely to be healthy and physically active throughout their lives.

Remember That Young Children . . .

Are in the process of acquiring many basic motor skills, including gross motor skills and fine motor skills.

Gross (large muscle) motor skills. Young children are learning how to run; walk on their tiptoes; stand on one foot; hop on both feet; ride a tricycle; walk down a series of steps, unsupported, with both feet on one step; and jump down from various locations including playground equipment at a park. They proceed to gallop; walk up and down steps unsupported, alternating their feet; and they may even perform tricks on a tricycle. In addition, you may see them hopping on one foot, two or more times.

Fine (small muscle) motor skills. Young children begin to make snips with scissors; hold crayons with a more adultlike grasp; and draw scribbles, straight lines, and simple shapes. They learn to eat by themselves with few spills; and they can dress themselves, although they require assistance with pullover shirts and some fasteners. They can brush their teeth by themselves and they like to brush their own hair. Older preschoolers enjoy cutting straight lines, working on 10- to 12-piece puzzles, stringing beads, and building a nine- or 10-block tower.

Keys to Effective Home-Based Child Care

Provide children with daily opportunities to engage in these experiences and activities:

- Experiences in which they use their senses—visual, auditory, taste, smell, and touch
- Large motor activities such as crawling, walking, climbing, running, jumping, dancing, balancing, throwing, and catching
- Small motor activities such as grasping, scribbling, cutting with scissors, buttoning, tying shoes, using art materials, or playing with objects

108

CHAPTER 3
Developing a
Home-Based
Curriculum

Physical and Motor
Development

Considerations When Infants and Toddlers Are Present

For infants and toddlers, learning is very physical; younger children learn a great deal through their senses and motor skills. For instance, two warm arms that rock a child to sleep teach trust and comfort, and a teething ring teaches the properties of objects. Because young children often mouth objects and grab for things within their reach, be aware of small items that could be choking hazards, or larger items that could be pulled over. Like preschoolers, infants and toddlers are learning fine motor skills (such as grasping their fingers and tracking objects with their eyes) and gross motor skills (for example, sitting up, climbing, and walking).

Motor skills do not need to be taught to typically developing infants. Infants instinctively learn to roll, balance, and crawl; and eventually they sit, stand, and walk. Trying to teach motor skills can actually interfere with a child's sense of balance and motivation. Instead, stay near the infants and toddlers, observe them, and encourage older children to respect each infant's unique way of moving.

GUIDELINES IN THIS SECTION

1. Observe all areas of motor-skill development, including gross motor, fine motor, oral motor, and sensorimotor skills.
2. Remember that children differ in their development of skills and abilities.
3. Provide many opportunities for safe and active play.

PHYSICAL AND MOTOR DEVELOPMENT
Observe all areas of motor-skill development, including gross motor, fine motor, oral motor, and sensorimotor skills.

Encourage children to develop all of their physical skills and abilities through a variety of learning activities and experiences. Children often have preferences for particular skills and will naturally focus on areas in which they feel the most comfortable.

For example, a boy who loves to make detailed clay figures may be reluctant to try walking on a balance beam. A girl who can do expert cartwheels may need help in fine motor activities such as cutting with scissors. All children should be encouraged to test their physical limitations without ridicule or fear of failure. Always acknowledge and value each child's strengths.

Practices to Facilitate Development of Motor Skills

*   Provide time for the children to practice the following skills:
    *   **Gross motor skills**—running, jumping, climbing, skipping, dancing

109

CHAPTER 3
Developing a
Home-Based
Curriculum

Physical and Motor
Development

- **Fine motor skills**—cutting, painting, threading, pouring, molding, buttoning, zipping, tying, constructing with play dough or clay, doing fingerplays
  - **Sensorimotor skills**—catching, pointing, matching, touching, clapping
  - **Oral motor skills**—talking, singing, imitating sounds, rhyming
- *When infants and toddlers are present,* allow them time to practice the following skills:
  - **Gross motor skills**—crawling, standing, walking
  - **Fine motor skills**—feeding self, using thumb and forefinger to pick up small items
  - **Sensorimotor skills**—pointing, touching, clapping
  - **Oral motor skills**—babbling, talking, singing, imitating sounds
- *When infants are present,* observe them as they work on these skills:
  - **Gross motor skills**—rolling over, lifting the head, crawling, sitting up
  - **Fine motor skills**—tracking objects and turning eyes toward sounds, grasping your finger
  - **Sensorimotor skills**—pointing, touching, clapping
  - **Oral motor skills**—opening and closing the mouth, imitating sounds

2 PHYSICAL AND MOTOR DEVELOPMENT
Remember that children differ in their development of skills and abilities.

Children acquire motor skills at different rates. Focus on the steady progression of physical development rather than the age at which a child develops a particular skill. Just as children must learn to walk before they can run, they must scribble before they can write. By building on acquired skills, you can guide children through their unique stages of physical development.

Practices That Enable Development at Different Rates

- Observe children to identify their levels of physical development.
- Encourage children—but do not pressure them—to attempt new tasks.
- Provide opportunities for safe, age-appropriate, and challenging gross motor activity, both inside and outside your home.
- Celebrate the children's achievements.
- Help children establish their own limits.
- To model skills and to provide motivation, pair children who have different abilities.
- Avoid making statements that point out differences in children's abilities.
- Offer physical activities that meet the needs of each child, including those who have disabilities or other special needs.

110

CHAPTER 3
Developing a
Home-Based
Curriculum

**Physical and Motor
Development**

Activities and Experiences

- Provide materials that allow for different skill levels and mixed-age group play. For example, younger children often mouth or handle large blocks; older children like to stack them or use them to build things. Blocks of varying colors allow young children to play but also allow older children to engage in more complex play (such as making designs or patterns).
- Provide equipment for motor-skill development that enables children to get on and off the equipment on their own. For example, preschool children may be able to climb on and off a jungle gym, toddlers can use a platform two inches off the ground, and infants and toddlers can use pillows.

When infants and toddlers are present

- Allow infants and toddlers ample time and safe spaces to move freely on the floor.
- Be aware of the mobility of older children and the limited mobility of infants. Protect the younger children from the older children's active play and wheeled toys.

3 PHYSICAL AND MOTOR DEVELOPMENT
Provide many opportunities for safe and active play.

Children should have opportunities to test their physical abilities freely in a safe, structured environment. Safe and active play is essential to each child's development of gross and fine motor skills. Use play periods to observe the children and to identify skills that may need further development. Help preschool-age children develop their skills by guiding their learning activities and experiences.

Practices to Promote Safe and Active Play

- Offer materials and equipment that support safe and active play; examples include a sandbox, bean bags to throw and catch, riding toys, and accessories for dramatic play such as clothes, hats, masks, and scarves.
- Provide music and musical instruments to inspire dancing. Play different styles of music (e.g., classical, jazz, rhythm and blues, salsa, country) with varying tempos and beats. Infants can repeat simple movements such as opening and closing their mouths, and older children can march to the music while beating sticks or a drum.
- Look for physical-play opportunities that involve nature. Walk to the nearest park, visit a nature museum, or enjoy the natural surroundings of your own yard.

111

CHAPTER 3
Developing a
Home-Based
Curriculum

Physical and Motor
Development

- Organize individual and group physical activities that allow for varying levels of development and moods. If children feel overwhelmed, sad, or angry, solitary playtime may help them relax and feel better.
- Be available during playtimes to offer support and encouragement.
- Help children learn to be safe and to take reasonable risks.
- Talk with families about active-play activities that their children enjoy at home, and offer those activities if possible.
- If you have climbing equipment, make sure it meets safety regulations and that the fall zone underneath it is properly cushioned.
- Observe children as they engage in active play. Assess each child's skills and needs.

When infants and toddlers are present

- Allow infants and toddlers ample time and safe spaces to move freely on the floor.
- When you offer times for active play, observe the younger children; if they spend most of their time watching the older children, adjust the activities so infants and toddlers feel safe and free to explore.

Ages and Stages on Wheels

When you have children of all ages in your care—and even if all the children are close in age—it can be difficult to plan activities that involve everyone and take into account varying rates of development and abilities. Children often love anything with wheels—and wheeled riding toys allow children to exercise, fine-tune their motor skills, and play cooperatively with others.

Young infants can be wheeled about in strollers, mobile infants can push wheeled toys, toddlers can learn to ride tricycles, preschoolers can ride scooters, and older preschoolers can ride bikes with training wheels. If you have only one or two bikes or scooters, you can teach preschoolers to take turns and share. You can also show preschoolers that toddlers take more time to get on and off the equipment—and the toddlers may have just as much fun getting on and off tricycles as they do riding them! Keep in mind that if you provide care for children with special needs or developmental delays, you may have to provide adaptive bicycles. Regardless of your situation, wheeled riding toys can allow you to offer physical activity for each child in your care.

112

CHAPTER 3
Developing a
Home-Based
Curriculum

Physical and Motor
Development

Summary of an Effective Curriculum

An effective home-based child care curriculum involves many different elements, including balance, inclusiveness, flexibility, and creativity. When you develop the curriculum for your home, strive to meet the following goals:

- Involve children and their family members in the selection, planning, and evaluation of activities.
- Reflect diversity of cultures and communities, especially those of the children for whom you provide care.
- Make sure your home and curriculum can include children with disabilities or other special needs.
- Accommodate different learning styles and abilities.
- Provide time for play and exploration.
- Introduce the children to new ideas and learning experiences on a regular basis.
- Offer choices to children.
- Include content that is interesting and meaningful to children.
- Balance adult-initiated and child-initiated learning activities and experiences.
- Provide alternating periods of active and quiet activities.
- Offer learning activities in individual, small-group, and large-group formats.

Notes

1. Hart and Risley 1995.
2. Garcia 1994.
3. Goodwyn et al. 2000.
4. Daniels 1994.
5. See also *Preschool English Learners: Principles and Practices to Promote Language, Literacy, and Learning* (Sacramento: California Department of Education, 2007).
6. International Child Art Foundation. http://www.icaf.org.

Professional Development for Home-Based Child Care Providers

$\mathscr{P}$ROFESSIONAL DEVELOPMENT ACTIVITIES SUCH AS TRAINING AND WORKSHOPS can help you remain current on important child care–related issues, including how to help children prepare for formal schooling, how to strengthen your partnerships with families, and how to include children with special needs. In addition, interacting with other child care professionals during training sessions or other professional development activities can be gratifying and can relieve feelings of isolation that you may experience as a provider.

114

CHAPTER 4
Professional
Development
for Home-Based
Child Care
Providers

This chapter is designed to assist you with professional development. It includes information on the following topics:

- Meeting other providers through family child care organizations, associations, and networks
- Becoming licensed and/or accredited
- Receiving training and support at child care resource and referral (R&R) agencies, community colleges, family child care associations, or through the Internet
- Earning a Child Development Associate (CDA) credential or other degree
- Qualifying for a California child development permit: Assistant, Associate Teacher, Teacher, Master Teacher, Site Supervisor, or Program Director
- Adopting or improving professional business practices

Why Is This Important?

As a home-based child care provider, you fill three important and challenging roles: caregiver, teacher, and family partner. Professional development includes learning about how to work with families to ensure consistency between a child's home and your child care setting—and one of the many benefits of home-based care is that families often keep their children with the same provider for many years. Whether you participate in workshops and meetings with other child care providers or pursue more formal education, the skills you learn will help you become a more effective provider.

Remember That Young Children . . .

- Have unique needs and abilities that are easier to address when you gain professional knowledge and experience.
- Benefit from providers who strive to learn, grow, and improve their child care environments.

Keys to Effective Home-Based Child Care

- Seek training and educational opportunities.
- Develop a support network consisting of other providers, a local child care association, or a national child care association.
- Keep up-to-date on a variety of topics including child development, health and safety, curriculum, cultural issues, family partnerships, and the inclusion of children with disabilities or other special needs.

Considerations When Infants and Toddlers Are Present

Infants and toddlers have different needs than older children. Look for training and other professional development opportunities that can help you integrate infants and toddlers with older children. You also may want to

115

CHAPTER 4
Professional
Development
for Home-Based
Child Care
Providers

search the Internet for information on how to provide high-quality care for mixed-age groups.

1. Make the children your top priority.
2. Be aware of legal requirements and responsibilities.
3. Consider the benefits of ongoing training and education.
4. Participate in a child care association and/or a network of home-based child care providers.
5. Develop a plan for improving your child care program.
6. Follow Best Business Practices.
7. Take care of yourself.

PROFESSIONAL DEVELOPMENT

Make the children your top priority.

You play an important role in the life of every child for whom you provide care. Each day, you have the opportunity to influence every child in positive ways. The children will watch you closely, learn from you, and model what they see, hear, and experience in your home. If they see joy in your face, if they hear kindness in your voice, and if they feel at ease in your home, their experiences will benefit them for the rest of their lives. Be sure the example you set is one you want the children to imitate!

To be an effective provider, the children must be your top priority. Your energy and attention should be directed toward the children at all times (whenever they are in your care). This mindset applies to all child care providers—those who provide care for the children of family members and friends, and individuals who operate small or large family child care homes licensed by the state.

Practices for Focusing on the Children in Your Care

- Give your full attention to the children during child care hours. Care of the children takes priority over personal telephone calls and any other activities unrelated to child care.
- Recognize that each child is unique, and provide responsive, individualized care. Reflect on what happens each day and address any special concerns that arise.
- Respect the confidentiality and privacy of the children and their families. The only exception to this is when you are legally required to report suspected child abuse or neglect.

116

CHAPTER 4
Professional
Development
for Home-Based
Child Care
Providers

2 Be aware of legal requirements and responsibilities.

If you provide care for children who come from more than one family and who are not related to you, California law requires you to have a child care license. The California Department of Social Services (CDSS), Community Care Licensing Division (CCLD), licenses family child care homes. There are two categories of family child care homes:

Small Family Child Care Homes. Provide child care for up to eight children, including the provider's own children who are under age 10. The maximum number of children allowed varies according to the ages of the children. For example, a provider may care for a maximum of four infants; or six children, no more than three of whom may be infants. Additionally, a provider may care for up to eight children if at least two of the children are over age six and if other conditions are met.[*]

Large Family Child Care Homes. Provide child care for up to 14 children, including the provider's own children under the age of 10, with two adults (the provider and an assistant) available to provide care and supervision at all times. If a provider chooses to care for as many as 12 children, no more than four of the children may be infants. A group of 13 or 14 children may include up to three infants and must include at least two children over the age of six; other conditions must be met as well.[†] Operators of large family child care homes must have at least one year of experience as a licensed small family child care home provider; or one year as an administrator, director, or teacher at a licensed child care center.

You do not need a license if you provide care for children from only one other family in addition to your own children. However, being exempt from licensure does not mean that you cannot be licensed. You still may want to apply for a license. The purpose of licensure is to promote the minimum standards necessary to protect children's health and safety.

Practices That Promote Compliance with Licensing Regulations

- *For all home-based child care providers:* Determine if you need a child care license. California law requires you to be licensed if you provide care for children from more than one family and if those children are not related to you.

---

[*]Section 102416.5(b) of the *California Code of Regulations, Title 22 (22 CCR),* provides detailed licensing requirements for Small Family Child Care Homes. For more information, visit the CDSS Community Care Licensing Division Web site at http://www.ccld.ca.gov.

[†]*22 CCR* Section 102416.5(c) provides detailed licensing requirements for Large Family Child Care Homes. For more information, visit the CDSS Community Care Licensing Division Web site at http://www.ccld.ca.gov.

117

CHAPTER 4
Professional
Development
for Home-Based
Child Care
Providers

- *For providers who must have a license:* Contact the Department of Social Services' CCLD for information on how to become licensed. You may visit http://www.ccld.ca.gov/PG487.htm, or you may call 916-651-8848. The section following these practices also presents licensing information.
- *For license-exempt providers:* The term "license-exempt" means that you do not need a license to provide child care in your home. **However, if you receive public funds for providing child care, you must register with TrustLine,** a database of in-home child care providers who have cleared criminal background checks in California. (Further information on TrustLine is presented in the next section.) Your TrustLine registration can help family members feel secure about you as a provider. It may also make you eligible for benefits offered by the Child and Adult Care Food Program (CACFP), which reimburses child care providers for serving healthy meals and snacks to the children in their care.

Licensing Benefits and Requirements

As discussed previously, if you provide care for children who come from more than one family and who are not related to you, California law requires you to have a child care license. By obtaining and maintaining a family child care license, you assure parents that you and your home meet health and safety standards established by the State of California. The CDSS visits each child care home before issuing a license; performs criminal background checks on all adults who live in the home; requires a tuberculosis (TB) clearance for all providers; makes unannounced visits to homes after licenses have been issued; investigates complaints; and denies and revokes licenses when necessary. Because the state regulates child care providers in these ways, parents can be assured that licensed providers have been carefully screened—and providers like you can feel proud of and confident about the care you offer.

To obtain a Family Child Care Home license, you must:

- Be 18 years of age or older.
- Attend an orientation session (if you have not completed a Family Child Care Home Orientation within the last 12 months).
- Submit the required forms from the CDSS application booklet.
- Submit payment for orientation and application fees.
- Pass a criminal record and Child Abuse Index check. All other adults who live or work in your home must pass these checks as well.

(continues on next page)

118

CHAPTER 4
Professional
Development
for Home-Based
Child Care
Providers

- Obtain a tuberculosis clearance (not more than one year old) for you and all adults who live or work in your home.
- Complete at least 15 hours of training in preventive health practices. This includes training in pediatric CPR and first aid in addition to a preventive-health-practices class that uses curriculum approved by the California Emergency Medical Services Authority (EMSA).
- Pass a home inspection conducted by a licensing analyst.
- Meet experience requirements if you will be operating a Large Family Child Care Home.
- Comply with all city, county, or other local ordinances.
- Inform your landlord (if you rent or lease your home) of your decision to operate a Family Child Care Home.

Note: You do not need formal education to qualify for a Family Child Care Home license. However, if you want to be accredited by the National Association for Family Child Care, you need a high school diploma or GED credential. Further information on accreditation appears later in this chapter.

To find a child care licensing office near you, contact the CDSS:

California Department of Social Services
Community Care Licensing Division, Child Care Offices
Telephone: 916-229-4500
http://ccld.ca.gov/PG513.htm

TrustLine Background Checks

TrustLine is California's registry of in-home child care providers, tutors, and in-home counselors who have passed criminal background checks. In California, all licensed child care providers must pass a TrustLine screening. **Additionally, license-exempt providers who receive government funds for providing care—with the exception of aunts, uncles, and grandparents—must pass a TrustLine screening.**

TrustLine is the only background screening authorized by California law to use the following three databases to check an individual's personal history: fingerprint records from the California Department of Justice's California Criminal History System; the Child Abuse Central Index of California; and fingerprint records from the FBI Criminal History System. The general public—including private investigators and background-check companies—does not have access to these databases. A person who has passed a TrustLine screening has no disqualifying criminal convictions or substantiated child abuse reports in California. **For more information, contact TrustLine at 1-800-822-8490, or visit http://www.trustline.org.**

119

CHAPTER 4
Professional
Development
for Home-Based
Child Care
Providers

Findings on Educational Qualifications of Family Child Care Providers*

According to the California Early Care and Education Workforce Study, family child care providers are more likely than the state's overall female population to have attended and completed some college.

The Center for the Study of Child Care Employment (CSCCE) at the University of California, Berkeley, in collaboration with the California Child Care Resource and Referral Network and with support from First 5 California, completed telephone surveys with a randomly selected sample of 1,800 licensed family child care home providers in four regions throughout California. The survey identified the number of home-based providers and staff members working in licensed family child care, and the educational qualifications of this workforce. Here are some of the survey findings:

- Compared with California's overall female population, surveyed licensed family child care providers were more likely to have attended college and/or completed a two-year college degree.
- Slightly more than 25 percent of surveyed licensed family child care providers had obtained a two-year, four-year, or graduate degree typically not related to early childhood development.
- Approximately 50 percent of all surveyed licensed providers reported that they had earned at least one college credit related to early childhood development. Two-thirds reported that they had participated in noncredit training related to that subject.
- Approximately 50 percent of paid assistants had participated in noncredit training or college courses in early childhood development.

 PROFESSIONAL DEVELOPMENT
3 Consider the benefits of ongoing training and education.

This book has emphasized that on many levels, child care providers are teachers. But teaching can be difficult if you do not have opportunities to advance your education. Your teaching practices can be enriched when you take classes and receive training. Establish a professional development plan that allows for an ongoing cycle of reading, learning, reflection, and practice. Your plan should include a coherent series of professional development experiences that build in succession and that offer you opportunities to reflect on and practice what you learn.

Home-based child care providers have varying educational levels. The amount of formal education you need depends on factors such as the type of home-based care you aim to provide and your desire to gain more

---

*Whitebook et al. 2006.

120

CHAPTER 4
Professional
Development
for Home-Based
Child Care
Providers

knowledge. As government policymakers increasingly look to early care and education to prepare children for school, providers may need additional education to qualify for participation in state and federal programs.

Practices That Support Professional Development

- Establish a professional development plan and set realistic goals. Your plan should take into account your current levels of knowledge, formal education, and child care experience; your energy level; and the demands of your own family.
- Reinforce and increase your knowledge of language and literacy, mathematics and science, social and emotional learning, physical and motor development, the arts, creative play, technology, conflict management, and effective communication. You can do this by reading, attending workshops and classes, and having discussions with other providers.
- Attend training on the inclusion of children with disabilities or other special needs. Additionally, learn about community resources that are available to these children and their families.
- Participate in activities in which you discuss, reflect upon, and observe teaching methods.
- Develop a curriculum for your child care program. Set aside time to reflect on your program and the children in your care; ask yourself what is working and what is not. Pick a time when you have few or no distractions, perhaps on Saturday mornings or Sunday evenings. It may also help to talk with other providers and members of child care associations or networks.
- Be aware of and seek resources to advance your skills.

  Read books, magazines, and journals related to early childhood education. The "References" section at the end of this publication lists numerous books, journal articles, and other written material that can help you grow as a child care provider.

  Use electronic media such as the Internet (including online courses), e-mail, DVDs, and audiobooks to advance your knowledge. References to helpful Web sites appear throughout this book. In addition, Appendix A ("Additional Resources") includes several organizations, Web sites, and DVDs that can help you expand your knowledge of early childhood care and education.

  Learn from other professionals and seek support from them. Join e-mail support groups and communicate regularly with other providers to learn new techniques and strategies. Take advantage of local, statewide, and national conferences such as those given by the National Association for the Education of Young Children (NAEYC); the California Association

121

CHAPTER 4
Professional
Development
for Home-Based
Child Care
Providers

for the Education of Young Children (CAEYC); and the California Association for Family Child Care (CAFCC).

- Look for opportunities to develop or expand your cultural competence.
- Participate in activities that focus on building partnerships with families. Attend workshops and join support groups that can help you improve your communication with children's family members. Whenever possible and appropriate, invite parents to workshops and information sessions that you attend or have attended.
- Consider the benefits of obtaining a California child development permit. Details on permits follow in this chapter.
- If you operate a large family child care home, include your assistants in professional development planning.

When infants and toddlers are present

Look for professional development opportunities that focus on the unique needs of infants and toddlers.

Where to Receive Training

California Child Care Resource and Referral Network. An association of R&R agencies located throughout the state. Child care R&R agencies are located in every county in California. These agencies provide information about training, insurance, immunization, and other resources. They also offer support to parents, caregivers, other community-based agencies, employers, and government policymakers. To find the agency in your county, contact the network:

> **California Child Care Resource and Referral Network**
> 111 New Montgomery Street, 7th Floor
> San Francisco, CA 94105
> Telephone: 415-882-0234
> http://www.rrnetwork.org

Local school districts. Provide information about how to earn a GED credential or high school diploma.

Community colleges. Offer a variety of classes in early childhood development and education. To find the community college(s) in your area, contact the California Community College System office:

> **California Community Colleges**
> 1102 Q Street, 4th Floor
> Sacramento, CA 95811
> Telephone: 916-445-8752
> http://www.cccco.edu

122

CHAPTER 4
Professional
Development
for Home-Based
Child Care
Providers

California Preschool Instructional Network (CPIN). Provides professional development and technical assistance to preschool teachers and administrators. The CPIN aims to ensure that preschool children are ready for school. It consists of 11 regions in California and disseminates information, training, and resources in each region.

> **California Preschool Instructional Network**
> Telephone: 1-800-770-6339
> http://www.cpin.us

Family Child Care at Its Best. A series of workshops that emphasize the needs of children from birth to age five. Workshops are offered statewide, free of charge. Participants can earn continuing education and child development units through the University of California, Davis (UC Davis), and they receive a certificate of completion documenting the hours attended. For information on workshops in your area, contact the UC Davis Extension, Center for Excellence in Child Development:

> **Center for Excellence in Child Development**
> Telephone: 530-757-8643
> http://humanservices.ucdavis.edu/childdev

Program for Infant/Toddler Care (PITC). Offers a variety of training opportunities, including the PITC Partners for Quality program (a subsidized on-site training and mentoring program for infant/toddler–center staff and family child care providers). For more information, contact the PITC:

> PITC
> 180 Harbor Drive, Suite 112
> Sausalito, CA 94965
> Telephone: 415-289-2300
> http://www.pitc.org

Child Development Training Consortium (CDTC). Provides financial and technical assistance to child development students and professionals. In addition to its other services, the CDTC assists individuals who are seeking a new, or maintaining a currently held, child development permit; it reimburses eligible students for costs such as tuition, enrollment fees, and textbooks. For more information, contact the CDTC:

> **Child Development Training Consortium**
> 1620 North Carpenter Road, Suite C-16
> Modesto, CA 95351
> Telephone: 209-572-6080
> http://www.childdevelopment.org

123

CHAPTER 4
Professional
Development
for Home-Based
Child Care
Providers

Family child care associations. Offer many resources for child care providers, including training and workshops. To find an association in your area, contact the California Association for Family Child Care (CAFCC):

California Association for Family Child Care
PO Box 8754
Emeryville, CA 94662
Telephone: 510-928-2273
http://www.cafcc.org

Child Development Permits

The California Commission on Teacher Credentialing (CTC) issues child development permits, which authorize individuals to perform different levels of service—assisting, teaching, or supervising—in child development programs. Permits are required for all child care and development teaching or administration positions that are funded by the CDE's Child Development Division (CDD). Additionally, programs not funded by the CDE/CDD may require a permit to document an individual's educational progress.

California offers six child development permits: (1) Assistant, (2) Associate Teacher, (3) Teacher, (4) Master Teacher, (5) Site Supervisor, and (6) Program Director. Each permit has specific education and experience requirements (see table 4.1 on the next page). Contact a professional growth advisor or college counselor to learn more about permits and to determine if you have qualifying education and experience. You can also obtain complete permit details from the CTC:

California Commission on Teacher Credentialing
PO Box 944270
Sacramento, CA 94244-2700
Telephone: 1-888-921-2682
http://www.ctc.ca.gov

124

CHAPTER 4
Professional
Development
for Home-Based
Child Care
Providers

Table 4.1 Education and experience requirements for California child development permits (summary)

Permit level	Education requirements	Experience requirements	Alternative qualifications
Assistant	6 units of early childhood education (ECE) or child development (CD) course work	None	Completion of approved HERO[a] or ROP[b] program in child development–related occupations
Associate Teacher	12 units ECE or CD course work, including core courses	50 days (3+ hours per day) in instructional role at child care and development program within last 2 years	Child Development Associate (CDA) credential
Teacher	24 units ECE or CD course work, including core courses; and 16 general education (GE) units	175 days (3+ hours per day) in instructional role at child care and development program within last 4 years	Associate in Arts (AA) degree or higher in ECE, CD, or related field; and 3 units supervised field experience in ECE setting
Master Teacher	24 units ECE or CD course work, including core courses; 16 GE units; 6 units in area of specialization; and 2 units adult supervision course work	350 days (3+ hours per day) in instructional role at child care and development program within last 4 years	Bachelor of Arts (BA) degree or higher; 12 units ECE or CD course work; and 3 units supervised field experience in ECE or CD setting
Site Supervisor	24 units ECE or CD course work, including core courses; AA degree (or 60 units); 6 units administration and supervision of child care and development programs; and 2 units adult supervision course work	350 days (3+ hours per day) in instructional role at child care and development program within last 4 years, including at least 100 days supervising adults	BA degree or higher with 12 units ECE or CD course work and 3 units supervised field experience in ECE setting; or a teaching or administrative services credential with specific education and experience requirements
Program Director	BA degree or higher; 24 units ECE or CD course work, including core courses; 6 units administration and supervision of child care and development programs; and 2 units adult supervision course work	Site Supervisor status and one program year of Site Supervisor experience	Master's degree or higher in ECE, CD, or related field; or a combination of specific course work and a credential in administrative services, Single Subject Teaching in home economics, or Multiple Subject Teaching

Note: The permit requirements listed above were accurate at the time this publication was developed.
[a]HERO: Home Economics and Related Occupations
[b]ROP: Regional Occupation Program

125

CHAPTER 4
Professional
Development
for Home-Based
Child Care
Providers

Child Development Associate (CDA) Credential

A Child Development Associate (CDA) is an individual who has successfully completed a CDA assessment and has earned a CDA credential.* A person with a CDA credential is qualified to meet the specific needs of children and to work with parents and other adults to nurture children's physical, social, emotional, and intellectual growth in a child development framework. A CDA credential can give you a solid foundation for professional development in child care and can show families that you are committed to high-quality care.

The CDA National Credentialing Program is administered by the Council for Professional Recognition, a nonprofit organization located in Washington, DC. The Council promotes improved performance and recognition of professionals who work with children from birth through age five in child care centers, family child care homes, and as home visitors. The Council's CDA program focuses on the skills of early care and education professionals and is designed to improve the quality of child care. The program provides performance-based training, assessment, and credentialing of child care staff, home visitors, and family child care providers.

A CDA credential is valid for three years from the issuance date, after which the credential may be renewed every five years. To be eligible for the program, you must meet the following requirements:

Personal

- Be eighteen years of age or older.
- Hold a high school diploma or GED credential.
- Be able to speak, read, and write well enough in English to understand and be understood by children and adults. Applicants for Bilingual Endorsements must meet these requirements in English and another language.

Child care setting

- The home meets at least the minimum requirements of state and/or local regulations.
- You must work with at least two children who are five years old or younger and who are not related to you by blood or marriage.
- If you are not the owner or operator of the family child care home, you must obtain written permission from the owner, operator, or person in authority.

---

*The CDA credential should not be confused with a Child Development Associate Teacher permit, which is issued by the California Commission on Teacher Credentialing. However, earning a CDA credential is one way to qualify for a Child Development Associate Teacher permit.

126

CHAPTER 4
Professional
Development
for Home-Based
Child Care
Providers

Child care experience and education

- Within the last five years, you must have gained at least 480 hours of experience working with children from birth through age five in a group setting.
- Within the last five years, you must have completed 120 clock hours of formal child care education, with no fewer than 10 hours in each of eight subject areas. This requirement may be met through participation in the wide variety of training available in the field, including in-service and association-sponsored workshops. Training obtained at conferences or from individual consultants is not acceptable. The formal-education hours can be credit or noncredit, but the hours must be completed through an agency or organization with expertise in early childhood teacher preparation.

If you meet all of the eligibility requirements and would like more information on the CDA credential program, contact the Council for Professional Recognition:

Council for Professional Recognition
2460 16th Street NW
Washington, DC 20009
Telephone: 1-800-424-4310 or 202-265-9090
http://www.cdacouncil.org

 4 PROFESSIONAL DEVELOPMENT
Participate in a child care association and/or a network of home-based child care providers.

Professional development involves more than training and education. It also involves participating in a community of peers for mutual support. Like all professions, family child care has its own professional organizations. These include state and local family child care associations.

Participating in family child care organizations can help you grow professionally and can link you with people who are interested in the growth and development of children. It can also help reduce the sense of isolation you may experience as a home-based provider.

State or local family child care associations may offer special benefits such as health insurance, homeowner insurance, discounts on business liability insurance, credit union memberships, representation on the local planning council, access to substitute caregivers, and retirement plans. Contact your county R&R agency or local planning council to learn about the family child care associations in your area and the benefits they may offer.

Family child care networks provide many of the same professional development benefits that are offered by family child care associations. For

127

CHAPTER 4
Professional
Development
for Home-Based
Child Care
Providers

example, networks introduce home-based child care providers to one another and enable providers to learn new child care strategies and methods. Networks can also help providers learn how to take care of themselves. Additionally, networks may offer training, and they can connect providers with important resources and services such as book and toy lending libraries, access to the Child and Adult Care Food Program (CACFP), centralized supply purchasing, purchase of liability insurance, and transportation options.

Practices That Promote Professionalism

- Seek information about regional support groups. These are similar to family child care associations but are not yet established as nonprofit organizations.
- If possible, locate and contact culturally diverse family child care associations (for example, an association whose members speak Chinese). Interacting with providers from different cultures can help you incorporate diversity into your child care setting.
- Find out if there is a network of family child care homes in your community.
- Establish ties with the larger child care community—such as family child care providers, center-based providers, kindergarten teachers, R&R agency staff, community college instructors, and pediatricians—to get a broad range of ideas and feedback.

What Can Family Child Care Organizations Do for You?

Home-based child care is a highly rewarding but very demanding profession. Working with children all day requires a lot of energy and patience, and interacting with children's parents and family members can be stressful. At the end of each day you may feel physically and emotionally drained, less able to love and care for your own family members. Additionally, spending much of your time at home can cause you to feel isolated.

Family child care organizations, both formal and informal, can link you with other people who understand the daily joys and struggles you experience as a home-based child care provider. Meeting with other providers can help you develop new friendships, give you opportunities to learn from and help peers, expose you to educational and training resources, and enable you to feel more connected to the world outside your home.

You may wonder how any home-based provider has time to meet with other providers—yet there are vibrant family child care organizations throughout California. It is true that forming and sustaining a family child care organization is challenging; it is easier to think about developing a provider group than it is to launch one and keep it going. To start a new group, you may need help from a community organization such as a child care R&R agency, the United Way, a church group, or local educational

128

CHAPTER 4
Professional
Development
for Home-Based
Child Care
Providers

institution. Regardless of whether you establish or join a family child care organization, you can benefit greatly by becoming involved with other home-based providers.

Family Child Care Associations

Family child care associations—national, state, and local—work to meet the child care and development needs of children, parents, child care providers, and the community. These associations help recruit licensed family child care providers; foster provider training and education; promote continuing interest in licensed family child care; create communication paths with licensing agencies; share information about state and federal policies, laws, and regulations; and bring together the broader child care community.

For more information, contact these organizations:

National Association for Family Child Care (NAFCC)
1743 West Alexander Street
Salt Lake City, UT 84119
Telephone: 1-800-359-3817 or 801-886-2322
http://www.nafcc.org

California Association for Family Child Care (CAFCC)
P.O. Box 8754
Emeryville, CA 94662
Telephone: 510-928-2273
http://www.cafcc.org

To find the family child care association(s) in your area, visit http://www.cafcc.org/alclfcca.html.

Family Child Care Home Networks

A family child care home network is a cluster of licensed providers working under an administering agency that contracts with the State of California to provide subsidized child care and development services in home care settings. An administering agency might be a school district, a Head Start grantee, a local church, the military, or a private, nonprofit child care agency. Networks have program directors who supervise and visit network providers on a regular basis. Additionally, networks are required to provide many of the same program components offered by subsidized center-based programs. In contrast, family child care associations link providers for professional development and support activities without providing subsidies for child care costs.

The State of California recognizes family child care home networks as distinct entities. Family child care networks operated by an administering agency that is under contract with the CDE to provide subsidized child care

129

CHAPTER 4
Professional
Development
for Home-Based
Child Care
Providers

and development programs are subject to the same legal requirements that center-based programs are. For example, family child care networks must participate in the Desired Results system, which documents progress made by children and families toward six desired results and provides information to help practitioners improve their child care and development services. This means that network staff members are expected to complete Desired Results Developmental Profiles (DRDPs) periodically—as required by the *California Code of Regulations, Title 5*—and to evaluate program quality by using the Family Child Care Environment Rating Scale. In addition, the individual who manages the network must have a Child Development Program Director Permit in order to supervise two or more sites. Individual providers are not required to hold permits to provide care for enrolled children. For more information on the Desired Results system, see Chapter 5, and visit http://www.cde.ca.gov/sp/cd/ci/desiredresults.asp.

Why be a provider in a family child care home network? Family child care home networks offer many of the professional development benefits that are available through family child care associations. For example, networks introduce home-based child care providers to one another and enable providers to learn new strategies and methods for caring for children—and for themselves. Networks also may offer training, and they can link providers with support services such as book and toy lending libraries, access to the CACFP, centralized supply purchasing, purchase of liability insurance, and transportation options.

Family child care home networks also offer subsidized payments for eligible families for child care costs; technical assistance; monitoring; and fiscal management. Additionally, networks sometimes arrange substitute caregivers for providers who are ill, on vacation, or temporarily unavailable. Family child care networks can be formed around specific needs such as after-school care, care for special populations (for example, children with special needs), and so forth.

Where can you obtain more information? Networks are not available in every community. To find out if there is a network in your area, contact your local R&R agency or call the CDE/CDD at 916-322-6233.

PROFESSIONAL DEVELOPMENT
Develop a plan for improving your child care program.

In addition to training, education, and peer support, professional development in home-based child care involves setting short- and long-term goals for improving your child care program. Every person who provides care and education for other people's children should establish ongoing plans to improve service quality, and there are specific professional standards for measuring that improvement.

130

CHAPTER 4
Professional
Development
for Home-Based
Child Care
Providers

Practices to Support Continuous Program Improvement

- Seek local resources that offer training and peer support. Start by contacting your local R&R agency.
- Take classes in early childhood education (ECE) and child development (CD) at your local community college, and attend workshops offered by your local R&R agency. These steps can improve your business and can increase your self-confidence and self-esteem.

For Licensed Providers

- Learn how to conduct a self-assessment of your child care program by using the revised Family Child Care Environment Rating Scale (FCCERS-R). The FCCERS-R can help you identify successful areas of your program and those that need improvement. Further information on the FCCERS-R follows in this chapter.
- Consider applying for or working toward accreditation by the National Association for Family Child Care (NAFCC). NAFCC accreditation is designed to promote and recognize high-quality family child care.

For License-Exempt Providers

- Consider the benefits of licensure. Earning and maintaining a license indicates to families that your home is safe and healthy for children—which can help your business thrive. Another possible benefit of licensure is membership in a family child care association.
- Even if you decide not to pursue licensure, consider using licensing regulations to assess your child care setting on a regular basis. Performing frequent self-assessments will help ensure that your child care home meets health and safety standards.
- Find out if your local R&R agency offers grants or other financial assistance for health and safety training (such as pediatric first aid and CPR).

The Child and Adult Care Food Program (CACFP)

The Child and Adult Care Food Program (CACFP) is sponsored by the U.S. Department of Agriculture (USDA) as part of the National School Lunch Act. The CACFP child care component is a state and federally funded program that gives financial aid to licensed child care centers and child care homes. The program aims to improve the diets of children under age 13 by providing nutritious, well-balanced meals, and it strives to foster good eating habits that children can practice throughout their lives.

The CACFP enables family child care providers to have a positive impact on the eating habits of growing children, and to be reimbursed for meals and snacks they serve. Meals are available free of charge to enrolled children

131

CHAPTER 4
Professional
Development
for Home-Based
Child Care
Providers

in participating licensed family child care homes. All children in attendance are offered the same meals, with no physical segregation or other discrimination against any child for any reason.

Benefits for participating providers include reduced costs for feeding children and the assurance that children receive healthy foods. Children benefit from the CACFP by receiving nutritious meals and snacks that support healthy growth and development. The program also helps children establish good eating habits that can last a lifetime. Finally, the CACFP helps control costs of child care and assures parents that their children are eating healthy and nutritious foods during the day.

The CACFP requires you to keep records. You must complete and submit monthly attendance records and menus to be reimbursed for meals served to children. Enrollment forms, signed by parents, are required for all children participating in the program—but you will need only about five minutes each day to complete the required paperwork. For more information about the CACFP, contact the CDE Nutrition Services Division:

Child and Adult Care Food Program—Child Care Component
CDE Nutrition Services Division
Telephone: 1-800-952-5609
http://www.cde.ca.gov/ls/nu/cc/ccc.asp

The Family Child Care Environment Rating Scale—Revised (FCCERS-R)

The revised Family Child Care Environment Rating Scale (FCCERS-R) is a resource that home-based child care providers can use to assess their programs. It is a self-evaluation that appraises the overall quality of a family child care environment. The 38 items of the scale are grouped into seven categories: (1) Space and Furnishings; (2) Personal Care Routines; (3) Listening and Talking; (4) Activities; (5) Interaction; (6) Program Structure; and (7) Parents and Provider. Each item is described by one of four levels of quality: Inadequate (does not even meet custodial-care needs); Minimal (meets custodial needs and, to some degree, basic developmental needs); Good (meets developmental needs); or Excellent (high-quality personalized care). The FCCERS-R is available for purchase from Teachers College Press:

Family Child Care Environment Rating Scale: Revised Edition
Authors: Thelma Harms, Debby Cryer, and Richard M. Clifford
Teachers College Press
Telephone: 1-800-575-6566
http://www.teacherscollegepress.com

132

CHAPTER 4
Professional
Development
for Home-Based
Child Care
Providers

National Association for Family Child Care (NAFCC) Accreditation

Accreditation is a process used in many industries to identify model practices in a specific field. The National Association for Family Child Care (NAFCC) sponsors the only nationally recognized accreditation system for family child care providers. NAFCC accreditation promotes and recognizes professional, high-quality family child care. It helps providers set and reach quality-improvement goals and it assists parents and policymakers in identifying high-quality family child care. Accreditation also helps providers, parents, and policymakers by:

- Defining standards of quality in family child care in five areas: relationships, environment, developmental learning activities, safety and health, and professional and business practices.
- Promoting provider self-assessments and professional development.
- Motivating providers to put training into practice.
- Serving as a cornerstone in state professional development systems.

Ten Reasons Why Home-Based Child Care Providers Like Accreditation*

Accredited home-based child care providers throughout the United States have reported that accreditation offers many benefits. Accreditation helps providers:

1. Gain more knowledge about their child care homes and about how they interact with children.
2. Increase their self-esteem.
3. Feel more professional.
4. Gain a more concrete definition of quality family child care.
5. Stay excited about their work.
6. Become motivated to pursue ongoing training and support.
7. Strive for higher quality in their programs than what is required by the state.
8. Become leaders in their profession.
9. Learn how to market their programs to parents.
10. Learn how to earn more money.

Who May Apply for Accreditation?

To apply for accreditation, you must:

- Be at least 21 years of age.
- Have a high school diploma or GED credential.
- Provide care to children for a minimum of 15 hours per week.
- Provide care to a minimum of three children in a home environment. At least one child must live outside the provider's home.
- Be the primary caregiver, spending at least 80 percent of the operating hours actively involved with the children. If individuals apply as

---

*Based on Cohen 2002.

133

CHAPTER 4
Professional
Development
for Home-Based
Child Care
Providers

coproviders, each provider must spend at least 60 percent of the operating hours actively involved with the children.

- Have at least 12 months of experience as a family child care provider.
- Meet the highest level of regulation necessary to operate a family child care program.
- Comply with all requirements of the authorized regulatory body.
- Have favorable state and federal criminal histories.
- Be in good health.
- Maintain a current Pediatric First Aid and CPR certification.
- Adhere to the National Association for the Education of Young Children (NAEYC) Code of Ethical Conduct.

If you meet these qualifications and would like more information about the accreditation process, visit the NAFCC Web site at http://www.nafcc.org, or call 1-800-359-3817.

PROFESSIONAL DEVELOPMENT
6 Follow Best Business Practices.

Another important component of professional development is learning to adopt sound business practices. Establishing clear policies for and contracts with the families of the children in your care will provide a solid foundation for high-quality service.

Business Practices for All Providers

- Work to form partnerships with children's families. Discuss topics such as eating, toileting, naps, and discipline, and be sure there is a good fit between parents' wishes and what you offer in your program.
- Ensure that families have a clear understanding of the boundaries in your home; this can help the children's families respect and value your needs and those of your family. For example, tell parents if certain areas of your home are off-limits to the children.
- Maintain current records regarding the children and your child care home:

  Children's medical information. Documentation of allergies, chronic illnesses, other health-related issues, and immunizations (and whether parents object to immunizations); documents signed by parents granting permission for their children to receive emergency medical treatment if necessary.*

  Personal and cultural information for each child. Food preferences; likes and dislikes; holidays and traditions observed by the child's family.

  Other business-related documents. Certificates showing your child care–related training and education; documents signed by parents granting

---

*Immunization documents and signed statements authorizing emergency medical treatment are required for licensure.

134

CHAPTER 4
Professional
Development
for Home-Based
Child Care
Providers

permission for their children to be transported for field trips or other reasons (if applicable); state and federal criminal-background clearances for you, for anyone in your home who works with the children in your care, and for each person over age 18 who lives in your home.

- Ask parents for advance notice of their vacation schedules so you will know when children will be absent. Likewise, give parents advance notice of your vacation plans so they can make other child care arrangements.

Business Practices for Licensed Providers

- Give written policies to parents covering issues such as your hours of service; payment of fees (including any overtime fees); health, safety, and emergency procedures (including CPR); discipline; vacation; your provision of substitute care; people who are authorized to pick up each child from your home; transportation and field trips; and so forth.
- Maintain liability insurance for your program. The insurance should cover injuries to children, assistants, and visitors to your home. Additionally, maintain vehicle insurance if you transport children.
- Issue receipts to parents when they pay for your services.

PROFESSIONAL DEVELOPMENT
Take care of yourself.

To provide high-quality child care, you need to take care of yourself. This may sound simple, but providers often neglect their own health because they spend so much time and energy meeting other people's needs. Taking time to care for yourself will benefit everyone: you, your family, and the children in your care.

Practices That Support Care of Your Own Needs

- Set aside time for regular health exams. Schedule a physical with an internist or primary-care physician at least once a year.
- Make time to talk with other child care professionals, family members, and adults. Remember that you can gain support from a variety of sources.
- Acknowledge that taking care of young children can be difficult—physically, mentally, and emotionally. Set aside time each day for meditation, quiet reflection, or other ways to help you stay centered and focused.
- Exercise regularly to stay in shape and relieve stress.
- Eat a balanced diet that includes a variety of healthy foods.
- Learn from your mistakes; they can help you become a better person and a better child care provider.
- Develop your own hobbies and passions. Fulfilling your needs and dreams will make you a happier person and a more interesting provider.

CHAPTER 5

Home-Based Child Care as Part of an Early Learning System

*H*OME-BASED CHILD CARE PROVIDERS HAVE A VERY IMPORTANT ROLE TO PLAY IN EARLY LEARNING. Previous chapters have focused on how to make your home a caring and learning environment, how to provide developmentally appropriate learning activities, and how to find professional development opportunities. This chapter provides a broad view of the role of home-based child care across the nation—especially in California—and reviews several of the major initiatives in California designed to provide resources for home-based providers.

136

CHAPTER 5
Home-Based
Child Care
as Part of an
Early Learning
System

The achievement gap is the disparity in academic performance between groups of students, particularly between white and Asian students and their African American and Hispanic peers; English learners and native English speakers; socioeconomically disadvantaged and nondisadvantaged students; and students with disabilities and those without disabilities.

 # Growing Emphasis on Home-Based Care

The Achievement Gap

Across the nation, concern about the achievement gap is the primary reason for increased attention to the quality of early child care, including family child care and exempt care as well as center- and school-based programs. The achievement gap for children from low-income families has been well documented. However, as many as a third of children from middle-income and a fourth of those from upper-middle-income homes also lack key pre-literacy skills when they enter school.[1]

High-quality early childhood programs have been found to narrow the achievement gap. Research demonstrates that high-quality preschool services improve children's school readiness and school completion rates while reducing costly expenditures for grade repetition, compensatory education, delinquency, and crime. Unfortunately, many families lack access to quality child care programs, whether home-, center-, or school-based. Either no such options exist in the community or families cannot afford them.[2]

Demographic factors make the achievement gap a special concern in California. California has the largest population of any state in the nation, and it has the largest number of noncitizen immigrants of any state.[3] Additionally, the state's population of young children has grown dramatically in the last decade. According to the California Department of Finance, the population of four-year-olds is projected to increase by 11 percent between 2008 and 2018.[4]

Trends in California's Kindergarten Population

From 1996–97 to 2006–07, the number of Hispanic kindergartners in California's public schools increased by 7 percent (see table 5.1). During the same time period, there was a 1 percent increase in the number of Asian kindergartners. In contrast, the number of White (non-Hispanic) kindergartners decreased by 8 percent, and the number of African American

Table 5.1 Breakdown of California's kindergarten population, by ethnicity, 1996–2009: four largest groups

Ethnicity	1996–97	2006–07	2008–09
Hispanic	46%	53%	51%
White (non-Hispanic)	35%	27%	26%
Asian	7%	8%	8%
African American	8%	7%	6%

Source: DataQuest, California Department of Education. http://dq.cde.ca.gov/dataquest/.

137

CHAPTER 5
Home-Based
Child Care
as Part of an
Early Learning
System

kindergartners decreased by 1 percent.[5] By 2008–09, Hispanics accounted for 51 percent of all kindergartners enrolled in California's public schools, and White (non-Hispanic) students accounted for 26 percent—a 9 percent decrease from 1996–97. Asians accounted for 8 percent of kindergarten enrollment by 2008–09, and African American enrollment was at 6 percent.

In 2006–07, for nearly 42 percent of California's public school kindergartners, English was not their home language. Of those children, 84 percent spoke Spanish and 3 percent spoke Vietnamese. Seven percent spoke one of 11 other Asian languages, 1 percent spoke Tagalog, 1 percent spoke Russian, and 1 percent spoke Arabic.[6] Additionally, in 2000, one in four families with children under six years old was headed by a single parent.[7]

All of these factors—the large number of children entering kindergarten, the high percentage of immigrants (for whom English is not their home language), the number of children growing up in single-parent families, and the diversity of cultures in California—point to the need for special attention and resources from the state's public education system. These factors also underscore the need to ensure that children receive quality early care, which is an important part of preparing children for kindergarten and for success in school.

Child Care Assistance for Working Parents

Major changes in the welfare system, and the growth of publicly funded child care—including programs based in homes, centers, and schools—have contributed to the increased interest in early care and education. In response to federal welfare-reform legislation, states have established programs that include child care assistance to help families move from welfare dependency to work. In California, the Legislature established the California Work Opportunity and Responsibility to Kids (CalWORKs) program.

Research suggests that families' selection of home-based caregivers reflects a variety of considerations. The strengths of family child care and exempt care include their flexibility to accommodate nontraditional work hours and unpredictable schedules, their ability to serve siblings of multiple ages in a single setting, and families' ability to choose providers with linguistic and cultural backgrounds similar to their own.

In addition, family child care and exempt care are often the primary child care options in rural areas. Rural families with children under age five are therefore more likely than urban families to use home-based care that is not provided by relatives.[8]

High Utilization of Home-Based Care

Home-based child care, including license-exempt and licensed family child care, is a major source of child care across the United States. Although the majority of investments to expand and improve early childhood pro-

138

CHAPTER 5
Home-Based
Child Care
as Part of an
Early Learning
System

grams have been directed to formal child care and preschool systems, there is growing recognition that at least half of the young children in the nation are in "family, friend, and neighbor" care—a term referring to license-exempt care.[9]

Working parents in California use relatively more home-based care, and less center-based care, than their counterparts in other states. Approximately 80 percent of the children in publicly funded child care voucher programs in California are served either in licensed family child care or exempt care, and half of the families in CalWORKs choose license-exempt arrangements.[10] According to the Center for Law and Social Policy, national statistics for children who were enrolled in voucher programs in 2005 were significantly different from California's: 58 percent of children were served in center-based care, and only 27 percent had license-exempt arrangements.[11]

Families cite a number of reasons for using home-based care. Parents frequently report that they know and trust their family members, friends, and neighbors, and feel that their children will be safe and receive individualized attention in home-based care.[12] Family, friend, and neighbor care also may offer a convenient location, a small number of children, a suitable environment for children's naps, and support for the neighborhood and family economy.[13]

Home-based care can be a particularly attractive form of child care for immigrant families.[14] First, it may be easier for those families to find a home-based provider who speaks their home language and comes from a similar cultural background. Finding a provider with the same cultural and linguistic background "creates a familiar, accessible point of entry for both the immigrant parents and their young children, reducing stress and strangeness."[15] A culturally supportive environment also may foster a child's sense of security and his or her self-concept.[16]

Additionally, family child care can help immigrant families form a bridge to their new culture. Providers may serve as partners and mentors for the children's parents, introducing them to community resources and helping them make the transition from home-based child care to the more formal educational setting of kindergarten. Depending on their knowledge of languages, providers also may play a variety of roles in helping the children learn English. Non-English-speaking providers can take English classes and can bring children to the library, thereby serving as role models for the children and their families. Providers who do not speak a child's home language can support their teaching and improve communication with the child's family by drawing on the language skills of assistants, family members, and members of the community.[17]

139

CHAPTER 5
Home-Based
Child Care
as Part of an
Early Learning
System

California's Early Learning and Development System

For more than a decade, educators and policymakers at the state and national level have been working to create early learning standards that set forth expectations for young children's learning and development prior to school entry. These standards can range from specific content knowledge to skills and attributes that should be strengthened through early care and education.

When the California Department of Education (CDE) initiated an effort to create preschool learning standards, the initial emphasis was to align those standards with kindergarten academic content standards. However, the CDE widened its focus to include a full range of learning and development domains, and the term "foundations" was used rather than "standards." This terminology also conveys that learning across all of the developmental domains builds young children's readiness for school.

As the CDE moved forward with publishing guidelines and began developing learning foundations for the preschool age span, the Department determined that comparable materials should be developed for infants and toddlers to show the importance of a child's earliest years and the links with the preschool years. At this time, all states have some form of early learning guidelines or standards for the preschool age span, and many have something similar for infants and toddlers.

In 2004, the National Association for the Education of Young Children (NAEYC) and the National Association of Early Childhood Specialists in State Departments of Education (NAECS–SDE) issued a position statement, "Where We Stand on Early Learning Standards," which reads as follows:

> Early learning standards define the desired outcomes and content of young children's education. Most states have developed such standards for children below kindergarten age. The [NAEYC and NAECS–SDE] believe that *early learning standards can be a valuable part of a comprehensive, high-quality system of services for young children.* But we caution that early learning standards support positive development and learning *only* if they:
> - emphasize significant, developmentally appropriate content and outcomes;
> - are developed and reviewed through informed, inclusive processes;
> - are implemented and assessed in ways that support all young children's development; and
> - are accompanied by strong supports for early childhood programs, professionals, and families. (http://www.naeyc.org/files/naeyc/file/positions/earlyLearning Standards.pdf [updated 2009])

140

CHAPTER 5
Home-Based
Child Care
as Part of an
Early Learning
System

The CDE has worked to create a vision for the "what" and "how" of early childhood education and to think about the way the components of a professional development system would fit into that vision. What has emerged is an Early Learning and Development System specific to California.

At each step in the development process, the CDE has considered the unique developmental issues of children with disabilities or other special needs and of children who are dual-language learners. The system was designed to include all children. It is important for people who work with young children to be aware of this system and to recognize it as an important resource. The following sections provide an overview of the system and show some ways that providers in child care home settings may want to use the information.

System Components

To guide providers and teachers of young children, the CDE has produced a library of publications and resource materials as part of the Early Learning and Development System. All of these materials are available for purchase from CDE Press at http://www.cde.ca.gov/re/pn/rc/. The CDE's Child Development Division (CDD) developed the following descriptions to help practitioners understand this comprehensive, interrelated system that supports learning and development for California's youngest children. The system consists of five elements:

- Foundations
- Curriculum Frameworks
- Desired Results Assessment System
- Program Guidelines and Resources
- Professional Development

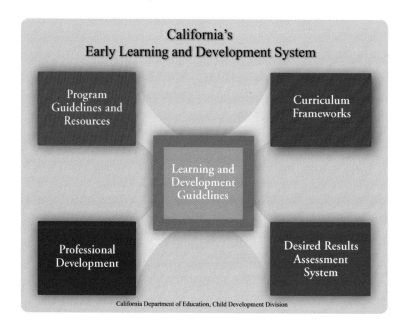

141

CHAPTER 5
Home-Based
Child Care
as Part of an
Early Learning
System

Central Role of Foundations

Although some elements of the Early Learning and Development System were developed prior to the publication of California's *Preschool Learning Foundations* and the *Infant/Toddler Learning and Development Foundations* (both referred to as foundations), the foundations are central to all the other components of the system. Foundations focus on the individual child. They describe the competencies (knowledge and skills) that we would expect to see in a child who is developing typically and who has had access to a quality early care and education setting. Foundations represent:

- Knowledge that children acquire.
- Skills they develop.
- Behavior they learn.
- Competencies they demonstrate.

The CDE has created a DVD series to illustrate the infant/toddler learning and development foundations. The series uses video clips of children's behavior to demonstrate each foundation for ages 8 months, 18 months, and 36 months. The footage shows children with disabilities or other special needs who demonstrate specific foundations or who are included with groups of children. This DVD set is available from CDE Press (item number 001700). The CDE also plans to develop a similar DVD series to illustrate the preschool learning foundations.

Curriculum Frameworks Facilitate Learning

Curriculum frameworks that correspond to the infant/toddler learning and development foundations and the preschool learning foundations are being finalized. Each framework will elaborate on the foundations and describe the curriculum and instruction necessary to help children achieve the levels of mastery. The frameworks will include teaching strategies, interactions with children and families, and guidance for setting up environments. They provide an overall approach for teachers to support children's learning through environments and experiences that are:

- Developmentally appropriate.
- Reflective of thoughtful observation and intentional planning.
- Individually and culturally meaningful.
- Inclusive of children with disabilities or other special needs.

Note that a framework is not a curriculum. Local programs choose specific curricula and instructional strategies.

Assessment to Inform Care

California uses a teacher-observation developmental assessment instrument in state-funded programs. The Desired Results Developmental Profile (DRDP) is a reliable tool with which teachers observe and assess children's

142

CHAPTER 5
Home-Based
Child Care
as Part of an
Early Learning
System

**Making the Most
of the Materials**

CDE resources
can be used by
individuals for
professional devel-
opment, by groups,
and for planning
and implementing
high-quality child
care programs.

learning. The DRDP is intended to document the progress made by children across the major domains of learning and development. It also provides information to help practitioners improve their child care and development services. Desired Results access is available for children with Individualized Education Programs (IEPs). Note that the distinction between foundations (or standards) and assessment instruments is important. The foundations describe what children typically learn with appropriate support, whereas the DRDP provides a way to document what individual children have learned.

Providers can gain general knowledge of young children's learning from the foundations, and ideas for supporting learning from curriculum frameworks, but neither of these resources will inform providers about individual children's learning and developmental progress. Documenting an individual child's learning with the DRDP is a key element of providers' efforts to understand how to support each child's learning and development. Information gained from the DRDP helps providers plan both for individual children and for small groups of children.

The DRDP instrument has been aligned with the infant/toddler and preschool foundations. The updated editions for each age span are available online at http://www.cde.ca.gov/sp/cd/ci/desiredresults.asp.

Learning and Development Program Guidelines

Learning and development program guidelines can help shape high-quality programs for infants, toddlers, and preschool children. Because the achievement of the knowledge and skills described in the foundations is based on experience in high-quality early care and education settings, the guidelines take on additional importance. Program guidelines present broad recommendations based on research, theory, and practice, and they inform programs seeking high-quality care and education for infant/toddler and preschool children. The *Prekindergarten Learning and Development Guidelines* were published in 2000 and remain relevant. The *Infant/Toddler Learning and Development Program Guidelines* were published in 2006. Together, these publications support the creation and implementation of high-quality early care and education programs for children from birth to age five.

The CDE's *Infant/Toddler Learning and Development Program Guidelines: The Workbook*—a companion to the *Infant/Toddler Learning and Development Program Guidelines* publication and DVD series—has many activities to help practitioners implement inclusive, high-quality early care and education programs. Although focused on center-based settings, much of the material is directly applicable to home-care settings.

A resource for working with children who have disabilities or special needs (and their families) is the CDE publication *Inclusion Works! Creating Child Care Programs That Promote Belonging for Children with Special Needs*. This publication provides guidance and proven strategies that promote

143

CHAPTER 5
Home-Based
Child Care
as Part of an
Early Learning
System

inclusion of children with disabilities and special needs. Building on research and many years of effective implementation, this book contains stories, examples, background information, and resources that support the creation of inclusive environments. This resource, as well as the others discussed in this section, can help you enhance the quality of care in your home setting and provide a learning environment that promotes school readiness.

Professional Development

Professional development gives providers many opportunities to learn about the components of California's Early Learning and Development System—namely, the foundations, program guidelines, curriculum frameworks, and assessment system.

There are numerous forms of professional development. They include pre-service training that early childhood educators receive in California's institutions of higher education, training provided for beginning teachers, and in-service training that is provided for experienced teachers to pursue ongoing improvement.

Professional development is provided by trainers at local child care resource and referral (R&R) agencies through the Child Care Initiative Project (CCIP) and the Growing, Learning, Caring (GLC) Project, both of which are described on the next page. Additional training for licensed family child care providers is offered through the Program for Infant/Toddler Care and "Family Child Care at Its Best" workshops given by the University of California, Davis. You also might want to ask your local R&R agency about family child care associations in your area. Associations provide opportunities for family child care providers to meet other providers in their area, discover resources to improve home learning environments, and gain a sense of professionalism about working with young children.

Recognizing the importance of home-based child care, California has been a leader in supporting family child care and exempt-care providers. The state has also included home-based care in its quality-improvement initiatives and has promoted school readiness through home-based as well as center- and school-based settings. The following is a summary of some of the state's major quality-improvement initiatives, which include resources for home-based providers. Using federal dollars from the Child Care and Developmental Block Grant (CCDBG), the CDE/CDD provides funding for its training partners to offer a variety of training opportunities to home-based providers.

California Child Care Initiative Project (CCIP)

The California Child Care Initiative Project (CCIP) was established in 1985 to address the shortage of licensed, high-quality child care in California communities. The program recruits and trains family child care

144

CHAPTER 5
Home-Based
Child Care
as Part of an
Early Learning
System

providers to help meet the great demand for child care services. The CCIP works through existing nonprofit, community-based child care R&R agencies.

A new funding source for CCIP projects was implemented in 1997. CCDBG grants provide funding for R&R agencies to develop family child care homes and to train family child care providers to care for infants and toddlers. This CCIP program does not require counties to raise local matching funds. For many R&R agencies, particularly those in rural and underserved areas, this funding has allowed them to implement a CCIP project, encourage new providers to become licensed, and train new and existing family child care providers. Further information about the CCIP is available at the California Child Care Resource and Referral Network Web site: http://www.rrnetwork.org/programs/child-care-initiative-project.html.

Growing, Learning, Caring Project (Informal Care Training)

In 2005, with funding from the CDE, the California Child Care Resource and Referral Network launched the Growing, Learning, Caring (GLC) Project, an outreach and training program for license-exempt child care providers. Every R&R agency in California now provides services for informal, license-exempt caregivers. Individuals who care for their own children and those from only one other family are exempt from licensure. Relatives (such as grandparents, aunts, and so on) who provide care for family members are also exempt. The GLC project gives priority to providers who care for children from families that receive financial assistance for child care.

GLC project training aims to show providers how to strengthen children's school readiness and instill a love of learning in young children. It teaches providers to offer fun, purposeful, and playful learning activities. The training focuses on topics such as these:

- Health and safety
- Nutrition
- Discipline and guidance
- Family support and communication
- Family literacy
- Learning through play
- Character development and education
- School success

The GLC project ensures that informal caregivers throughout California have access to quality training and to support services.

145

CHAPTER 5
Home-Based
Child Care
as Part of an
Early Learning
System

Preschool Education Program (PEP)

The Preschool Education Program is supported by the Public Broadcasting Service (PBS) and the CDE/CDD. PBS stations in Eureka, Fresno, Los Angeles, Redding, Sacramento, San Diego, San Francisco, and San Jose participate in this program. Caregivers of children who are over age two learn how to help the children actively view age-appropriate PBS programs. Providers also learn how to extend the children's viewing experiences by participating in local workshops that use children's books, television, and related materials.

Program for Infant/Toddler Care (PITC) Partners for Quality

PITC Partners for Quality, a project of WestEd's Center for Child and Family Studies, offers on-site training, mentoring, and coaching in the PITC philosophy for groups of infant/toddler care teachers, administrators, and family child care providers throughout California. Training covers six essential PITC policies, some of which exist naturally in child care home settings that support high-quality infant/toddler programs. Those policies are:

- Primary Care—assignment of a primary infant care teacher to each child and family
- Small Groups—creation of small groups of children and caregivers
- Continuity—continuity of teacher assignments and groups over time
- Personalized Care—responsiveness to individual needs, abilities, and schedules
- Cultural Continuity—cultural continuity between home and program through dialogue and collaboration with families
- Inclusion of Children with Special Needs—appropriate accommodations and support for children with disabilities or other special needs

The on-site training, conducted by experienced, PITC-certified infant/toddler specialists, is tailored to the individual needs of each participating program and includes a comprehensive series of videos and adult learning strategies. Trainers mentor and coach program staff on how to implement the PITC philosophy and essential policies. The program's goal is to promote responsive, high-quality, relationship-based infant and toddler care.

Family Child Care at Its Best

The Center for Excellence in Child Development at the University of California, Davis, recognizes that family child care providers are an important source of support for working families. The center's Family Child Care at Its Best program, which is funded by the CDE/CDD, delivers university-based continuing education to licensed and license-exempt providers.

146

CHAPTER 5
Home-Based
Child Care
as Part of an
Early Learning
System

Offered statewide, this series of classes helps providers improve their knowledge, skills, and quality of care. Providers can earn academic credit and continuing education units through the program.

The Family Child Care at Its Best program focuses on infant/toddler care, school readiness, and other special topics. Professional growth in these areas is designed to help providers and teachers become more intentional in their work with young children. Program courses are offered throughout California, with training sessions scheduled primarily at night and on weekends. Classes are taught in English, Spanish, Cantonese, and Russian, and simultaneous translation in other languages can be arranged. The courses are free of charge to family child care providers. Courses for licensed providers are coordinated through local host agencies. Providers who wish to attend classes in their area should contact their local R&R agency, family child care association, county office of education, or county First 5 Commission.

Students who are enrolled in academic-credit courses are evaluated through a formal process based on attendance, participation, and assignments. Students receive a "pass" or "no pass" grade. Upon receiving a passing grade, students earn one-tenth of a quarter unit for each hour of class attended; for example, a 10-hour class is equivalent to 1 quarter unit of academic credit. A quarter unit is equivalent to two-thirds of a semester unit.

 ## Concluding Thoughts

Now, more than ever, early childhood educators and policymakers recognize the importance of licensed family child care—and of unlicensed family, friend, and neighbor care—in meeting the child care and development needs of working families. As a provider in a child care home setting, you have an opportunity to define how you can offer families a safe, healthy environment that supports children's learning, development, and school readiness with intentional learning environments. As California develops a Quality Rating and Improvement System (QRIS) through the work of the California Early Learning Quality Improvement System (CAEL QIS) Advisory Committee, the role of family child care and license-exempt care will be discussed, and the committee will identify recommendations for including family child care in the system.

Many children spend as much time in family, friend, and neighbor care as they do in their own homes. Family child care and exempt-care providers have an important role in preparing children for school. As partners with children's parents, providers have an opportunity to promote the health and nutrition of the children in their care. They can help each child develop a sense of confidence and self-worth, which are the foundations for future learning. Providers can also promote language and literacy development

147

CHAPTER 5
Home-Based
Child Care
as Part of an
Early Learning
System

through a variety of language activities and by offering print-rich environments. And they can prepare children for future learning in mathematics by engaging them in problem solving, measurement, and sorting in the context of daily home activities.

You have many important decisions to make as you shape and evaluate your child care home setting. Your choices will help you develop a sense of professional satisfaction, create a sustainable livelihood for you and your family, and minimize issues that result in stress and challenges. May you find this publication helpful in defining how you will serve the children and families in your care.

Notes

1. Coley 2002.
2. Burton and Whitebook 1998.
3. Montgomery et al. 2002.
4. California Department of Finance. http://www.dof.ca.gov/html/demograp/dru_datafiles/race/racedata_2000-2050.
5. California Department of Education 2007a.
6. Ibid.
7. United States Census 2000.
8. Smith 2006.
9. O'Donnell and Morrissey 2005.
10. California Department of Education 2006b.
11. Center for Law and Social Policy 2006.
12. Schulman and Blank 2007.
13. Whelan 2007.
14. Schnur and Koffler 1995.
15. Ibid.
16. Washington 1985.
17. California Department of Education 2007b.

APPENDIX A

Additional Resources

The following is a compendium of organizations, publications, videos and DVDs, and other resources that can help you provide high-quality home-based child care. Many of these resources were listed or referred to earlier in this publication, but many were not. All of the listings can lead you to people and information that will help you advance as a home-based child care professional.

Americans with Disabilities Act (ADA) Information Line
Telephone: 1-800-514-0301 (voice)
TTY: 1-800-514-0383
http://www.ada.gov/infoline.htm

The United States Department of Justice operates the toll-free ADA Information Line. Specialists are available to answer general or specific questions about the ADA.

Beginning Together Institute
Telephone: 760-682-0271
http://www.cainclusivechildcare.org/bt

The purpose of Beginning Together is to ensure that children with special needs are incorporated, and appropriate inclusive practices are promoted, in the training and technical assistance provided by CDE/WestEd certified trainers in the Program for Infant/Toddler Care (PITC).

California Association for Family Child Care (CAFCC)
P.O. Box 8754
Emeryville, CA 94662
Telephone: 510-928-2273
http://www.cafcc.org

The CAFCC promotes the healthy growth and development of California's children and assists families and family child care providers through various means. The CAFCC Web site offers links to local/county, state, national, and international family child care associations. The site also provides resources on how to run your child care business; information about insurance (medical, dental, vision, liability, and other types) for licensed family child care providers; health and safety updates related to home-based child care settings; and links to government offices.

California Association for the Education of Young Children (CAEYC)
950 Glenn Drive, Suite 150
Folsom, CA 95630
Telephone: 916-486-7750
http://caeyc.org

Affiliated with the National Association for the Education of Young Children (NAEYC), CAEYC is a professional organization that offers services for early childhood educators. Membership in CAEYC automatically enrolls a person in NAEYC and in a local AEYC. Members can pursue accreditation through NAEYC; receive discounts on books, training materials, and professional-development conferences; obtain several industry-related publications free of charge; and gain access to local meetings, workshops, and newsletters.

California Child Care Healthline
1950 Addison Street, Suite 107
Berkeley, CA 94704
Telephone: 1-800-333-3212
http://www.ucsfchildcarehealth.org/html/healthline/healthlinemain.htm

The toll-free Healthline is a project of the California Childcare Health Program and is funded by the California Department of Education, Child Development Division. It was created for child care center staff, family child care providers, and parents who use child care settings in California. The Healthline is staffed by professional nurses and other specialists in the areas of child health and safety, public health, infant and toddler caregiving, child behavior and mental health, and inclusion of children who have chronic health conditions or other special needs. The Healthline provides telephone consultations free of charge to California early care and education programs and families.

California Child Care Resource and Referral Network
111 New Montgomery Street, 7th Floor
San Francisco, CA 94105
Telephone: 415-882-0234
http://www.rrnetwork.org

The California Child Care Resource and Referral Network was founded in 1980 as an association of resource and referral (R&R) agencies that can be found throughout California. These agencies provide information, training, and support for child care providers, parents, other community-based agencies, employers, and government policymakers. The Network has information about how to become a licensed provider, how to find the child care licensing office in your community, where to find technical assistance and support, and many other resources.

California Department of Education (CDE) Publications

CDE Press Sales Office
1430 N Street, Suite 3207
Sacramento, CA 95814
Telephone: 1-800-995-4099
http://www.cde.ca.gov/re/pn/rc

The CDE's *Educational Resources Catalog* features many publications and resources covering child development topics—including infant/toddler and preschool programs, school-age care, inclusion of children who have disabilities and special needs, and parent involvement. The catalog also offers publications on K–12 academic content standards, curriculum frameworks, and numerous educational subjects.

California Preschool Instructional Network (CPIN)

California Department of Education/WestEd
Telephone: 1-800-770-6339
http://www.cpin.us

The purpose of the CPIN is to provide professional development and technical assistance to early childhood educators and administrators, with the goal of ensuring that preschool children are ready for school. The CPIN is organized into 11 regions throughout California that disseminate information, training, and resources on topics such as early language and literacy, mathematics, school readiness, children with disabilities, English language learners, and others.

California Reading Association (CRA)

3186 D-1 Airway
Costa Mesa, CA 92626
Telephone: 714-435-1983
http://www.californiareads.org

The CRA is a nonprofit professional organization dedicated to increasing literacy and fostering a love for reading in children and adults. The CRA is composed of educators who are actively involved in all aspects of reading and language-arts education. The organization offers publications; information about professional development, networking, and policy issues; and other resources related to the promotion of literacy.

California Tomorrow

360 22nd Street, Suite 640
Oakland, CA 94612
Telephone: 510-496-0220
http://www.californiatomorrow.org/index.php

California Tomorrow is a nonprofit organization dedicated to building a more equitable, inclusive, multicultural society. The organization conducts research, produces publications, and offers technical assistance to community organizations, schools, policymakers, and others.

Center for Excellence in Child Development

University of California, Davis (UC Davis) Extension
Telephone: 530-757-8643
http://humanservices.ucdavis.edu/childdev

The Center for Excellence in Child Development offers resources—including educational and training opportunities—for educators, parents, and others who are interested in early childhood development.

Center for the Child Care Workforce (CCW)

555 New Jersey Avenue NW
Washington, DC 20001
Telephone: 202-662-8005
http://www.ccw.org

Affiliated with the American Federation of Teachers, CCW is a nonprofit organization that provides research, education, and advocacy for child care professionals. CCW aims to improve child care quality by promoting better compensation, working conditions, and training for child care teachers and family child care providers. The CCW Web site contains links to publications and training programs; wage data; and information on public policy.

Community Care Licensing Division (California Department of Social Services)

- *Child Care Licensing Web Site:* http://www.ccld.ca.gov/PG411.htm
- *Child Care Program Office:*
  California Department of Social Services
  744 P Street, MS 19-48
  Sacramento, CA 95814
  Telephone: 916-229-4500

Council for Exceptional Children (CEC)

1110 North Glebe Road, Suite 300
Arlington, VA 22201
Telephone: 703-620-3660 (voice)
TTY: 1-866-915-5000
http://www.cec.sped.org

The CEC is an international professional organization dedicated to improving the educational success of individuals with exceptionalities, disabilities, and special gifts or talents. The CEC publishes journals, newsletters, and special education materials.

English Learning for Preschoolers Project
http://www.cpin.us/p/pel

This project offers teaching strategies, materials, and training for individuals seeking optimal educational outcomes for preschool children who attend public preschool programs; are between the ages of three and five; arrive at school knowing a language other than English; or come from homes in which more than one language (one of which may be English) is spoken.

First 5 California (California Children and Families Commission)
2389 Gateway Oaks Drive, Suite 260
Sacramento, CA 95833
Telephone: 916-263-1050
http://www.first5california.com

First 5 California, also known as the California Children and Families Commission, provides a comprehensive, integrated system of early childhood development services for all children from birth through age five—including children with disabilities and special needs. First 5 California programs focus on education, health services, child care, and other issues that impact children during the early years of their lives.

International Child Art Foundation (ICAF)
P.O. Box 58133
Washington, DC 20037
Telephone: 202-530-1000
http://www.icaf.org

ICAF's mission is to integrate arts with science, athletics, and technology for the development of children's creativity and empathy. The ICAF Web site includes a variety of information and resources related to children's art.

Local Child Care and Development Planning Councils (LPCs)

Each county in California has an LPC whose mission is to provide child care and development services based on the needs of families in local communities. For more information about LPCs, visit the following California Department of Education Web site: http://www.cde.ca.gov/sp/cd/re/lpc.asp

National Association for Family Child Care (NAFCC)
1743 West Alexander Street
Salt Lake City, UT 84119
Telephone: 1-800-359-3817 or 801-886-2322
http://www.nafcc.org

• See Chapter 4 for information about NAFCC accreditation.

National Association for the Education of Young Children (NAEYC)

1313 L Street NW, Suite 500
Washington, DC 20005
Telephone: 1-800-424-2460 or 202-232-8777
http://www.naeyc.org

NAEYC is the world's largest organization that works on behalf of young children. NAEYC advocates high-quality early education and care for all young children, and one of its goals is to improve professional practice and working conditions in early childhood education. NAEYC offers a national, voluntary accreditation system that can identify your child care setting as a high-quality program.

National Child Care Information and Technical Assistance Center (NCCIC)

10530 Rosehaven Street, Suite 400
Fairfax, VA 22030
Telephone: 1-800-616-2242
http://nccic.acf.hhs.gov

NCCIC, a service of the U.S. Department of Health and Human Services' Child Care Bureau, is a national clearinghouse and technical assistance center that provides child care information resources to administrators, policymakers, national organizations, early care and school-age professionals, businesses, and the general public. NCCIC offers question-and-answer services (free of charge), an online library, a quarterly child care bulletin, and other pertinent information.

National Dissemination Center for Children with Disabilities (NICHCY)

1825 Connecticut Avenue NW, Suite 700
Washington, DC 20009
Telephone: 1-800-695-0285 (voice/TTY)
http://www.nichcy.org

The NICHCY provides information about children and youth disabilities; programs and services for infants, children, and youths with disabilities; effective, research-based practices for children with disabilities; and links to related materials and Web sites.

National Network for Child Care (NNCC)

Iowa State University Extension
1094 LeBaron Hall
Ames, IA 50001

The best way to contact someone at NNCC is through its Web site:
http://www.nncc.org

NNCC is an Internet source of over 1,000 publications and resources related to child care. NNCC also offers an e-mail Listserv called KIDCARE, which provides a way to communicate nationally and internationally with other individuals who value children and child care.

Program for Infant/Toddler Care (PITC)

http://www.pitc.org

A collaboration between the California Department of Education and WestEd, the PITC offers a variety of training opportunities, including the PITC Partners for Quality program (a subsidized on-site training and mentoring program for infant/toddler center staff and family child care providers). The PITC Web site also offers DVDs, audio and video presentations, guides, manuals, handouts, and other multimedia resources related to early childhood development.

Raising a Reader®

1700 South El Camino Real, Suite 300
San Mateo, CA 94402
Telephone: 650-581-4300
http://www.raisingareader.org/index.html

Raising a Reader® is a nationwide program that aims to foster healthy brain development, parent–child bonding, and early literacy skills in children from birth to age five. The program involves parents, librarians, and early childhood educators, and it features book bags filled with high-quality children's books that move from home to home.

Zero to Three (National Center for Infants, Toddlers and Families)

2000 M Street NW, Suite 200
Washington, DC 20036
Telephone: 202-638-1144 or 213-481-7279 (Western Office)
http://www.zerotothree.org

Zero to Three is a national nonprofit organization that promotes the health and development of infants and toddlers. The organization informs, trains, and supports professionals, policymakers, and parents who want to improve the lives of infants and toddlers. Zero to Three provides science-based information and tools to help parents and caregivers nurture their young children's development.

Regional Centers

Regional centers are private, nonprofit corporations that contract with the California Department of Developmental Services to provide or coordinate services for individuals with developmental disabilities and their families. California has 21 regional centers with more than 40 offices located throughout the state.

http://www.dds.cahwnet.gov/RC/Home.cfm

Videos/DVDS

A World Full of Language: Supporting Preschool English Learners. 2007. California Department of Education (Sacramento). http://www.cde.ca.gov/re/pn/rc.

Getting in Tune: Creating Nurturing Relationships with Infants and Toddlers. 1990. Lally, J. R.; P. L. Mangione; S. Signer; G. O. Butterfield; and S. Gilford. United States: The Program for Infant/Toddler Care (developed collaboratively by the California Department of Education and WestEd). http://www.pitc.org/cs/pitclib/view/pitc_res/88.

How Caring Relationships Support Self-Regulation. 1999. Goulet, M. National Association for the Education of Young Children (Washington, DC). http://www.naeyc.org/store/node/460.

Ingredients for a Good Start. 1994. Lally, J. R.; S. Signer; and G. O. Butterfield. United States: The Program for Infant/Toddler Care (developed collaboratively by the California Department of Education and WestEd). http://www.pitc.org/cs/pitclib/view/pitc_res/86.

Protective Urges: Working with the Feelings of Parents and Caregivers. 1996. Lally, J. R.; P. L. Mangione; S. Signer; and G. O. Butterfield. United States: The Program for Infant/Toddler Care (developed collaboratively by the California Department of Education and WestEd). http://www.pitc.org/cs/pitclib/view/pitc_res/820.

Today's Special: A Fresh Approach to Meals for Preschoolers. 1996. United States: The Program for Infant/Toddler Care (developed collaboratively by the California Department of Education and WestEd). http://www.pitc.org/cs/pitclib/view/pitc_res/546.

Together in Care: Meeting the Intimacy Needs of Infants and Toddlers in Groups. 1992. Lally, J. R.; P. L. Mangione; S. Signer; G. O. Butterfield; and S. Gilford. United States: The Program for Infant/Toddler Care (developed collaboratively by the California Department of Education and WestEd). http://www.pitc.org/cs/pitclib/view/pitc_res/598.

APPENDIX B
Applicable Laws

The Americans with Disabilities Act (ADA)

The Americans with Disabilities Act (ADA) is federal legislation that was passed in 1990. The ADA guarantees civil rights protection to people with disabilities in areas such as employment, transportation, public accommodations, and child care. Both child care centers and family child care homes must comply with the ADA, whether they are privately or publicly funded. The only exemptions allowed are for religious organizations operating child care programs. The ADA provides protection to a child or adult who meets any of the following criteria:

- Has a physical or mental impairment that substantially limits one of the "major life activities"
- Has a record of such an impairment
- Is regarded as having an impairment
- Is associated with an individual with a disability

The ADA mandates that "reasonable accommodations" be made in child care for children with disabilities. In most cases, the accommodations needed are quite simple and inexpensive to implement. For instance, a child with diabetes may need a snack at a different time or more frequently than other children; or a child who has difficulty making the transition to different activities may need a little extra time and support to do so. The ADA also makes it clear that the child care program may not charge families of children with disabilities higher fees than other families pay.

The ADA also mandates that architectural barriers to entering or using facilities be removed when this is "readily achievable." This phrase means that those necessary changes that do not place "an undue burden" on a provider need to be made ("an undue burden" is defined as a "significant difficulty or expense"). Examples of readily achievable designs could involve rearranging furniture for a child with visual impairments, installing a handrail in the bathroom for a child who uses a walker, changing door hinges, or other similarly minor accommodations. By making these relatively simple accommodations, a child care provider is complying with the ADA.

There are instances in which accommodations involve more significant changes. Fortunately, there are tax credits and other resources that can help offset the cost of these more extensive alterations to the child care setting (visit the ADA Web site at http://www.ada.gov/ for more information).

The ADA also acknowledges that there may be a situation in which a child may not be admitted to the child care program if the child would pose a direct threat to others, if the modification would fundamentally alter the program itself, or if the accommodation needed would be an undue hardship to the program. These exceptions are considered on an individual basis, and the law expects child care providers to work hard to include children with disabilities as often as possible.

California's Unruh Civil Rights Act

Every state has the option of enacting provisions that provide more protection than the ADA. California has the Unruh Civil Rights Act, *California Civil Code* Section 51, which is much more expansive than the ADA and offers even broader protection for children with special needs. Unlike the ADA, it provides protection from discrimination by *all* business establishments in California, including housing and public accommodations. California's law may apply even to religious entities, although there have not been published legal opinions where that has been tested.

The Individuals with Disabilities Education Act (IDEA) and Child Care

Both Part C and Part B of the Individuals with Disabilities Education Act (IDEA) strongly emphasize a collaborative relationship between parents and teachers/providers in the development of services. Parents may invite child care providers to participate in the development and implementation of IFSPs and IEPs. Participation in this process is an excellent opportunity for child care providers to share knowledge about the child in their care and to assist in coordinating services for that child. Families can also request that consultation or direct services from early intervention and special education programs be provided in the child care setting.

Additional Information About IDEA

The IDEA is federal legislation mandating special education for all eligible children. The Individuals with Disabilities Education Improvement Act of 2004 (IDEA 2004) is the most recent reauthorization of the statute. The IDEA guarantees children with disabilities a free, appropriate public education; an education in the least restrictive environment; related services; and fair assessment in the delivery of those special education services to children, from birth to age twenty-two. The law has four parts: Part A covers the general purpose of the law and definitions; Part B addresses the requirements for the education of all children with disabilities from age three through age twenty-one; Part C covers the specific requirements for services to infants and toddlers (children from birth to thirty-six months) with disabilities and their families; and Part D authorizes national activities to improve special education services (research, personnel development, technical assistance, and state improvement grants).

The IDEA makes it possible for states and localities to receive federal funds to assist in the education of infants, toddlers, preschoolers, children, and youths with disabilities. Essentially, in order to remain eligible for federal funds under the law, states must ensure the following:

- All children and youths with disabilities, regardless of the severity of their disability, will receive a free, appropriate public education (FAPE) at public expense.
- The education of children and youths with disabilities will be based on a complete and individual evaluation and assessment of the specific, unique needs of each student.
- An individualized education program (IEP) or an individualized family services plan (IFSP) will be drawn up for every child or youth found eligible for early intervention or special education, stating precisely what types of early intervention services or what kinds of special education and related services each infant, toddler, preschooler, child, or youth will receive.
- To the maximum extent appropriate, all children and youths with disabilities will be educated in the regular education environment. Children and youths receiving special education have the right to receive the related services they need to benefit from special education instruction.
- Parents have the right to participate in every decision related to the identification, evaluation, and placement of their child or youth with a disability.
- Parents must give consent for any initial evaluation, assessment, or placement; they must be notified of any change in placement that may occur; they must be included, along with teachers, in conferences and meetings held to draw up IFSPs or IEPs; and they must approve these IFSPs or IEPs before they go into effect for the first time.
- The right of parents to challenge and appeal any decision related to the identification, evaluation, and placement—or any issue concerning the provision of FAPE—of their child is fully protected by clearly spelled out due-process procedures.
- Parents have the right to have information kept confidential. No one may see a child's records unless the parents give written permission. Once a child has an IFSP or IEP, parental consent is needed for anyone to discuss the child with others. (The exception to this is school personnel who have legitimate educational interests.)

Part C in California: Early Start

As mentioned previously, Part C of the IDEA addresses services for infants and toddlers. California's state law that implements this component of the IDEA is the California Early Intervention Services Act. The state's early intervention program for infants and toddlers from birth through thirty-six months is known as Early Start. This state act is guided by both federal and state laws. The Department of Developmental Services is the lead agency for Early Start and collaborates with the California Department of Education, Department of Social Services, and several other state agencies to provide services to infants and toddlers who have a developmental delay or disability or who have an established risk condition.

Children and families eligible for the Early Start program qualify for early intervention services. Regional centers share primary responsibility with local educational agencies (LEAS)—school districts and county offices of education—for coordinating and providing these services at the local level. They may include specialized instruction, speech and language services, physical and/or occupational therapy, and transportation.

Infants and toddlers may be identified and referred to regional centers or LEAs through primary referral sources in their communities, including hospitals, health-care providers, child care providers, social service programs, or the child's family. Each infant or toddler referred to Early Start receives an evaluation to determine eligibility and, if eligible, an assessment to determine service needs. The IFSP is the legal document that describes the services the child is receiving. IFSPs are reviewed at least every six months, and child care providers are welcome to participate in these meetings as long as they have the permission of parents. The participation of child care providers in these meetings may be especially important if the child is receiving any early intervention services at the child care program's site.

Federal and state laws emphasize that early intervention services should be provided in "natural environments" whenever possible. Natural environments are those places where the child and family would be if the child did not have a disability, such as the home or a child care program. Therefore, a parent may approach service providers about providing intervention at their child care program itself. Welcoming a therapist or an early interventionist into a child care program is a positive way for a child care provider to promote inclusion and enrich the program as a whole.

Early Start also provides funding for over 50 family resource centers (FRCs) throughout the state that provide parent-to-parent support to families with infants and toddlers with special needs. These FRCs are staffed primarily by parents and provide support in nonclinical, family-centered environments. Specifically, FRCs provide referral information and outreach to underserved populations, they support child-find activities and family/ professional collaborative activities, and they assist families with transition.

Services for Children from Three to Twenty-Two Years of Age

As discussed briefly, Part B of the IDEA applies to children from three to twenty-two years of age who qualify for special education services. The California Department of Education oversees the implementation of Part B services in the state, as do departments of education in other states across the country.

There have been several revisions to the IDEA over the years, and the latest strengthens provisions concerning "least restrictive environments." This term means that, to whatever extent possible, children should be in the same classes as their typically developing peers. For children ages three to five, this means that specialized services are ideally provided in settings such as the home, child care center, or family child care home. For this age group, services are provided through the local school district, county office of education, or special education local planning area (SELPA).

Special education provides specific early education programs for children between the ages of three and five who have disabilities. These programs include individual and group services in a variety of typical, age-appropriate environments for young children, such as regular child care programs, the home, and special education preschool programs. Services are based upon ongoing consultations with the family, include related support services for the child and family, and are provided in the least restrictive environment.

California Special Education Programs: A Composite of Laws (Thirty-first edition)

The State of California has numerous laws and regulations related to programs for individuals with exceptional needs. The California Department of Education, with assistance from the Sacramento County Office of Education, offers a searchable database of the state's special education statutes; *California Code of Regulations, Title 5* (Education); provisions; and related laws and regulations affecting programs for individuals with exceptional needs. The database is available at http:// www3.scoe.net/speced/laws_search/searchLaws.cfm.

APPENDIX C
Talking with Parents When Concerns Arise
© Linda Brault, MA, and Janet Gonzalez-Mena, MA

Marta cared for six children in her home. Rashad, now nearly eight months old, was enrolled by his parents Maurice and Rosa when he was six months old. Rashad was their first child. Marta began to be concerned about Rashad's development. Rashad was a very happy, contented baby. However, he seemed almost too content to Marta. He would stay on a blanket either on his back or his stomach for hours without fussing. He could roll over, but hadn't shown much interest in moving by himself. When Marta asked Maurice or Rosa how things were going, they seemed very thankful for such a "good" baby. Marta wondered if she should say anything about her worries. Maybe Rashad was just a "good" baby.

Sarali attended ABC Child Care Center. She was nearly three years old and had been at the center for one year. Emily, her teacher, had just taken a class at the local community college about child development. During the class, she found herself thinking about Sarali who was always in need of adult attention. Sarali often was in the middle of things when other children were hurt or upset. Emily wondered what it was about Sarali that made her stand out. Her parents, Juan and Maria, had two older children and were always rushed during drop-off or pick-up. They certainly didn't seem worried. Why was she?

As a child care provider, you are often the first one to notice a child who learns or communicates differently than other children in your care. If your careful observation and efforts to work effectively with a particular child do not seem to be meeting the child's needs, it is time to look for help to foster belonging and appropriately support this child in your program. This help can come from the family, but more expertise may be needed, such as from the child's pediatrician or health care provider, a therapist or another specialist. When you recommend to the family that they seek help in this way, or if you get their permission to seek such help yourself, you are "making a referral." It is easiest if the parent or family member makes the referral, as they will have the information needed and can get the process started more quickly. In order for you to make a referral, you will need to talk to the parents of the child first. They must give their written permission (consent) before you seek other assistance.

Sometimes parents will notice the developmental differences on their own. Although comparing one child with another is a disservice to both, it often helps parents to have a broader view than they may have if their experience is limited to their own child. One mother of a baby who was born with a heart defect entered an infant/toddler program that had a parent observation component. She was shocked when she saw the difference in development between her son and the other children his age. Because of his fragile condition and several surgeries, his early experiences had been very different from other children his age in this program. This mother didn't need the caregiver to recommend a referral. She went immediately to the heart specialist and the pediatrician and asked for help with her son's developmental needs. She understood that when specialists are worried about saving a baby's life, their concerns about overall development go on hold sometimes. With the help of the caregiver and a developmental specialist, the child moved from being seen primarily as a heart patient to being a developing toddler.

That case was unusual because the parent didn't need a referral. She already had specialists to help her and ultimately the child care program as well. If the concern you have is for a child who isn't already defined as a child with special needs, you may not know how the parents will react when you share your concerns.

How do you decide when to have a formal conference to talk to parents about your concerns? If you have spent some time focusing on the child and clarifying your concerns, you can ask the parents to schedule an uninterrupted time for you to talk with them. If you have worked to establish a good relationship with the parents, you probably have been talking to them all along, so you know if the issues you are worried about are unique to your setting or if the parents have noticed the same at home. You may know that the parents are concerned as well, and that their concerns are the same as yours. You may also know if they have not expressed any worries and can take that into account in planning a conference.

Certainly if there have been regular small conversations, the conference itself won't come as a surprise to the parents. Nevertheless, if you decide that the time has come to get some outside help by making a referral, this conference may take on deeper significance than the usual parent-caregiver conference or the casual conversations you've been having with the parents and/or other family members.

Preparing for a Formal Conference

Prepare for the conference by making careful observations of the child. Observation of the child over time will give you information about specific behaviors that illustrate the concern. It will help you clarify a general concern (Rashad seems too easygoing; Sarali is always in the middle of trouble.)

with specific examples of behavior (Rashad stays in one position for up to 30 minutes and doesn't change positions on his own; Sarali has trouble sitting at the table during snack time and often hits children.). Note when and where those behaviors occur and under what circumstances. Also, with focused observation, you may get some insights into what is contributing to the behavior. See if changing the environment or your approach affects the behavior. Keep track of all the details of what you have tried and what happened. This record can contain important information to share with the parents.

Remember it is only appropriate for you to discuss what you have observed about *specific behaviors*. Avoid the urge to label or diagnose. Sometimes parents have noticed that their child's development is different from most children and they come to the conference feeling relief that someone has noticed. They may come anticipating that they will get the help and support they need. Other times, parents may be unaware of differences or unable to see them. Parents may have different expectations due to culture or experience. If parents haven't noticed anything, it may be a different situation.

Observations of Rashad

Marta thought about Rashad and what other infants his age were like. Marta decided to focus on Rashad's movement. She would make notes with the time and position in which Rashad was. She noticed that Rashad would stay in the position in which he started for at least 30 minutes. Rashad only rolled over from his back to his stomach one time in the three days Marta was keeping track. He did roll from his back to his side. Marta also noticed that Rashad spent time watching the other children and looking at toys, but rarely picked up toys or other objects that were in his reach. Marta came to realize that she had been changing Rashad's position without realizing it several times a day.

Observations of Sarali

When Emily asked her aide Tim about Sarali, he said Sarali "behaved badly and bothered other children" but Emily knew that would not be helpful to her parents. Emily decided to watch Sarali carefully so that she could give specifics. Emily noticed that Sarali had a harder time sitting still than other children and didn't cope well with transitions. She counted the times Sarali got up during snack and was able to give the actual figures of two times on Monday, Tuesday and Wednesday, five times on Thursday and one time on Friday. Emily could describe the behavior that indicated Sarali doesn't cope when there is a change. When it's time to come inside or to go down for a nap, she ran away from the teacher and grabbed toys from the shelf. When playing with more than one other child, Emily observed and recorded five incidents of hitting other children during the past week. She also noticed that Sarali had fewer words and phrases than other almost-three year olds.

Caregiver Responses

One thing to keep in mind is that YOU may have an emotional response to the possibility of a child having a delay or difference in development. Noticing a difference in development can make you sad, nervous, upset, or anxious to get help. Your own emotional response will impact the way you share the information with the family. If Marta's only exposure to children with motor delays had come from seeing children with Muscular Dystrophy on the television, she might be very sad and even scared about the potential for this disability in Rashad. If you are a person concerned about children growing up to be independent individuals, the idea that a child has a special need that might get in the way of that goal may seem tragic to you. On the other hand, if your background stressed interdependence more than independence, you may consider a child with a special need a gift, not a liability. The family may have entirely different feelings. For example, if Emily is anxious to get speech and language help for Sarali, Emily may not be able to listen fully to the parent's perspective, and may be especially discouraged if Sarali's family does not share her concern.

Caregivers need to take the time to uncover their own emotional responses before meeting with the family. It may be helpful to talk with a colleague or the director about your own feelings. Sharing about the situation should not contain specific information about the family unless the listener is part of the staff. The discussion also needs to occur in a private location, not a restaurant or crowded staff room. Knowing what your feelings are can help you anticipate what reactions you may have when sharing the information. For example, you may be surprised if the family agrees with your observations, yet is not very worried. Or, you may be especially frustrated if the family wants more time to observe on their own when you are sure that the child needs help. Once you realize your potential emotional reaction, you will be better able to keep it "out of the way" when conducting the conference. You may also be better prepared for the variety of ways that each family member may react.

When thinking about your feelings about your concerns for the child, the implications of those concerns, and about the family's response, keep in mind the positive feelings that you have for the child and all of the strengths that you've seen in the child. Regardless of your concerns, the child is still the wonderful being who is the focus of her family's love and your care.

Conducting the Conference

In the meeting itself, do what you can to make the parents feel comfortable and at ease as much as possible. Choose a seating arrangement that brings you together instead of separating you. Sitting behind a desk, for example, can make a psychological as well as a physical barrier between you and the parents or other family members. A warmer, friendlier arrangement may work better. Provide for privacy. This meeting is between you and the parents, not the business of the secretary or the rest of the staff. If you are a family child care provider you may need to meet outside of regular hours of care. Set aside enough time so that the meeting isn't rushed and you can talk things through. If this is the first such meeting the parents have had, they need to feel that you care and that they can trust you.

If you and the family members do not speak the same language, careful thought must be given to interpretation during the conference. This conversation generally has an emotional component, and therefore appropriate interpretation is critical. When sharing information about a child's development, it is likely that some of the words and nuances in phrasing will be challenging for inexperienced interpreters to translate. Additionally, some parents may understand another language, such as English, yet not be able to fully understand and participate in a conversation about their child. A family may use someone (such as another family member or older child) for routine interpretation; however, they might not feel comfortable putting that person in the position of interpreting for this conference. You may need to explore other community resources.

Start the conference by gathering information from the family about how they see their child. Ask open-ended questions. Truly listen and show an interest in all that they say. Give them a chance to talk without interruption. You'll learn more about the family and the child and may be able to identify concerns that you have in common with the family.

When it is your turn to share, start with what is going well. Sharing positive qualities that you've observed lets the family know that you're paying close attention to their child and that you care about their child. Both listening to the family and sharing positive things about the child helps the family to know that you are partners in meeting the needs of their child.

Ask about how the child behaves at home. If the family differs in their view of the child, be open to their perspective. Asking how the child behaves at home gives you information for comparison of your observations. You may also discover that there are different expectations due to the family's culture or values. When done respectfully, this communication can lead to a better exchange of ideas and ultimately be of most help to the child.

Before you share your concerns with the family, ask if they have any concerns that they haven't already indicated. Specifically asking the family if they have concerns that they haven't mentioned before gives the family another opportunity to voice their own observations or concerns and may provide information that supports what you've seen.

As you begin to talk about your concerns, let the family know that you are sharing your concerns to support their child's development and to get some ideas for how to best meet their child's needs. Be sure you communicate what you want to say clearly, without judgment and with concrete examples. It is especially important that you share your observations without labeling or diagnosing. DO NOT suggest that a child has a specific diagnosis (such as attention deficit disorder). Most child care providers are not qualified to provide such a diagnosis and doing so often gets in the way of the next steps in the referral process. On the other hand, your specific observations and descriptions of what is happening will be very helpful to any specialists who become involved.

Supporting the Family Who Wants to Access Resources

If the family is also concerned or agrees with your observations, you can move to a discussion of possible next steps. Support the family in getting help. Their biggest fear is often that you will reject their child or them if extra help is needed. Let them know that you are there to support their child and to incorporate any new ideas. You should have information ready about services within your program, local early intervention services, special education services, and other resources. By sharing your concrete observations, you will be able to help the family clarify their questions about their child and what the referral will accomplish.

When ready to refer to the early intervention program, local school district, or pediatrician/healthcare provider, let the family take the lead. Since many families will want to take action, be prepared to talk with them about resources for obtaining further assessment and/or possible services. This is the point at which you are "making a referral." It is generally appropriate to refer the family to their pediatrician at the same time you refer them to the local early intervention / special education resources.

Calling resource agencies ahead of time to gather general information can be very helpful. However, you cannot guarantee eligibility or services from another agency to a family. Rather, describe what might happen after the referral and what the possible outcomes might be based on what you've learned from the agency. You can also let the family know that you can be a source of information to the referral agency. Parents must give permission for you to talk about their child with referral sources, so you will want to carefully respect the family's confidentiality and be sure that you have clear, written consent.

When the family wants to access other resources, being aware of potential barriers can be very helpful. Some barriers include issues of insurance, spoken language, cultural practices, transportation, and discomfort, or previous negative experiences with authority figures such as teachers or doctors. It is not uncommon for a child care provider to help the families obtain services their child needs by setting the process in motion for them. Be careful not to do too much for the family, however. Rather than feeling responsible for overcoming the barrier, you can focus on supporting the family as they encounter a barrier. For example, a family can make the call to the referral source from your office, with you there to provide support and clarification if needed. Finding ways for the family to meet their child's needs will serve the family and their child best in the long run.

When the Family Chooses Not to Access Resources

If the parents don't understand what your concerns are, think they are not important, or disagree with your observation, they may be upset if you suggest that a referral is necessary. It's even possible that your observations will shock or anger them. In this case, sensitively supporting the parents' feelings is called for without getting caught up in them. When infants and toddlers are distressed, caregivers accept the feelings and empathize with the child. Parents need the same approach from caregivers. You are not a therapist, but some of the listening skills of a therapist can serve you well. For example, if the parents get angry, your immediate response may be to get defensive and argue your case. If you get caught up in your own feelings, you are less available to give parents the support they need at a time when they are vulnerable. Understanding that anger or blame are common responses for people in pain helps you accept the feelings without taking them personally. You may feel an urge to come back with your own feelings, but this is the time to focus on those of the parents and listen to what they have to say without minimizing their upset feelings or trying to talk them out of the feelings. Share with the parents that you see further assessment as a positive move and that both of you have the child's best interests at heart even if you don't see eye-to-eye at the moment.

Sometimes the family may not choose to access resources when you first share your concerns or they may be open to information, yet not take action immediately. Rather than label them as being "in denial" or something else, remember that everyone moves at a different pace and accepts information differently. The family's emotional response will affect what they are able to hear and understand. Processing and integrating this information will take varying amounts of time. The reality that life will have to change—that their child may be different than other children—is very hard for some families to hear. Unless behavior or other issues, such as medical urgency, will prevent you from caring for the child without assistance, allow the family to proceed on their own time line. Be prepared to support them in understanding what you have shared, repeating the information whenever necessary. Let them know that there is resource information available whenever they want it. If you find that your own judgment or emotions about this interfere with your ability to respect the family as the decision-maker, seek support for yourself and don't be afraid to suggest that the family discuss this with someone else as well. If you believe that not seeking help is an issue of neglect, then you do have an obligation to be clear with the family and make an appropriate referral to a child protective agency yourself. Referrals to child protective agencies do not require parent consent.

Resources for Families

Health and medical service systems

In many cases, it is appropriate to have a family talk about their concerns with their primary health care provider. Some issues faced by children with disabilities or other special needs are medical in nature and will require careful follow-up by a health care provider. Some health care providers specialize in working with children with special needs, while others have limited knowledge of the assessment and service issues. Parents and providers must be proactive to assure a good match between child and primary health care provider. It is often a good idea for the referral to be made to the special education/early intervention service system at the same time as the referral to the health care provider because the referral process takes time and referring only to one system (such as health care) may delay the entry to the other (such as early intervention). Remember, referrals are best made directly by the family. If a provider makes a referral, the family must have provided clear permission.

Local special education / early intervention service systems

Local special education and early intervention service systems are required by law to engage in "Child Find." In other words, there is supposed to be an active and ongoing effort on the part of the specialist system to identify children who may be eligible for services. Some areas may provide free screenings at local child care settings, while others may send outreach materials to child care and medical agencies. Not all children with differences in their development will qualify for services from special education or early intervention. This is determined after appropriate screening and assessment. This assessment is provided to families free of charge, as are most special education services. After referral, the special education or early intervention agency has 45 calendar days (50 for children over three) to complete the assessment, determine eligibility, and hold a meeting to plan for services if needed. Again, referrals are best made directly by the family.

Once a referral is received, representatives of those agencies will talk with the family and may schedule an assessment to see if the child qualifies for services. Knowing the best contact name and number in your local districts can be of great help to the family. Each state is required to have a *Central*

Directory of Services for early intervention services. There are legal timelines for responding to parent requests for consideration of early intervention or special education services. Parents may also put their request in writing if they are having difficulty getting a response. Parents must give written permission for the child to be tested and receive early intervention or special education. All services are confidential and many are provided at no cost to the family. Even if a child is not found eligible for early intervention or special education services, the team providing the assessment may have suggestions for ways to support the child's growth and development. Additionally, they will be able to give guidelines for monitoring the child's progress as the child becomes older, in case the family or you become concerned.

If the child referred is found eligible and begins to receive services, the child can benefit from your working with the specialists on his or her team. They can become consultants to you and the family. The open and ongoing communication you have established with the family will serve you well as you continue to exchange information and support the child.

The sooner concerns about a child's development or behavior are identified, the better the chance to provide effective help that may be important to the child's future development. You, as a care provider, are in a unique position to work with families to identify concerns and take advantage of the opportunity to access services and supports early. Together you and the family provide the love and support for the child to become all that she or he can be!

APPENDIX D
Summary of the Guidelines

Chapter 1. The Home-Based Child Care Provider: Roles and Relationships

The Home-Based Child Care Provider as Caregiver

1. Create a caring and nurturing environment where positive social and emotional development can take place.
2. Use caregiving routines as opportunities to meet children's social, emotional, and physical needs and to respond to their interests and abilities.

The Home-Based Child Care Provider as Teacher

1. Understand children's needs and capabilities. Pay attention to their behavior to provide responsive, individualized care.
2. Honor and encourage each child's curiosity and creativity, and make learning fun.
3. Balance adult-initiated and child-initiated learning activities and experiences.
4. Observe children regularly to support their growth and development.
5. Observe children in natural and familiar settings and during routines. Use multiple sources of information to get a complete picture of each child.
6. Keep families informed about, and involved in, observations and records of their children.

The Home-Based Child Care Provider as Family Partner

1. Encourage families to talk with you about their ideas for supporting their children's learning and about working with you to prepare their children for school.
2. Create an environment in which families feel comfortable about speaking up for their children.
3. Share information with families about activities and experiences in your home, and encourage them to continue these activities in their homes.
4. Establish partnerships with families to strengthen what children learn about math, reading, science, motor skills, and the arts.
5. Recognize that family members and adults other than parents may play a role in promoting children's development.
6. Support families in other ways, especially by connecting them with resources in their communities.

Chapter 2. The Home as a Caring and Learning Environment

Welcoming Children into a Safe and Healthy Home

1. Prepare and arrange your home in ways that welcome children and foster learning.
2. Focus on preventing illness and injuries.
3. Emphasize and model proper nutrition.
4. Provide interest areas, materials, and activities that are engaging and age-appropriate.

Addressing Cultural Diversity

1. Respect and show appreciation for all individuals and cultures, making the acceptance of diversity a central theme in your child care environment.
2. Understand your cultural beliefs and practices, and be aware of how your feelings and ideas about other cultures, ethnicities, communities, and religions affect the care you provide.
3. Learn about the history, beliefs, and practices of the children and families you serve.
4. To the extent possible, use caregiving practices that are consistent with children's experiences in their own homes.
5. Provide materials that reflect the characteristics, values, and practices of diverse cultural groups.
6. Teach children what to do when they experience social injustice, bias, and prejudice.

Including Children with Disabilities or Other Special Needs

1. Actively support the concept of inclusion by creating an environment in which all children and families feel welcome.
2. Partner with families by communicating frequently and by exchanging resources.
3. Be a part of the educational team that develops and implements IFSPs and IEPs for eligible children.
4. Work with family members and specialists to support children's daily learning activities, experiences, and environments.
5. Develop strategies to include children who have disabilities or other special needs by participating in training and by talking with family members and specialists.

Chapter 3. Developing a Home-Based Curriculum

Social and Emotional Development

1. Help each child develop a sense of self-esteem and self-confidence.
2. Be responsive to each child's emotional needs.
3. Teach children to express their emotions in socially acceptable ways.
4. Consider children's social and cultural backgrounds when interpreting their preferences and behaviors.
5. Help children form and maintain satisfying relationships with one another and with adults.
6. Help each child feel valued and included.
7. Understand that the goal of guidance and discipline is to promote greater social and emotional competence.
8. Create a sense of safety, security, and predictability through the culture, environment, and routines of your home.
9. Guide children's social behavior in the context of daily learning activities and experiences.

Language and Literacy Development

1. Listen to children, talk with them, and encourage them to talk with one another.
2. Read aloud to children and share stories with them.
3. Help children notice the sounds of spoken language.
4. Provide a wide variety of printed materials.
5. Model proper speech, grammar, and communication skills.
6. Respect children's home languages.
7. Support children's language and literacy development by working closely with the children's families.

Mathematics Learning and Development

1. Create a math-rich learning environment by integrating adult-guided and child-initiated learning activities and experiences.
2. Implement activities that lay the foundation for children's success in elementary-school mathematics.
3. Identify clear, age-appropriate goals for mathematics learning and development.

Cognitive Development (Thinking Skills)

1. Build on children's natural curiosity by providing opportunities to explore social studies and science.
2. Use computers and other forms of technology appropriately.

Creativity and Self-Expression

1. Offer a variety of opportunities for children to use their imagination and creativity.
2. Encourage children to express their feelings through art, music, dramatic play, and dance.

Physical and Motor Development

1. Observe all areas of motor-skill development, including gross motor, fine motor, oral motor, and sensorimotor skills.
2. Remember that children differ in their development of skills and abilities.
3. Provide many opportunities for safe and active play.

Chapter 4. Professional Development for Home-Based Child Care Providers

1. Make the children your top priority.
2. Be aware of legal requirements and responsibilities.
3. Consider the benefits of ongoing training and education.
4. Participate in a child care association and/or a network of home-based child care providers.
5. Develop a plan for improving your child care program.
6. Follow Best Business Practices.
7. Take care of yourself.

APPENDIX E
Summary of the California Infant/Toddler Learning and Development Foundations

SOCIAL-EMOTIONAL DEVELOPMENT

Interactions with Adults: The developing ability to respond to and engage with adults

Relationships with Adults: The development of close relationships with certain adults who provide consistent nurturance

Interactions with Peers: The developing ability to respond to and engage with other children

Relationships with Peers: The development of relationships with certain peers through interactions over time

Identity of Self in Relation to Others: The developing concept that the child is an individual operating within social relationships

Recognition of Ability: The developing understanding that the child can take action to influence the environment

Expression of Emotion: The developing ability to express a variety of feelings through facial expressions, movements, gestures, sounds, or words

Empathy: The developing ability to share in the emotional experiences of others

Emotion Regulation: The developing ability to manage emotional responses with assistance from others and independently

Impulse Control: The developing capacity to wait for needs to be met, to inhibit potentially hurtful behavior, and to act according to social expectations, including safety rules

Social Understanding: The developing understanding of the responses, communication, emotional expressions, and actions of other people

LANGUAGE DEVELOPMENT

Receptive Language: The developing ability to understand words and increasingly complex utterances

Expressive Language: The developing ability to produce the sounds of language and use vocabulary and increasingly complex utterances

175

APPENDIX E
Summary of the
California
Preschool Learning
Foundations

Communication Skills and Knowledge: The developing ability to communicate nonverbally and verbally

Interest in Print: The developing interest in engaging with print in books and in the environment

COGNITIVE DEVELOPMENT

Cause-and-Effect: The developing understanding that one event brings about another

Spatial Relationships: The developing understanding of how things move and fit in space

Problem Solving: The developing ability to engage in a purposeful effort to reach a goal or figure out how something works

Imitation: The developing ability to mirror, repeat, and practice the actions of others, either immediately or later

Memory: The developing ability to store and later retrieve information about past experiences

Number Sense: The developing understanding of number and quantity

Classification: The developing ability to group, sort, categorize, connect, and have expectations of objects and people according to their attributes

Symbolic Play: The developing ability to use actions, objects, or ideas to represent other actions, objects, or ideas

Attention Maintenance: The developing ability to attend to people and things while interacting with others and exploring the environment and play materials

Understanding of Personal Care Routines: The developing ability to understand and participate in personal care routines

PERCEPTUAL AND MOTOR DEVELOPMENT

Perceptual Development: The developing ability to become aware of the social and physical environment through the senses

Gross Motor: The developing ability to move the large muscles

Fine Motor: The developing ability to move the small muscles

Summary of the California Preschool Learning Foundations

In 2008, the California Department of Education (CDE) published *California Preschool Learning Foundations (Volume 1)*, a document that describes the knowledge and skills that four- and five-year-old children typically acquire in high-quality preschool programs. The preschool learning foundations cover topics such as self-awareness; social interaction and relationships; language and literacy (listening, speaking, reading, and writing); and mathematics. Being familiar with these foundations can help you develop an effective curriculum for preschool-age children in your care.

The preschool learning foundations are summarized in the following pages. For information on the complete *California Preschool Learning Foundations* publication, contact the CDE Press Sales Office at 1-800-995-4099, or visit http://www.cde.ca.gov/re/pn/rc.

SOCIAL-EMOTIONAL DEVELOPMENT

Self

1.0   Self-Awareness

At around 48 months of age	At around 60 months of age
1.1 Describe their physical characteristics, behavior, and abilities positively.	1.1 Compare their characteristics with those of others and display a growing awareness of their psychological characteristics, such as thoughts and feelings.

2.0   Self-Regulation

2.1 Need adult guidance in managing their attention, feelings, and impulses and show some effort at self-control.	2.1 Regulate their attention, thoughts, feelings, and impulses more consistently, although adult guidance is sometimes necessary.

3.0   Social and Emotional Understanding

3.1 Seek to understand people's feelings and behavior, notice diversity in human characteristics, and are interested in how people are similar and different.	3.1 Begin to comprehend the mental and psychological reasons people act as they do and how they contribute to differences between people.

4.0　Empathy and Caring

4.1 Demonstrate concern for the needs of others and people in distress.	4.1 Respond to another's distress and needs with sympathetic caring and are more likely to assist.

5.0　Initiative in Learning

5.1 Enjoy learning and are confident in their abilities to make new discoveries although may not persist at solving difficult problems.	5.1 Take greater initiative in making new discoveries, identifying new solutions, and persisting in trying to figure things out.

Social Interaction

1.0　Interactions with Familiar Adults

At around 48 months of age	*At around 60 months of age*
1.1 Interact with familiar adults comfortably and competently, especially in familiar settings.	1.1 Participate in longer and more reciprocal interactions with familiar adults and take greater initiative in social interaction.

2.0　Interactions with Peers

2.1 Interact easily with peers in shared activities that occasionally become cooperative efforts.	2.1 More actively and intentionally cooperate with each other.
2.2 Participate in simple sequences of pretend play.	2.2 Create more complex sequences of pretend play that involve planning, coordination of roles, and cooperation.
2.3 Seek assistance in resolving peer conflict, especially when disagreements have escalated into physical aggression.	2.3 Negotiate with each other, seeking adult assistance when needed, and increasingly use words to respond to conflict. Disagreements may be expressed with verbal taunting in addition to physical aggression.

Social-Emotional Development *(continued)*

3.0   Group Participation

3.1 Participate in group activities and are beginning to understand and cooperate with social expectations, group rules, and roles.	3.1 Participate positively and cooperatively as group members.

4.0   Cooperation and Responsibility

4.1 Seek to cooperate with adult instructions but their capacities for self-control are limited, especially when they are frustrated or upset.	4.1 Have growing capacities for self-control and are motivated to cooperate in order to receive adult approval and think approvingly of themselves.

Relationships

1.0   Attachments to Parents

At around 48 months of age	*At around 60 months of age*
1.1 Seek security and support from their primary family attachment figures.	1.1 Take greater initiative in seeking support from their primary family attachment figures.
1.2 Contribute to maintaining positive relationships with their primary family attachment figures.	1.2 Contribute to positive mutual cooperation with their primary family attachment figures.
1.3 After experience with out-of-home care, manage departures and separations from primary family attachment figures with the teacher's assistance.	1.3 After experience with out-of-home care, comfortably depart from their primary family attachment figures. Also maintain well-being while apart from primary family attachment figures during the day.

Social-Emotional Development *(continued)*

2.0 Close Relationships with Teachers and Caregivers

2.1 Seek security and support from their primary teachers and caregivers.	2.1 Take greater initiative in seeking the support of their primary teachers and caregivers.
2.2 Contribute to maintaining positive relationships with their primary teachers and caregivers.	2.2 Contribute to positive mutual cooperation with their primary teachers and caregivers.

3.0 Friendships

3.1 Choose to play with one or two special peers whom they identify as friends.	3.1 Friendships are more reciprocal, exclusive, and enduring.

LANGUAGE AND LITERACY

Listening and Speaking

1.0 Language Use and Conventions

At around 48 months of age	*At around 60 months of age*
1.1 Use language to communicate with others in familiar social situations for a variety of basic purposes, including describing, requesting, commenting, acknowledging, greeting, and rejecting.	1.1 Use language to communicate with others in both familiar and unfamiliar social situations for a variety of basic and advanced purposes, including reasoning, predicting, problem solving, and seeking new information.
1.2 Speak clearly enough to be understood by familiar adults and children.	1.2 Speak clearly enough to be understood by both familiar and unfamiliar adults and children.
1.3 Use accepted language and style during communication with familiar adults and children.	1.3 Use accepted language and style during communication with both familiar and unfamiliar adults and children.
1.4 Use language to construct short narratives that are real or fictional.	1.4 Use language to construct extended narratives that are real or fictional.

Language and Literacy *(continued)*

2.0 Vocabulary

2.1 Understand and use accepted words for objects, actions, and attributes encountered frequently in both real and symbolic contexts.	2.1 Understand and use an increasing variety and specificity of accepted words for objects, actions, and attributes encountered in both real and symbolic contexts.
2.2 Understand and use accepted words for categories of objects encountered and used frequently in everyday life.	2.2 Understand and use accepted words for categories of objects encountered in everyday life.
2.3 Understand and use simple words that describe the relations between objects.	2.3 Understand and use both simple and complex words that describe the relations between objects.

3.0 Grammar

At around 48 months of age	*At around 60 months of age*
3.1 Understand and use increasingly complex and longer sentences, including sentences that combine two phrases or two to three concepts to communicate ideas.	3.1 Understand and use increasingly complex and longer sentences, including sentences that combine two to three phrases or three to four concepts to communicate ideas.
3.2 Understand and typically use age-appropriate grammar, including accepted word forms, such as subject-verb agreement, progressive tense, regular past tense, regular plurals, pronouns, and possessives.	3.2 Understand and typically use age-appropriate grammar, including accepted word forms, such as subject-verb agreement, progressive tense, regular and irregular past tense, regular and irregular plurals, pronouns, and possessives.

Language and Literacy *(continued)*

Reading

1.0   Concepts about Print

At around 48 months of age	*At around 60 months of age*
1.1 Begin to display appropriate book-handling behaviors and begin to recognize print conventions.	1.1 Display appropriate book-handling behaviors and knowledge of print conventions.
1.2 Recognize print as something that can be read.	1.2 Understand that print is something that is read and has specific meaning.

2.0   Phonological Awareness

	2.1 Orally blend and delete words and syllables without the support of pictures or objects.
	2.2 Orally blend the onsets, rimes, and phonemes of words and orally delete the onsets of words, <u>with</u> the support of pictures or objects.

3.0   Alphabetics and Word/Print Recognition

At around 48 months of age	*At around 60 months of age*
3.1 Recognize the first letter of own name.	3.1 Recognize own name or other common words in print.
3.2 Match some letter names to their printed form.	3.2 Match more than half of uppercase letter names and more than half of lowercase letter names to their printed form.
	3.3 Begin to recognize that letters have sounds.

Language and Literacy *(continued)*

4.0 Comprehension and Analysis of Age-Appropriate Text

4.1 Demonstrate knowledge of main characters or events in a familiar story (e.g., who, what, where) through answering questions (e.g., recall and simple inferencing), retelling, reenacting, or creating artwork.	4.1 Demonstrate knowledge of details in a familiar story, including characters, events, and ordering of events through answering questions (particularly summarizing, predicting, and inferencing), retelling, reenacting, or creating artwork.
4.2 Demonstrate knowledge from informational text through labeling, describing, playing, or creating artwork.	4.2 Use information from informational text in a variety of ways, including describing, relating, categorizing, or comparing and contrasting.

5.0 Literacy Interest and Response

5.1 Demonstrate enjoyment of literacy and literacy-related activities.	5.1 Demonstrate, with increasing independence, enjoyment of literacy and literacy-related activities.
5.2 Engage in routines associated with literacy activities.	5.2 Engage in more complex routines associated with literacy activities.

Writing

1.0 Writing Strategies

At around 48 months of age	*At around 60 months of age*
1.1 Experiment with grasp and body position using a variety of drawing and writing tools.	1.1 Adjust grasp and body position for increased control in drawing and writing.
1.2 Write using scribbles that are different from pictures.	1.2 Write letters or letter-like shapes to represent words or ideas.
1.3 Write marks to represent own name.	1.3 Write first name nearly correctly.

ENGLISH-LANGUAGE DEVELOPMENT

Listening

1.0   Children listen with understanding.

Focus: Beginning words

Beginning	Middle	Later
1.1 Attend to English oral language in both real and pretend activity, relying on intonation, facial expressions, or the gestures of the speaker.	1.1 Demonstrate understanding of words in English for objects and actions as well as phrases encountered frequently in both real and pretend activity.	1.1 Begin to demonstrate an understanding of a larger set of words in English (for objects and actions, personal pronouns, and possessives) in both real and pretend activity.

Focus: Requests and directions

1.2 Begin to follow simple directions in English, especially when there are contextual cues.	1.2 Respond appropriately to requests involving one step when personally directed by others, which may occur with or without contextual cues.	1.2 Follow directions that involve a one- or two-step sequence, relying less on contextual cues.

Focus: Basic and advanced concepts

1.3 Demonstrate an understanding of words related to basic and advanced concepts in the home language that are appropriate for the age (as reported by parents, teachers, assistants, or others, with the assistance of an interpreter if necessary).	1.3 Begin to demonstrate an understanding of words in English related to basic concepts.	1.3 Demonstrate an understanding of words in English related to more advanced concepts.

English-Language Development *(continued)*

Speaking

1.0 Children use nonverbal and verbal strategies to communicate with others.

Focus: Communication of needs

Beginning	Middle	Later
1.1 Use nonverbal communication, such as gestures or behaviors, to seek attention, request objects, or initiate a response from others.	1.1 Combine nonverbal and some verbal communication to be understood by others (may code-switch—that is, use the home language and English—and use telegraphic and/or formulaic speech).	1.1 Show increasing reliance on verbal communication in English to be understood by others.

Focus: Vocabulary production

1.2 Use vocabulary in the home language that is age-appropriate (as reported by parents, teachers, assistants, or others and with the assistance of an interpreter if necessary).	1.2 Begin to use English vocabulary, mainly consisting of concrete nouns and with some verbs and pronouns (telegraphic speech).	1.2 Use new English vocabulary to share knowledge of concepts.

Focus: Conversation

1.3 Converse in the home language (as reported by parents, teachers, assistants, or others, with the assistance of an interpreter if necessary).	1.3 Begin to converse with others, using English vocabulary but may code-switch (i.e., use the home language and English).	1.3 Sustain a conversation in English about a variety of topics.

English-Language Development *(continued)*

1.0 Children use nonverbal and verbal strategies to communicate with others.

Focus: Utterance length and complexity

Beginning	Middle	Later
1.4 Use a range of utterance lengths in the home language that is age-appropriate (as reported by parents, teachers, assistants, or others, with the assistance of an interpreter if necessary).	1.4 Use two- and three-word utterances in English to communicate.	1.4 Increase utterance length in English by adding appropriate possessive pronouns (e.g., his, her); conjunctions (e.g., and, or); or other elements (e.g., adjectives, adverbs).

Focus: Grammar

1.5 Use age-appropriate grammar in the home language (e.g., plurals; simple past tense; use of subject, verb, object), sometimes with errors (as reported by parents, teachers, assistants, or others, with the assistance of an interpreter if necessary).	1.5 Begin to use some English grammatical markers (e.g., *-ing* or plural *–s*) and, at times, apply the rules of grammar of the home language to English.	1.5 Expand the use of different forms of grammar in English (e.g., plurals; simple past tense; use of subject, verb and object), sometimes with errors.

Focus: Inquiry

1.6 Ask a variety of types of questions (e.g., "what," "why," "how," "when," and "where") in the home language (as reported by parents, teachers, assistants, or others, with the assistance of an interpreter if necessary.	1.6 Begin to use "what" and "why" questions in English, sometimes with errors.	1.6 Begin to use "what," "why," "how," "when," and "where" questions in more complete forms in English, sometimes with errors.

English-Language Development *(continued)*

2.0 Children begin to understand and use social conventions in English.

Focus: Social conventions

Beginning	Middle	Later
2.1 Use social conventions of the home language (as reported by teachers, parents, assistants, or others, with the assistance of an interpreter if necessary).	2.1 Demonstrate a beginning understanding of English social conventions.	2.1 Appropriately use words and tone of voice associated with social conventions in English.

3.0 Children use language to create oral narratives about their personal experiences.

Focus: Narrative development

Beginning	Middle	Later
3.1 Create a narrative in the home language (as reported by parents, teachers, assistants, or others, with the assistance of an interpreter if necessary).	3.1 Begin to use English to talk about personal experiences; may complete a narrative in the home language while using some English (i.e., code-switching).	3.1 Produce simple narratives in English that are real or fictional.

Reading

1.0 Children demonstrate an appreciation and enjoyment of reading and literature.

Focus: Participate in read-aloud activity

Beginning	Middle	Later
1.1 Attend to an adult reading a short storybook written in the home language or a storybook written in English if the story has been read in the home language.	1.1 Begin to participate in reading activities, using books written in English when the language is predictable.	1.1 Participate in reading activities, using a variety of genres that are written in English (e.g., poetry, fairy tales, concept books, and informational books).

Focus: Interest in books and reading

1.2 "Read" familiar books written in the home language or in English when encouraged by others and, in the home language, talk about the books.	1.2 Choose to "read" familiar books written in the home language or in English with increasing independence and, in the home language or in English, talk about the books.	1.2 Choose to "read" familiar books written in English with increasing independence and talk about the books in English.

English-Language Development *(continued)*

2.0 Children show an increasing understanding of book reading.

Focus: Personal connections to the story

Beginning	Middle	Later
2.1 Begin to identify and relate to a story from their own life experiences in the home language (as reported by parents, teachers, assistants, or others, with the assistance of an interpreter if necessary).	2.1 Describe their own experiences related to the topic of the story, using telegraphic and/or formulaic speech in English.	2.1 Begin to engage in extended conversations in English about stories.

Focus: Story structure

Beginning	Middle	Later
2.2 Retell a story in the home language when read or told a story in the home language (as reported by parents, teachers, assistants, or others, with the assistance of an interpreter if necessary).	2.2 Retell a story using the home language and some English when read or told a story in English.	2.2 Retell in English the majority of a story read or told in English.

3.0 Children demonstrate an understanding of print conventions.

Focus: Book handling

Beginning	Middle	Later
3.1 Begin to understand that books are read in a consistent manner (e.g., in English, pages are turned from right to left and the print is read from top to bottom, left to right; this may vary in other languages).	3.1 Continue to develop an understanding of how to read a book, sometimes applying knowledge of print conventions from the home language.	3.1 Demonstrate an understanding that print in English is organized from left to right, top to bottom, and that pages are turned from right to left when a book is read.

English-Language Development *(continued)*

4.0 Children demonstrate awareness that print carries meaning.

Focus: Environmental print

Beginning	Middle	Later
4.1 Begin to recognize that symbols in the environment (classroom, community, or home) carry a consistent meaning in the home language or in English.	4.1 Recognize in the environment (classroom, community, or home) some familiar symbols, words, and print labels in the home language or in English.	4.1 Recognize in the environment (classroom, community, or home) an increasing number of familiar symbols, words, and print labels in English.

5.0 Children demonstrate progress in their knowledge of the alphabet in English.

Focus: Letter awareness

Beginning	Middle	Later
5.1 Interact with material representing the letters of the English alphabet.	5.1 Begin to talk about the letters of the English alphabet while playing and interacting with them; may code-switch (use the home language and English).	5.1 Begin to demonstrate understanding that the letters of the English alphabet are symbols used to make words.

Focus: Letter recognition

Beginning	Middle	Later
5.2 Begin to recognize the first letter in their own name or the character for their own name in the home language or English.	5.2 Identify some letters of the alphabet in English.	5.2 Identify ten or more letters of the alphabet in English.

English-Language Development *(continued)*

6.0 Children demonstrate phonological awareness.

Focus: Rhyming

Beginning	Middle	Later
6.1 Listen attentively and begin to participate in simple songs, poems, and finger plays that emphasize rhyme in the home language or in English.	6.1 Begin to repeat or recite simple songs, poems, and finger plays that emphasize rhyme in the home language or in English.	6.1 Repeat, recite, produce, or initiate simple songs, poems, and finger plays that emphasize rhyme in English.

Focus: Onset (initial sound)

Beginning	Middle	Later
6.2 Listen attentively and begin to participate in simple songs, poems, and finger plays in the home language or in English.	6.2 Begin to recognize words that have a similar onset (initial sound) in the home language or in English, with support.	6.2 Recognize and produce words that have a similar onset (initial sound) in English.

Focus: Sound differences in the home language and English

Beginning	Middle	Later
6.3 Attend to and manipulate different sounds or tones in words in the home language (as reported by parents, teachers, assistants, or others, with the assistance of an interpreter if necessary.)	6.3 Begin to use words in English with phonemes (individual units of meaningful sound in a word or syllable) that are different from the home language.	6.3 Begin to orally manipulate sounds (onsets, rimes, and phonemes) in words in English, with support.

Writing

1.0   Children use writing to communicate their ideas.

Focus: Writing as communication

Beginning	Middle	Later
1.1 Begin to understand that writing can be used to communicate.	1.1 Begin to understand that what is said in the home language or in English can be written down and read by others.	1.1 Develop an increasing understanding that what is said in English can be written down and read by others.

Focus: Writing to represent words or ideas

1.2 Begin to demonstrate an awareness that written language can be in the home language or in English.	1.2 Begin to use marks or symbols to represent spoken language in the home language or in English.	1.2 Continue to develop writing by using letters or letter-like marks to represent their ideas in English.

Focus: Writing their name

1.3 Write marks to represent their own name in a way that may resemble how it is written in the home language.	1.3 Attempt to copy their own name in English or in the writing system of their home language.	1.3 Write their first name on their own in English nearly correctly, using letters of the English alphabet to accurately represent pronunciation in their home language.

MATHEMATICS

Number Sense

At around 48 months of age	*At around 60 months of age*
1.0 Children begin to understand numbers and quantities in their everyday environment.	**1.0 Children expand their understanding of numbers and quantities in their everyday environment.**
1.1 Recite numbers in order to ten with increasing accuracy.	1.1 Recite numbers in order to twenty with increasing accuracy.
1.2 Begin to recognize and name a few written numerals.	1.2 Recognize and know the name of some written numerals.
1.3 Identify, without counting, the number of objects in a collection of up to three objects (i.e., subitize).	1.3 Identify, without counting, the number of objects in a collection of up to four objects (i.e., subitize).
1.4 Count up to five objects, using one-to-one correspondence (one object for each number word) with increasing accuracy.	1.4 Count up to ten objects, using one-to-one correspondence (one object for each number word) with increasing accuracy.
1.5 Use the number name of the last object counted to answer the question, "How many . . . ?"	1.5 Understand, when counting, that the number name of the last object counted represents the total number of objects in the group (i.e., cardinality).
2.0 Children begin to understand number relationships and operations in their everyday environment.	**2.0 Children expand their understanding of number relationships and operations in their everyday environment.**
2.1 Compare visually (with or without counting) two groups of objects that are obviously equal or nonequal and communicate, "more" or "same."	2.1 Compare, by counting or matching, two groups of up to five objects and communicate, "more," "same as," or "fewer" (or "less").
2.2 Understand that adding to (or taking away) one or more objects from a group will increase (or decrease) the number of objects in the group.	2.2 Understand that adding one or taking away one changes the number in a small group of objects by exactly one.

Mathematics *(continued)*

At around 48 months of age	*At around 60 months of age*
2.3 Understand that putting two groups of objects together will make a bigger group.	2.3 Understand that putting two groups of objects together will make a bigger group and that a group of objects can be taken apart into smaller groups.
2.4 Solve simple addition and subtraction problems nonverbally (and often verbally) with a very small number of objects (sums up to 4 or 5).	2.4 Solve simple addition and subtraction problems with a small number of objects (sums up to 10), usually by counting.

Algebra and Functions
(Classification and Patterning)

At around 48 months of age	*At around 60 months of age*
1.0 Children begin to sort and classify objects in their everyday environment.	**1.0 Children expand their understanding of sorting and classifying objects in their everyday environment.**
1.1 Sort and classify objects by one attribute into two or more groups, with increasing accuracy.	1.1 Sort and classify objects by one or more attributes, into two or more groups, with increasing accuracy (e.g., may sort first by one attribute and then by another attribute).
2.0 Children begin to recognize simple, repeating patterns.	**2.0 Children expand their understanding of simple, repeating patterns.**
2.1 Begin to identify or recognize a simple repeating pattern.	2.1 Recognize and duplicate simple repeating patterns.
2.2 Attempt to create a simple repeating pattern or participate in making one.	2.2 Begin to extend and create simple repeating patterns.

Mathematics *(continued)*

Measurement

At around 48 months of age	*At around 60 months of age*
1.0 Children begin to compare and order objects.	**1.0 Children expand their understanding of comparing, ordering, and measuring objects.**
1.1 Demonstrate awareness that objects can be compared by length, weight, or capacity, by noting gross differences, using words such as *bigger, longer, heavier,* or *taller,* or by placing objects side by side to compare length.	1.1 Compare two objects by length, weight, or capacity directly (e.g., putting objects side by side) or indirectly (e.g., using a third object).
1.2 Order three objects by size.	1.2 Order four or more objects by size.
	1.3 Measure length using multiple duplicates of the same-size concrete units laid end to end.

Geometry

At around 48 months of age	*At around 60 months of age*
1.0 Children begin to identify and use common shapes in their everyday environment.	**1.0 Children identify and use a variety of shapes in their everyday environment.**
1.1 Identify simple two-dimensional shapes, such as a circle and square.	1.1 Identify, describe, and construct a variety of different shapes, including variations of a circle, triangle, rectangle, square, and other shapes.
1.2 Use individual shapes to represent different elements of a picture or design.	1.2 Combine different shapes to create a picture or design.
2.0 Children begin to understand positions in space.	**2.0 Children expand their understanding of positions in space.**
2.1 Identify positions of objects and people in space, such as in/on/under, up/down, and inside/outside.	2.1 Identify positions of objects and people in space, including in/on/under, up/down, inside/outside, beside/between, and in front/behind.

Mathematical Reasoning

At around 48 months of age	*At around 60 months of age*
1.0 Children use mathematical thinking to solve problems that arise in their everyday environment.	**1.0 Children expand the use of mathematical thinking to solve problems that arise in their everyday environment.**
1.1 Begin to apply simple mathematical strategies to solve problems in their environment.	1.1 Identify and apply a variety of mathematical strategies to solve problems in their environment.

References

American Academy of Child and Adolescent Psychiatry. 2002. "Facts for Families: Children and TV Violence." No. 13, updated November 2002. http://www.aacap.org/page.ww?section=Facts%20for%20Families&name=Children%20And%20TV%20Violence (accessed June 12, 2009).

American Academy of Pediatrics, American Public Health Association, and the National Resource Center for Health and Safety in Child Care. 2002. *Caring for Our Children: National Health and Safety Performance Standards—Guidelines for Out-of-Home Child Care.* 2nd ed. http://nrc.uchsc.edu/CFOC/XMLVersion/Title.xml (accessed September 12, 2007).

Berrueta-Clement, J. R.; L. J. Schweinhart; W. S. Barnett; A. S. Epstein; and D. P. Weikart. 1984. *Changed Lives: The Effects of the Perry Preschool Program on Youths Through Age 19.* Ypsilanti, MI: HighScope Press.

Bryant, D.; K. Maxwell; K. Taylor; M. Poe; E. Peisner-Feinberg; and K. Bernier. 2003. *Smart Start and Preschool Child Care Quality in North Carolina: Change Over Time and Relation to Children's School Readiness.* Chapel Hill, NC: Frank Porter Graham Institute.

Burchinal, M.; C. Howes; and S. Kontos. 2002. "Structural Predictors of Child Care Quality in Child Care Homes." *Early Childhood Research Quarterly* 17(1): 87–105.

Burchinal, M. R.; M. Lee; and C. Ramey. 1989. "Type of Day Care and Preschool Intellectual Development in Disadvantaged Children." *Child Development* 60:128–37.

Burton, A., and M. Whitebook. 1998. *Child Care Staff Compensation Guidelines for California 1998.* Washington, DC: Center for the Child Care Workforce (prepared for the California Department of Education).

California Child Care Resource & Referral Network. 2005. *The 2005 California Child Care Portfolio.* San Francisco: California Child Care Resource & Referral Network. http://www.rrnetwork.org/our-research/2005Portfolio.html.

California Child Care Resource & Referral Network Web site. http://www.rrnetwork.org/programs/child-care-initiative-project.html (accessed August 17, 2007).

CARES Training and Technical Assistance Project Web site. http://cares.edgateway.net.

California Department of Education. 1996. *Project EXCEPTIONAL: A Guide for Training and Recruiting Child Care Providers to Serve Young Children with Disabilities* (Vol. 1). Sacramento: California Department of Education.

———. 1998. *Ready to Learn: Quality Preschools for California in the 21st Century.* The Report of the Superintendent's Universal Preschool Task Force. Sacramento: California Department of Education.

———. 1999a. "Early Warning Signs That Your Child or a Child in Your Care May Need Help." Sacramento: California Department of Education.

———. 1999b. *First Class: A Guide for Early Primary Education*. Sacramento: California Department of Education.

———. 2000. *Prekindergarten Learning and Development Guidelines*. Sacramento: California Department of Education.

———. 2005a. Desired Results Developmental Profile (DRDP-R). *Infant Toddler Instrument*. http://www.wested.org/desiredresults/training/forms.htm (accessed September 19, 2007).

———. 2005b. Desired Results Developmental Profile (DRDP-R). *Preschool Instrument*. http://www.wested.org/desiredresults/training/forms.htm (accessed September 19, 2007).

———. 2006a. *Infant/Toddler Learning and Development Program Guidelines*. Sacramento: California Department of Education.

———. 2006b. "Monthly Child Care Population Information (CDD-801A)." Data file. Sacramento: California Department of Education.

———. 2007a. *DataQuest* (database). Sacramento: California Department of Education. http://dq.cde.ca.gov/dataquest/.

———. 2007b. *Preschool English Learners: Principles and Practices to Promote Language, Literacy, and Learning*. Sacramento: California Department of Education.

California Department of Education, in collaboration with WestEd Center for Child and Family Studies. 1992. *Together in Care: Meeting the Intimacy Needs of Infants and Toddlers in Groups*. Video/DVD. Sacramento: The Program for Infant/Toddler Care. http://www.pitc.org/cs/pitclib/view/pitc_res/830.

California Department of Finance. 2007. "Race/Ethnic Population with Age and Sex Detail, 2000-2050." Data files. Sacramento: California Department of Finance. http://www.dof.ca.gov/html/Demograp/DRU_datafiles/Race/RaceData_ 2000-2050/.

California Department of Social Services. "License Application and Instructions for Family Child Care Homes." Sacramento: California Department of Social Services. http://ccld.ca.gov/FamilyChil_1887.htm (accessed September 12, 2007).

Campbell, F. A., and C. Ramey. 1994. "Effects of Early Intervention on Intellectual and Academic Achievement: A Follow-up Study of Children from Low-Income Families." *Child Development* 65:669–84.

Center for Human Services. 2002. *Family Child Care at Its Best* (series). Davis, CA: University of California, Davis; UC Davis Extension.

Center for Law and Social Policy (CLASP). 2006. *Child Care and Development Block Grant Participation in 2005*. Washington, DC: Center for Law and Social Policy. http://www.clasp.org/.

Chalufour, Ingrid, et al. 1988. "As I Am" (curriculum guide). Washington, DC: U.S. Department of Health and Human Services, Office of Human Development Services, Head Start Bureau.

Child Welfare League of America (CWLA). "Family Child Care Systems." Arlington, VA: Child Welfare League of America. http://www.cwla.org/programs/daycare/fccsoverview.htm (accessed January 12, 2004).

Cohen, N. 2002. *Ten Reasons Why Family Child Care Providers Like Accreditation.* National Association for Family Child Care. http://www.wccip.org/ Accreditation_&_Quality/NAFCC/Ten_Reasons.html (accessed August 19, 2009).

Coley, R. 2002. *An Uneven Start.* Princeton, NJ: Educational Testing Service.

Crary, E. 1994. *Kids Can Cooperate.* Seattle, WA: Parenting Press, Inc. http://www. parentingpress.com/index.html.

Daniels, M. 1994. "The Effects of Sign Language on Hearing Children's Language Development." *Communication Education* 43, no. 4 (October): 291(8).

Early Head Start National Resource Center. 2003. "The Child Development Associate: National Credentialing Program Information." Washington, DC: U.S. Department of Health and Human Services. http://www.childcareinc.org/ fcc/providers.php (accessed November 13, 2003).

Fischer, J. L., and B. K. Eheart. 1991. "Family Day Care: A Theoretical Basis for Improving Quality." *Early Childhood Research Quarterly* 6(4): 549–563.

Fromboluti, C. S., and N. Rinck. 1999. *Early Childhood: Where Learning Begins— Mathematics.* Washington, DC: U.S. Department of Education, Office of Educational Research and Improvement.

Galinsky, E.; C. Howes; and S. Kontos. 1995. *The Family Child Care Training Study.* New York: Families and Work Institute.

Garcia, J. 1994. *Toddler Talk: The First Signs of Intelligent Life.* Stratton Kehl Publications.

Goelman, H., and A. R. Pence. 1987. "Effects of Child Care, Family, and Individual Characteristics on Children's Language Development: The Victoria Day Care Research Project." From Phillips, D. *Quality in Child Care: What Does the Research Tell Us? (Research Monographs of the National Association for the Education of Young Children)*, pp. 43–56. Washington, DC: National Association for the Education of Young Children.

Gonzalez-Mena, J. 1993. *Tips and Tidbits—A Book for Family Child Care Providers.* Washington, DC: National Association for the Education of Young Children.

Goodwyn, S. W.; L. P. Acredolo; and C. Brown. 2000. "Impact of Symbolic Gesturing on Early Language Development." *Journal of Nonverbal Behavior* 24:81–103.

Gormley Jr., W.; T. Gayer; D. Phillips; and B. Dawson. 2004. *The Effects of Oklahoma's Universal Pre-K Program on School Readiness.* Georgetown University Center for Research on Children in the U.S.

Hancox, R.; B. Milne; and R. Poulton. July 2004. "Association Between Child and Adolescent Television Viewing and Adult Health: A Longitudinal Birth Cohort Study." *The Lancet* 364, no. 9430: 257–262. http://www.thelancet. com/journals/lancet/article/PIIS0140-6736(04)16675-0/fulltext (accessed June 12, 2009).

Hart, B. and T. Risley. 1995. *Meaningful Differences in Everyday Parenting and Intellectual Development in Young American Children.* Baltimore: Paul H. Brookes Publishing Co.

Healy, J. M. 1998. "Understanding TV's Effects on the Developing Brain." *AAP News*, American Academy of Pediatrics.

Heckman, J. J. 2006. "Investing in Disadvantaged Young Children is an Economically Efficient Policy." Paper presented at the Committee for Economic Development/Pew Charitable Trusts/PNC Financial Services Group forum on "Building the Economic Case for Investments in Preschool." New York: January 10, 2006.

Howes, C., and C. E. Hamilton. 1993. "Child Care for Young Children," in *Handbook of Research on the Education of Young Children*, pp. 322–36 (edited by B. Spodek). New York: Macmillan.

International Child Art Foundation. (No date.) *Why ChildArt*. Washington, DC: International Child Art Foundation. http://www.icaf.org/.

Karoly, L. A. 2005. *County-Level Estimates of the Effects of a Universal Preschool Program in California*. RAND Technical Report. http://www.rand.org/pubs/technical_reports/TR340/.

Karoly, L. A., and J. H. Bigelow. 2005. *The Economics of Investigating in Universal Preschool Education in California*. Santa Monica, CA: RAND Corporation.

Katz, Lilian G.; E. Demetra; and J. A. Hartman. 1990. *The Case for Mixed-age Grouping in Early Education*. Washington, DC: National Association for the Education of Young Children.

Kontos, S. 1994. "The Ecology of Family Day Care." *Early Childhood Research Quarterly* 9(1): 87–110.

Kontos, S.; C. Howes; M. Shinn; and E. Galinsky. 1995. *Quality in Family Child Care and Relative Care*. New York: Teachers College Press.

Lally, J. R.; P. L. Mangione; S. Signer; G.O. Butterfield; and S. Gilford. 1992. *Discoveries of Infancy: Cognitive Development and Learning*. Video/DVD. United States: The Program for Infant/Toddler Care (developed collaboratively by the California Department of Education and WestEd).

Lally, J. R.; S. Signer; and G.O. Butterfield. 1994. *Ingredients for a Good Start*. Video/DVD. United States: The Program for Infant/Toddler Care (developed collaboratively by the California Department of Education and WestEd).

Layzer, J. I.; B. D. Goodson; and M. Moss. 1993. *Life in Preschool: Observational Study of Early Childhood Programs, Final Report*. Vol. 1. Cambridge, MA: Abt Associates, Developmental Assistance Corporation, and RMC Research Corporation.

Lewit, E. M., and L. S. Baker. 1995. "School Readiness." *The Future of Children* 5:128–139.

Montgomery, D.; L. K. Kaye; R. Geen; and K. Martinson. 2002. *Recent Changes in California Welfare and Work, Child Care, and Child Welfare Systems*. Washington, DC: The Urban Institute.

National Academy of Sciences. 2001. *Eager to Learn: Educating Our Preschoolers*. National Research Council Committee on Early Childhood Pedagogy. Bowman, B.; M. Donovan; and M. Burns, eds. Washington, DC: National Academy Press.

National Academy Press. 1990. *Who Cares for America's Children: Child Care Policy for the 1990s*. Edited by S. Hayes, F. Palmer, and M. Zaslow. Washington, DC: National Academy Press.

National Association for Family Child Care. 2005. *Quality Standards for NAFCC Accreditation.* 4th ed. Salt Lake City, UT: National Association for Family Child Care.

National Research Council and Institute of Medicine. 2000. *From Neurons to Neighborhoods: The Science of Early Childhood Development.* Committee on Integrating the Science of Early Childhood Development. Jack P. Shonkoff and Deborah A. Phillips, eds. Washington, DC: National Academy Press. http://www.nap.edu/openbook.php?record_id=9824&page=R1 (accessed January 8, 2009).

O'Donnell, N. S., and T. W. Morrissey. 2005. "Family, Friend and Neighbor Care and Early Systems: Issues and Recommendations." New York: Families and Work Institute. http://www.familiesandwork.org/sparking/pdf/FFN_Care_and_Early_Learning_Systems.pdf (accessed August 21, 2007).

Reynolds, A. J.; J. A. Temple; D. L. Robertson; and E. A. Mann. 2001 (June). "Long-Term Effects of Early Intervention on Educational Achievement and Juvenile Arrest: A 15-Year Follow-Up of Low-Income Children in Public School." *Journal of the American Medical Association* 285:2339–346.

Rimm-Kaufman, S. E.; R. B. Pianta; and M. J. Cox. 2000. "Teachers' Judgments of Problems in the Transition to Kindergarten." *Early Childhood Research Quarterly* 15:146–166.

Schnur, E., and R. Koffler. 1995 (November/December). "Family Child Care and New Immigrants: Cultural Bridge and Support." *Child Welfare* 74:6.

Schulman, K., and H. Blank. 2007. *State Strategies to Strengthen and Support Family, Friend, and Neighbor Care.* Washington, DC: National Women's Law Center.

Schweinhart, L., and D. Weikart. 1997. *Lasting Differences: The High/Scope Preschool Curriculum Comparison Study Through Age 23.* Ypsilanti, MI: HighScope Press.

Smith, K. 2006. *Rural Families Choose Home-Based Child Care for their Preschool-Aged Children.* Policy Brief No. 3:1–2. Durham, NH: Carsey Institute. http://www.carseyinstitute.unh.edu/documents/ChildCare_final.pdf. As cited in *Close to Home: State Strategies to Strengthen and Support Family, Friend, and Neighbor Care,* by Karen Schulman and Helen Blank. National Women's Law Center, February 2007.

Solnit Sale, J. 1998a. "How Children Catch Colds." *UCLA Working Parents Newsletter* 4(3).

———. 1998b. "Rhyming: Verbal Toys for Children." *UCLA Working Parents Newsletter* 22.

United States Census. 2000. U.S. Census Bureau. http://www.census.gov.

United States Department of Education, Early Childhood-Head Start Task Force. 2002. *Teaching Our Youngest: A Guide for Preschool Teachers and Child Care and Family Providers* (18).

United States Department of Education, Office of Educational Research and Improvement. 1993. *Helping Your Child Get Ready for School.* http://readyweb.crc.uiuc.edu/library/1992/getready/getready.html (accessed April 1, 2004).

Washington, V. 1985. "Head Start: How Appropriate for Minority Families in the 1980s?" *American Journal of Orthopsychiatry* 55(4): 577–590.

WestEd. The Program for Infant/Toddler Care (PITC). 1997. *The Program for Infant/Toddler Caregivers' Training Manual, Module IV: Culture, Family, and Providers.* Sacramento: California Department of Education.

Whelan, M. 2007. "Strengthening Family, Friend & Neighbor Child Care." Webinar. National Women's Law Center. http://www.nwlc.org/pdf/ StrengtheningFFNCareWebinar1.pdf (accessed July 13, 2009).

Whitebook, M.; L. Sakai; F. Kipnis; Y. Lee; D. Bellm; R. Speiglman; M. Almaraz; L. Stubbs; and P. Tran. 2006. *California Early Care and Education Workforce Study: Licensed Family Child Care Providers, Statewide 2006.* Berkeley, CA: Center for the Study of Child Care Employment; and San Francisco, CA: California Child Care Resource and Referral Network.

Zetes, K. 1998. *Look Who's Coming to Family Child Care: Infants and Toddlers, Birth to 24 Months.* San Francisco: The California Child Care Initiative Project.

Further Reading and References

Anderson, M. P. 1998. *Families Matter: Parent-Provider Partnerships.* Cambridge, MA: Harvard Family Research Project.

Annie E. Casey Foundation. 2006. *KIDS COUNT Data Book.* Baltimore, MD: Annie E. Casey Foundation.

Baker, A. C., and L. A. Manfredi-Pteitt. 1998. *Circle of Love: Relationships Between Parents, Providers, and Children in Child Care.* St. Paul, MN: Redleaf Press.

Belshé, S., and T. Mitchell. 2006. *Family Child Care Homes: Manual of Policies and Procedures.* Sacramento: State of California Health and Welfare Agency and Department of Social Services. http://www.cdss.ca.gov/getinfo/pdf/fcc.PDF.

Berman, C., and J. Fromer. 1997. *Meals without Squeals.* Palo Alto, CA: Bull Publishing Company.

Brandon, R. N.; E. J. Haher; J. M. Joesch; and S. Doyle. 2002. *Understanding Family, Friend and Neighborhood Care in Washington State: Developing Appropriate Training and Support.* Seattle, WA: Human Services Policy Center, University of Washington.

Brazelton, T. B. 1992. *Touchpoints: Your Child's Emotional and Behavioral Development.* Reading, MA: Addison-Wesley Publishing Company.

Bredekamp, S., and C. Copple, eds. 1997. *Developmentally Appropriate Practice in Early Childhood Programs.* Washington, DC: National Association for the Education of Young Children.

California Child Care Health Program. 1998. *Health and Safety in the Child Care Setting: Prevention of Infectious Disease.* 1st ed. San Diego, CA: California Child Care Health Program.

California Department of Education. 1996. *Teaching Reading: A Balanced, Comprehensive Approach to Teaching Reading in Prekindergarten Through Grade Three.* Sacramento: California Department of Education.

———. 1997. *Continuity for Young Children: Positive Transitions to Elementary School.* Sacramento: California Department of Education.

————. 1998a. *Observing Preschoolers: Assessing First and Second Language Development.* Video/DVD. Sacramento: California Department of Education.

————. 1998b. *English–Language Arts Content Standards for California Public Schools: Kindergarten Through Grade Twelve.* Sacramento: California Department of Education.

————. 1999. *Mathematics Content Standards for California Public Schools: Kindergarten Through Grade Twelve.* Sacramento: California Department of Education.

————. 2001. *Visual and Performing Arts Standards for California Public Schools: Kindergarten Through Grade Twelve.* Sacramento: California Department of Education.

————. 2002. *English-Language Development Standards: Kindergarten Through Grade Twelve.* Sacramento: California Department of Education.

————. 2006. *Mathematics Framework for California Public Schools: Kindergarten Through Grade Twelve.* Sacramento: California Department of Education.

————. 2007c. *Reading/Language Arts Framework for California Public Schools: Kindergarten Through Grade Twelve.* Sacramento: California Department of Education.

————. 2007d. *A World Full of Language: Supporting Preschool English Learners.* DVD. Sacramento: California Department of Education.

Carnegie Task Force on Meeting the Needs of Young Children. 1994. *Starting Points: Meeting the Needs of Our Youngest Children.* New York: Carnegie Corporation of New York.

Chandler, P. A. 1994. *A Place for Me: Including Children with Special Needs in Early Care and Education Settings.* Washington, DC: National Association for the Education of Young Children.

Chang, H. N. 1996. *Affirming Children's Roots: Cultural and Linguistic Diversity in Early Care and Education.* San Francisco: California Tomorrow.

Chang, H. N.; Muckelroy, A.; and D. Pulido-Tobiassen. 1996. *Looking in, Looking out: Redefining Child Care and Early Education in a Diverse Society.* San Francisco: California Tomorrow.

Child Care Coordinating Council of San Mateo, in collaboration with the California Child Care Resource and Referral Network and the Center for the Study of Child Care Employment at the University of California, Berkeley. 2004. *Preschool for All: Supply and Demand Study.*

Children's Foundation. 1990. *Helping Children Love Themselves and Others: A Professional Handbook for Family Day Care.* Washington, DC: Children's Foundation.

Copeland, T. 1991. *Family Child Care Contracts and Policies: How to be Businesslike in a Caring Profession.* St. Paul, MN: Redleaf Press.

————. 1999. *Family Child Care Marketing Guide: How to Build Enrollment and Promote Your Business as a Child Care Professional.* St. Paul, MN: Redleaf Press.

Copely, J., ed. 1999. *Mathematics in the Early Years.* Reston, VA: National Council of Teachers of Mathematics; and Washington, DC: National Association for the Education of Young Children.

Denton, K.; E. Germino-Hausken; and J. West. 2000. "America's Kindergartners: Early Childhood Longitudinal Study, Kindergarten Class of 1998-99, Fall 1998." *Education Statistics* Quarterly 2(1): 7–13. Washington, DC: U.S. Department of Education, National Center for Education Statistics.

Derman-Sparks, L. 1989. *Anti-Bias Curriculum: Tools for Empowering Young Children.* Washington, DC: National Association for the Education of Young Children.

Diamond, M., and J. Hopson. 1998. *Magic Trees of the Mind: How to Nurture Your Child's Intelligence, Creativity, and Healthy Emotions from Birth Through Adolescence.* New York: E. P. Dutton.

Diffily, D., and K. Morrison, eds. 1997. *Family-friendly Communication for Early Childhood Programs.* Washington, DC: National Association for the Education of Young Children.

Engel, B. S. 1995. *Considering Children's Art: Why and How to Value Their Works.* Washington, DC: National Association for the Education of Young Children.

Ewen, D., and H. Matthews. 2007. *Families Forgotten: Administration's Priorities Put Child Care Low on the List.* Washington, DC: Center for Law and Social Policy.

Florida Children's Forum. 2001. *Understanding Inclusion and the Americans with Disabilities Act (ADA): A Resource to Assist Families, Child Care Providers and Advocates in Planning and Delivering Child Care for Children with Special Needs.* Tallahassee, FL: Florida Children's Forum.

Florida Institute of Education. 2000. *Florida School Readiness Performance Standards.* Tallahassee, FL: Florida Institute of Education.

Fromboluti, C. S., and C. Seefeldt. 1999. *Early Childhood: Where Learning Begins—Geography.* Washington, DC: U.S. Department of Education, Office of Educational Research and Improvement.

Gerber, M. 2003. *Dear Parent: Caring for Infants with Respect.* Edited by Joan Weaver. Los Angeles: Resources for Infant Educators.

Gonzalez-Mena, J. 2008. *Diversity in Early Care and Education: Honoring Differences.* New York: McGraw-Hill.

Goulet, M. 1999. *How Caring Relationships Support Self-Regulation.* Video/DVD. Washington, DC: National Association for the Education of Young Children.

Hawley, T. 1998. *Starting Smart: How Early Experiences Affect Brain Development.* Washington, DC: Zero to Three National Center for Infants, Toddlers, and Families.

Head Start. 2007. *NHSA Survey: Over Half of Head Start Programs Forced to Reduce Services to Children in Face of 11 Percent in Federal Cuts That Could Grow to 13 Percent in Fiscal Year 2008.* Washington, DC: National Head Start Association. http://www.supportheadstart.org/News/releases2.cfm?releaseID=45.

Hernandez, D. J. 1995. "Changing Demographics: Past and Future Demands for Early Childhood Programs." *The Future of Children* 5 (winter).

Hodges, S. 1997. *Celebrating Likes and Differences: Fun and Easy Theme Units for Exploring Diversity with Young Children.* Torrance, CA: Totline Publications.

Holt, B. G. 1993. *Science with Young Children.* Washington, DC: National Association for the Education of Young Children.

Hyson, M. C. 1994. *The Emotional Development of Young Children: Building an Emotion-centered Curriculum.* New York: Teachers College Press.

Isenberg, J. P., and N. Quisenberry. 2002. *Play: Essential for All Children* (a position paper). Olney, MD: Association for Childhood Education International.

Jones, E., and G. Reynolds. 1992. *The Play's the Thing: Teacher's Role in Children's Play.* New York: Teachers College Press.

Kaeser, G. 1999. *Love Makes a Family: Portraits of Lesbian, Gay, Bisexual and Transgender Parents.* Amherst, MA: University of Massachusetts Press.

Kamii, C. 1995. *Numbers in Preschool and Kindergarten.* Washington, DC: National Association for the Education of Young Children.

Katz, L. G., and D. E. McClellan. 1997. *Fostering Children's Social Competence: The Teacher's Role.* Washington, DC: National Association for the Education of Young Children.

Kauffman Early Education Exchange. 2002. *Set for Success: Building a Strong Foundation for School Readiness Based on the Social-Emotional Development of Young Children.* Kansas City, MO: The Ewing Marion Kauffman Foundation.

Kendall, F. 1996. *Diversity in the Classroom: New Approaches to the Education of Young Children.* 2nd ed. New York: Teachers College Press.

Krementz, J. 1992. *How it Feels to Live with a Physical Disability.* New York: Simon and Schuster.

Lally, J. R. 1997. "Brain Development in Infancy: A Critical Period." *Bridges* 3(1).

Lally, J. R.; P. L. Mangione; S. Signer; and G. O. Butterfield. 1996. *Protective Urges: Working with the Feelings of Parents and Caregivers.* Video/DVD. United States: The Program for Infant/Toddler Care (developed collaboratively by the California Department of Education and WestEd).

———. 2001. *The Next Step: Including the Infant in the Curriculum.* Video/DVD. United States: The Program for Infant/Toddler Care (developed collaboratively by the California Department of Education and WestEd).

Lally, J. R.; P. L. Mangione; S. Signer; G.O. Butterfield; and S. Gilford. 1990. *Getting in Tune: Creating Nurturing Relationships with Infants and Toddlers.* Video/DVD. United States: The Program for Infant/Toddler Care (developed collaboratively by the California Department of Education and WestEd).

———. 1992. *Together in Care: Meeting the Intimacy Needs of Infants and Toddlers in Groups.* Video/DVD. United States: The Program for Infant/Toddler Care (developed collaboratively by the California Department of Education and WestEd).

Lally, J. R.; S. Signer; and G. O. Butterfield. 1996. *Today's Special: A Fresh Approach to Meals for Preschoolers.* Video/DVD. United States: The Program for Infant/Toddler Care (developed collaboratively by the California Department of Education and WestEd).

Lane, M., and S. Signer. 1990. *A Guide to Creating Partnerships with Parents.* Booklet. Sacramento: California Department of Education and WestEd.

Lombardi, J. 2003. *Time to Care: Redesigning Child Care to Promote Education, Support Families and Build Communities.* Philadelphia, PA: Temple University Press.

Matiella, A. C. 1992. *Positively Different: Creating a Bias-free Environment for Young Children.* Santa Cruz, CA: ETR Associates/Network Publications.

McCartney, S. 1992. *Active Learning in a Family Day Care Setting.* Glenview, IL: Good Year Books.

McLaughlin, B. 1995. *Fostering Second Language Development in Young Children: Principles and Practices.* Santa Cruz, CA: National Center for Research on Cultural Diversity and Second Language Learning.

Miller, K. 1995. *The Crisis Manual for Early Childhood Teachers: How to Handle the Really Difficult Problems.* St Paul, MN: Redleaf Press.

Modigliani, K., and J. Bromer. 1996. "What Does 'Quality Family Child Care' Mean? How Can Quality Be Identified?" *Child Care Bulletin* 8 (March/April). Fairfax, VA: National Child Care Information and Technical Assistance Center. http://nccic.acf.hhs.gov/ccb/issue8.html (accessed August 5, 2009).

Modigliani, K.; M. Reiff; and S. Jones. 1985. *Opening Your Door to Children: How to Start a Family Day Care Program.* Washington, DC: National Association for the Education of Young Children.

National Association for the Education of Young Children. 1986. *Helping Children Learn Self-control: A Guide to Discipline.* Washington, DC: National Association for the Education of Young Children.

National Center for Education Statistics. 1993. *Public School Kindergarten Teachers' Views on Children's Readiness for School.* Washington, DC: U.S. Department of Education, Office of Educational Research and Improvement. http://nces.ed.gov/pubs93/93410.pdf.

National Education Goals Panel. 1991. *The National Education Goals Report: Building a Nation of Learners.* Washington, DC: National Education Goals Panel.

Neugebauer, B., ed. 1992. *Alike and Different: Exploring Our Humanity with Young Children.* Washington, DC: National Association for the Education of Young Children.

Nieto, L. 1999. *The Light in Their Eyes: Creating Multicultural Learning Communities.* New York: Teachers College Press.

Odom, S. L., ed. 2002. *Widening the Circle: Including Children with Disabilities in Preschool Programs.* New York: Teachers College Press.

Paley, V. G. 1993. *You Can't Say You Can't Play.* Cambridge, MA: Harvard University Press.

Powell, E. S. 1990. *Heart to Heart Caregiving: A Sourcebook of Family Day Care Activities, Projects, and Practical Provider Support.* St. Paul, MN: Toys 'n Things Press.

Preschool California. 2005. *Praise for Preschool: California Kindergarten Teachers Say All Children Will Benefit.* Oakland, CA: Preschool California.

Pruissen, C. M. 1999. *Start and Run a Profitable Home Day Care.* 2nd ed., Self-Counsel business series. Bellingham, WA: Self-Counsel Press.

Quibb, B., and J. King. 1994. *Play in Home Spaces in Family Child Care.* Augusta, ME: University of Maine.

Shade, D. 1997. *Computers in Early Childhood: A World of Discovery*. New York: Prentice Hall.

Snyder, K., and G. Adams. 2001. *State Child Care Profile for Children with Employed Mothers: California. Assessing the New Federalism: An Urban Institute Program to Assess Changing Social Policies*. Washington, DC: The Urban Institute.

Solnit Sale, J., ed. 1999. *Family Child Care Handbook*. 6th ed. San Francisco: California Child Care Resource and Referral Network.

Solter, A. J. 1998. *Tears and Tantrums*. Goleta, CA: Shining Star Press.

Thompson, B. 2002. *The Home Day Care Complete Recordkeeping System: A System to Help You Reduce Your Taxable Income*. Williston, VT: Datamaster, LLC.

Trister Dodge, D., and L. Colker. 2003. *The Creative Curriculum for Family Child Care*. 3rd ed. Washington, DC: Teaching Strategies, Inc.

Valdes, G. 1996. *Con Respeto: Bridging the Distances Between Culturally Diverse Families and Schools*. New York: Teachers College Press.

Washington, V.; F. Johnson; and J. B. McCracken. 1995. *Grassroots Success: Preparing Schools and Families for Each Other*. Washington, DC: National Association for the Education of Young Children.

Waugh, L., and L. Sweitzer. 2000. *Tired of Yelling: Teaching Our Children to Resolve Conflict*. Atlanta, GA: Pocket Books.

Westridge Young Writers Workshop. 1996a. *Kids Explore America's African American Heritage*. Santa Fe, NM: John Muir Publications.

———. 1996b. *Kids Explore America's Hispanic Heritage*. Santa Fe, NM: John Muir Publications.

Worley, M., and J. S. Wilbers, eds. 1994. *Including Children with Special Needs in Early Childhood Programs*. Washington, DC: National Association for the Education of Young Children.

Yolan, J., ed. 1992. *Street Rhymes Around the World*. Honesdale, PA: Wordsong/Boyds Mills Press.

———. 1994. *Sleep Rhymes Around the World*. Honesdale, PA: Wordsong/Boyds Mills Press.

Zero to Three. 1992. *Heart Start: The Emotional Foundations of School Readiness*. Arlington, VA: National Center for Clinical Infant Programs.